Given for you

To Alan

Given for you

A FRESH LOOK AT COMMUNION

Eleanor Kreider

inter-varsity press

INTER-VARSITY PRESS
38 De Montfort Street, Leicester LE1 7GP, England

First British edition 1998

British Library Cataloguing in Publication Data
A catalogue record for this book is available from the British Library.

ISBN 0–85111–582–9

Set in Garamond
Printed and bound in Great Britain

Inter-Varsity Press is the book-publishing division of the Universities and Colleges Christian Fellowship (formerly the Inter-Varsity Fellowship), a student movement linking Christian Unions in universities and colleges throughout the United Kingdom and the Republic of Ireland, and a member movement of the International Fellowship of Evangelical Students. For information about local and national activities write to UCCF, 38 De Montfort Street, Leicester LE1 7GP.

Contents

Foreword by Robert Webber	7
Preface	9

Introduction 11

Communion Across the Centuries 15
1. Last Supper to Church Supper 17
2. Jewish Blessings and Roman Banquets 25
3. Love Feasts 34
4. Early Christian Eucharist 40
5. Medieval Mass and Divine Liturgy 46
6. Reformation: A Communion Revolution 57
7. Modern Developments: Innovation and Recovery 67

Communion: Variations on the Theme 87
Introduction to the Variations 89
8. Historic Themes Come Alive 90
9. Christ Is Present, the Mystery Is Revealed 99
10. Communion Themes for Life in the Congregation 106
11. Communion Themes for Mission 119

Communion Shapes Character 133
Introduction: Communion That Nurtures 135
12. The Language of Ritual 136
13. Thanksgiving Sets the Tone 145
14. An Open Table? 150
15. A Community of Many Tables 167
16. Words and Stories at the Table 173
17. Singing Our Communion Theology 181
18. Offering Ourselves and Our Gifts 190
19. An Environment for Thanksgiving 194
20. Praying at the Table 201

What Comes from Communion?   211
21. Character   213
22. Unity   216
23. Mission   220

Appendixes:
A. Planning a Communion Service   228
  1. The Basic Design of Christian Eucharist   228
  2. A Baptist Pattern in England   229
  3. An Informal Breaking of Bread   230
  4. Breaking Bread at a Conference   230

B. Service Resources   233
  1. A Seder Service   233
  2. A Didache Service   236
  3. A Sixteenth-Century Anabaptist Communion Service   239

Notes   244
Index   253

Foreword

TODAY CHURCH-GROWTH specialists suggest that the megachurch movement with its large space, multiple staff, and entertainment worship is the dominant church model of the future. To survive, pastors are told to develop seeker-driven churches, purpose-driven churches, or music-driven churches. In none of these church-growth writings do we find any significant reference to the Lord's table. There seems to be an implicit assumption: "Why bother? It's a foreign idea. It has no relevance to our current world."

Another small group of Christian leaders is saying the opposite. These scholars, ministers, worship leaders, and laypersons are rediscovering the biblical and ancient way of worship, the way of the Word and the table. Eleanor Kreider is one of these scholars who stands against the popular trends and calls us to return to Bible-driven worship.

Kreider's discussion of table worship in the early church is a solid contribution to the recovery of historic worship in our time. She has taken the fruit of current scholarship on communion and expressed it in the language of the people. Her work is particularly enlightening because she shows us both the biblical and the Greek roots of the early-Christian common meal. Obviously, any worship change that we make in our table worship must be informed by the biblical and early-Christian practice.

Her insights into the history of worship are equally helpful. Historical studies have a way of opening new windows and providing a connection with the past. Because the past is the road that leads into the future, we dare not move into the future without a critical assessment of where our worship came from and how it took on its present shape.

Having set the stage for our contemporary study of communion, Kreider shifts the focus of the book to the modern practice of communion. Her treatment of the meaning of communion through a study of its images is a delight. She refuses to follow the approach that insists "we are a breaking-of-the-bread church," or "we are a Eucharist church," or "we are a Lord's Supper church," or "we are a communion church." Instead, she leads us into a compelling study of the fullness of table worship that draws on the variety of images in the New Testament.

Kreider's openness to the fullness of table worship lays the groundwork

7

for the most creative and profound aspect of the book – how communion shapes character. Her emphasis is reminiscent of a Latin maxim that has been applied to the early church: *lex orandi lex credendi est* (the rule of prayer is the rule of faith). Prayer shapes character and affirms faith. Kreider recaptures this ancient insight for us and opens us up to a whole new (or old!) way of seeing communion.

It was a treat for me to read *Given for you*. I found it to be a work that roots our understanding in Scripture, a writing keenly aware of historical development, and a valuable guide to contemporary practice.

Don't just read this book. Devour it! Read it again and again. It sets us back on the right track and sends us into the future on the same road that connects us to the past.

Robert Webber
Professor of Theology, Wheaton College
Director, Institute for Worship Studies

Preface

FOR YEARS I stood back from communion. Along with many others from my church, I was awed by the sober solemnity of the service. Its infrequency had a double effect. If one had the flu in November and missed communion, it was necessary to wait until spring for the next one. During all those weeks, it was easy to forget about it altogether. But then on spring communion Sunday, everyone approached the service with extreme care and preparation. It was obviously important, yet my understandings, even as a young adult, were childlike, more reactive attitudes than positive convictions. I was puzzled by communion but not really engaged with it.

For a long time, in fact, I actively resisted thinking about communion. Didn't we have enough problems in the Christian churches, enough disagreements and dilemmas for our own times? Why take on the conflicts and debates of former generations? Who wants to refight centuries-old doctrinal battles? Fenced tables, excommunication, transubstantiation, the ban – all those words tasted bad.

But gradually I changed. Something drew me to communion, to the focus of Christ's love and presence among those who regularly and often gathered at his table. Christians I knew – Anglicans, Reformed, Baptists, Brethren, and more – were experiencing the grace and energy of the Spirit flowing through more frequent communion. I was drawn to the Lord's table. Through my own deeper experience of communion, I became willing to consider it more closely. This book charts my path of discoveries.

Several kinds of questions became urgent for me. I wanted to understand the basics of the communion controversies that plague the church and the backgrounds to the practices that drive Christians apart. I needed to learn some history.

I wanted to think theologically about communion, and to grasp more of its meanings. I needed to study more carefully the Bible's themes of redemption, atonement, justice, sacrifice, and healing – all of which focus on the table.

I wanted to imagine how churches might "do" communion, so it could become a living sign of God's reign, a magnet of God's love, and an engine for God's mission. I needed to observe other Christians and find practical ways to enrich communion observance.

I don't try to reinvent communion. The Christian church as a whole has preserved the service as its most precious treasure and tradition. But in this book I do want gently to remind us who have forgotten or sidelined communion. I want to nudge us back toward the table. I want to help us to listen to the Lord's welcome and to respond to the love, healing, and joy of his table fellowship. The eucharist is Christ's gift to the church. Let's open our hearts to receive it anew.

In this journey toward deeper communion I particularly acknowledge Alan, my companion in rediscovery. How many hours we have walked and talked about these things! I owe much to my North American Mennonite home congregations, even though they are so far away from my current arena of ministry. The memories and the values lie deeply grounded. I mention the Wood Green Mennonite Church (London), the Post Green Community (Dorset), and the Communaut, de Grandchamp (Switzerland) as places of special focus for my eucharistic experience and learning. In communion the Lord meets his communities, and it is especially in communities that I have grown.

I pray this book will help us toward a fresh look at communion. As we lay aside prejudices and distortions, may we allow this rich service of thanksgiving to reclaim its place at the heart of our worship.

Eleanor Kreider
Oxford, England

Introduction

FROM EARLIEST times, Christians worshiped God through Word and meal. Soon a two-part form emerged, made up of a service of the Word and a service of the table. Sunday worship focused on all aspects of the church's life – its teaching, its prayers, its economic sharing, its nurture, and its disciplines of thanksgiving and praise. Through Word and meal, Christians retold the great story of creation and redemption, they communed with their Lord (crucified and risen), and they looked for his coming again.

But today the worship of many Christians has a different focus. To answer the question "Is a communion service central to your church's worship?" many would say, "Central? Not particularly. We do observe it, of course. After all, the Lord commanded it. But no, it's not the primary focus for our church's worship or its spiritual and practical life."

Across the centuries many factors account for significant changes in the perception and practice of communion. Pulled apart from its material reality, communion in some places has become a personal devotional exercise. Such "spiritualized" communion might be a reaction against a perceived "super-sacramentalism" in which everything depends on the physical bread and wine. Yet a highly charged, individualist piety may grow out of the opposite – a sacramental perception of Christ's action and presence in the eucharistic bread and wine. At its worst, an undue focus on personal feelings has, for some people, reduced communion to a purely emotional experience. We might say that it becomes overly subjective.

But distortions have also come about through an overly objective approach. Some conceive the eucharist as a liturgical rite conveying grace to individuals as a result of a "qualified" person "validly" saying certain words over "the elements." This has placed too much emphasis on objective features, including valid office, verbal formulas, and the physical substances of bread and wine.

During the eighteenth century, many Western Christians, steeped in a rationalist worldview, reduced communion to a pious exercise which might encourage participants, in light of what Christ had gone through, to try harder to be good. For them it had become merely a mental and moral exercise.

11

Churches continue to struggle with this legacy. When we consider these distortions, we are tempted to have strong reactions and narrowed perspectives. It is easy to react to a reaction. Maybe we escape into personal experience or emotional feelings. Or we revere the bread and wine, taking no account of the community around us. Or we stop going to communion altogether, considering it optional or even irrelevant. In so many ways we can miss the mark and debase communion. We need a broader perspective.

Communion piety has often expressed an interplay between mystical and sacramental understandings. It has also expressed and shaped Christians' understandings of the church, and of Christ's relationship to his people.

What is communion for, anyway? As a gift of worship, communion brings glory to God. It is Christ's gift to the church, so that through it the great story of incarnation and salvation may be told and retold. God, Creator and Redeemer, reaches into history in loving presence, healing, restoring, and energizing. The Lord's table is for us a place of focus, a place of meeting, a place of communication. Here, where individuals and communities grasp a cruciform vision for true life, the glory of God shines through. The cross of Christ casts its shadow and its light across the table, alternately darkening and illuminating the way.

Most of us don't use that kind of language. It sounds high-flown! Sunday after Sunday, not thinking too much about why, we just go to church. Better buildings, better musicians, and better children's programs attract more people to attend. A plethora of how-to books and evangelistic schemes urge our churches toward numerical growth. Some grow bigger. Some flourish.

But what visible difference does all the churchgoing make in the quality of a community's life or in the Christian character of its members? New Christians, like old Christians, live so much like everyone else. All too often they are superficially hospitable, secretive about financial giving, more willing to gossip than to pursue truth in a loving way, careless about inequities, and undisciplined in prayer. These are marks of an immature church.

The thesis of this book is that full-orbed Christian worship, Sunday upon Sunday, uniting the services of the Word and of the Lord's Supper, has a life-giving, maturing effect on our churches, not least on their visible character. This is a book about community character-building, not as an aim in itself but as a by-product of true worship. Worship does not need to get stuck in a sanctuary; throughout the week its energy can be set free to transform and shape our everyday lives.

Churches will be renewed when the Lord's Supper, graced by God's presence and Word, oriented to the living Lord and empowered by the

Spirit, is fully restored to the place it had in the early centuries – as the central communal Christian act of worship.

As gifts of grace from Jesus Christ, the marks of his character will imprint themselves on the Christian community. Everyone looking at our corporate life will recognize his love, graciousness, mercy, courage, faithfulness, dedication to the Father's will, and self-giving humility. For us, just as for Peter and John, it will happen: observers "recognized them as companions of Jesus" (Acts 4:13).

How have communion practices over the centuries shaped Christian communities? Have they made a difference, either for good or ill, in how Christians have understood and celebrated communion? Yes, sometimes communion practices have shaped a crosslike character; other times they have had perverse and contradictory consequences. As we will explore, there are historical questions to consider.

What actually happens in communion? What does it mean? There are many biblical themes the table can bring into focus. The cross of Christ is central to these themes. As the church explores and prays through a wider range of biblical material in the context of the meal, the meaning and way of the cross become clearer.

The temptation is to look only at our own perceptions, our own actions, and our own experience. We thankfully remember the Lord, we signify our bond with one another, we reenact the Lord's meal, we experience his presence, we place ourselves in solidarity with other Christians, and we glimpse the future. All of these are commendable activities. But there is more to communion than this. Big questions remain: What is the Spirit's part? What is God longing to do? Is communion with Christ more than warm feelings? There are theological questions to consider.

How can churches enrich their communion celebrations? Are there practical ways of honoring and yet enriching eucharistic tradition so that the Lord is freed to enter in and shape the church's character? Can we develop our rites, prayers, settings, and songs so a lively and dynamic communion shapes the character of the church? There are practical questions to consider.

My intention is that, dealing with these questions – historical, theological, and practical – I will point in a positive and hopeful direction. That trajectory I chart in the book's final section. Through our worship at the Lord's table, let us allow God to shape the character of our churches so we enter into the gift of Christian unity and go out with joy into the task of Christian mission.

COMMUNION ACROSS
THE CENTURIES

1

Last Supper
to Church Supper

IN SIMPLEST TERMS, communion is the celebration of a joyful community gathered around a table, remembering and meeting its Lord, who is both host and guest. As we explore layers of significance, we will always come back to these powerful symbols – the shared meal and the common table. A community chooses its symbols and develops its rites. The rites, in turn, shape the character of the community.

Christians in all places and in all times have believed that their communion service is based on events and words at a particular table on a particular evening in Jesus' life. The Gospels recount details vivid in the memory of those friends of Jesus who were present at that unforgettable meal.

We can almost see the action. The gestures are familiar. Leonardo da Vinci's painting flickers on our memory monitor. Jesus and his friends, around a table, are celebrating a Jewish festival, with its typical foods and prescribed prayers. But Jesus adds strange words to the familiar blessings. He seems to have a foreboding of his own death. Jesus' friends glance at one another, bewildered and alarmed. Judas abruptly goes out, apparently to distribute alms for the poor. They sing psalms together and follow Jesus into the night.

Last Supper – Prototype for the Church's Supper?

The Last Supper is the meal table which people usually consider as the model for their church's Sunday communion service. It's the "mother of all tables." But consider – how similar to that Last Supper is a typical Sunday communion? Which of these features of the historical Last Supper correspond?

A domestic setting? An evening meal-hour? A dozen people? A real meal, with proper courses of food? A worrying disruption as a trusted member abruptly departs? A foreboding mood? Brief, puzzling sayings ascribed to Jesus, along with certain gestures? Prescribed questions and answers, story and song woven into an ancient ceremony? Psalm-singing?

If I were asked to describe a modern communion service to a non-Christian inquirer, I would choose virtually none of those qualities and

17

actions of the Last Supper. Only the few words and gestures of Jesus himself, in blessing the bread and cup, persist to link us to that Last Supper in the upper room. But those precise words and gestures are indispensable, central to Christian communion services.

In spite of many differences in their ritual, all Christian traditions have this in common: they repeat the institution narrative, the biblical words which retell the heart of the Last Supper story. Besides these words in common, most churches also agree at one other but negative point. The service, though it might be called the Lord's Supper, has little resemblance to a real meal.

Early Christians Ate Together and Gave Thanks

In the Last Supper accounts, Jesus said, "Do this" (Luke 22:19; 1 Cor. 11:24-25). The New Testament indicates that his followers obeyed. But we might ask, What did they really do? Did they disperse in domestic groups of a dozen to perform (once a year) the ceremonies of the Jewish Passover? Did they repeat those baffling blessing-words of Jesus over bread and wine? Did they relive the sorrow, dread, betrayal, and fear of that terrible Friday night?

Whatever else they did, they ate together. New Testament accounts give us clues as to how the first generations of Christians assembled. They met in homes and shared meals. They just continued doing what they had done when Jesus was with them.

In Acts we read of the early Jesus-community growing in numbers and developing distinctive ways of worshiping. They met frequently for meals in their homes, they prayed, they shared their goods (Acts 2). They searched the Scriptures to understand more fully who Jesus the Messiah was, and to figure out what they should do in light of his life, teaching, death, and resurrection. It was an exciting time.

These Christian meals were not patterned on an annual Passover feast, although Jewish Christians continued to observe Passover as well. Frequently eating together simply continued a way of being together so familiar from Jesus' days with his disciples. They called it "breaking bread," the typical Jewish designation of shared meals, similar to an Irish idiom for everyday meals, "taking potatoes."

Breaking bread before every meal, the Jewish host began the meal in a ritualized form: "Blessed be God, our Lord, King of the Universe, who brings forth bread from the earth." Saying the blessing, breaking and sharing the bread – both set a tone of thanksgiving and conviviality, two marked features of early Christian assemblies.

Remembering Jesus, the Life of the Party

There can be no doubt that the disciples treasured memories and retold anecdotes of their days and months in Jesus' company. In Luke 8 we read of generous friends' donations for Jesus and his roving band. He so often taught them after a shared meal, in their own homes, out in the open, or sometimes in the homes of other hosts – rich ones, powerful ones, even despised ones. In fact, critics scoffed at Jesus as one who enjoyed too much the delights of the table. He loved to tell stories about feasts and banquets, hosts and guests. Maligned as a man too much given to the delights of food and drink, Jesus at table evoked potent memories.

Jesus practiced the roles both of host and guest at meals. In both he surprised and sometimes scandalized people. He accepted invitations from sinners. He generously provided for the poor. And always he pushed at the boundaries. "Invite those who can't invite you back." "East and West will sit at the table in the kingdom." He challenged Jewish purity laws surrounding eating and drinking. "What comes out of the mouth proceeds from the heart, and this is what defiles" (Luke 14:12; Matt. 8:11; 15:18).

Watching and listening to Jesus at table, people had glimpsed the heart of God. Through eating with others and through his stories of feasts and banquets, Jesus showed God's mercy toward all humans. "God is not a respecter of persons," Jesus said. God invites all to the great banquet. Yet people come by their own volition, without coercion. Jesus stretched their imagination, jolted their hearts. He was their immensely attractive, yet maddeningly difficult rabbi.

Life in Common

How could they not remember him when they met for a shared meal? On the simplest level of meal fellowship, in obeying his "Do this," they fulfilled what Jesus most desired. He had gathered around him and nurtured a small community. He wanted them to continue their common life, sharing their provisions as they shared their common destiny as his followers. The common meal was primary to their common life, both physically and symbolically. They met in their homes to "break bread" together, and they shared their food with joy and generosity (Acts 2:46).

More Than a Memory – Jesus Was Truly Present

Among the meal memories of Jesus' disciples, surely the most potent were those of his unpredictable comings and goings at their post-resurrection common meals. However strong their emotions of disbelief, amazement, or unalloyed joy, the disciples' consistent witness was that Jesus himself was there. From the very earliest times, when Christians gathered to "do this in remembrance," they were confident that the risen Christ, more than a memory, was truly with them.

For many of us, the presence of Christ at communion is too often a matter of dogma or of conflicting opinions. We may hesitate simply to anticipate and to delight in communion without having to explain it in rational detail. But if we follow our earliest Christian brothers and sister, we will embrace the unabashed joy and cleansing release of Jesus' encounter with us at his table. Jesus' words "Do this" are not so much command as invitation to his friendship and to vulnerable fellowship at his table. As we come to his table again and again, we learn to bring more of ourselves, to receive more of him, to experience the deeply joyful solidarity with others at the Lord's table with us.

It may be hard to do this. But if we can read this story proceeding forward, from the Last Supper through the post-resurrection meals and the common meals of the early Christians, we can see that Jesus' "Do this" carried a simple invitation: "My disciples, continue to enjoy *eating together,* continue to *bless God* and *share your food.* And especially *remember me, your Master.* Remember my life, my teaching, my compassion, my conflicts, my faithfulness to the Father's will, my love for you." With that message the disciples remembered Jesus' promise to be with them "always, to the end of the age." He would be with them at table, and he would be with them as they went out, carrying on the Lord's discipling mission (Matt. 28:19).

Real Meals – But a Variety of Traditions

Early Christian worship meals were real meals. Like the Passover meal in the upper room, like the picnics and banquets Jesus had eaten with his friends and his disparagers, these were face-to-face intimate occasions. Often they must have been like family reunions.

When we look more closely at these common meals and at the varied Gospel accounts, we realize there were actually a number of meal traditions. If we hope to find a prototype Lord's Supper, a true original, with one "correct" form of words and actions, we will be disappointed.[1] Various Christian communities faced particular struggles. These the emphases of the separate Gospels clearly reveal. Some of the emphases are discipleship, covenant, service, humility, economic justice, and care for the poor and weak.

If each Gospel carried a distinctive focus on the story and meaning of Jesus, then it is likely that each presentation of the Lord's Supper revealed a particular angle on the struggles, values, and aspirations of each community's experience.[2]

God's Love Shines Through

The fact that they nicknamed their shared meals "agape" reveals that these earliest Christians put into practice Jesus' invitation to "love one another as I have loved you." Their common meals became practical expressions of love. It was at these meals that they made the daily distribution of the necessities of life. In this everyday mutual help, at the meals shared "first in one home, then another," they undoubtedly experienced a powerful bond, both spiritual and material. More meaningful than a mere food line, the agape meals expressed God's love among them (Jude 12; John 15:12; Acts 6:11ff.; 2:46).

Contempt for the Church

But things did not always turn out well. Paul gives a vivid vignette of the agape gone terribly wrong. In the church at Corinth there was trouble at the Lord's table. Paul heard rumors about it and was incensed. There are hardly sharper words in the whole New Testament than in Paul's rebuke. The Corinthian Christians' worship is "not for the better but for the worse ... It is not ... the Lord's supper" (1 Cor. 11:17, 20). Their worship was a travesty, doing more harm than good. What on earth was going on?

In a plausible reconstruction, it would seem the fellowship meal, to which people brought baskets of food to share, had become a two-tier social event. The richer folk, perhaps having visited the baths, arrived in the early evening. They went ahead with their eating and drinking. They did not wait for the working people, some of whom were probably slaves. By the time the later ones came, there was little to eat. All the best places in the dining room were occupied. They had to remain out in the courtyard.[3] Paul calls this impatient behavior of the rich "contempt for the church of God" and "humiliation" of the poor. It was a complete repudiation of the Lord in whose name they met.

Just as there was trouble at the church's table, so Paul finds a solution at the true table of the Lord. Jesus had spoken and acted out a parable about his life-giving love, broken and poured out like bread and wine. In the story (the tradition) of Jesus at table, as well as in that tradition's deep history, rooted in Passover, the Corinthians could find the inner dynamic for keeping Jesus' true memory alive in their community. This is what Paul means when he reminds them of Jesus' words, "Do this to remember me." In meal-practice true to his story and character, they would authentically "*do*" the memory of Jesus.

Paul states that in "doing" the memory of Christ, they should discern the body (1 Cor. 11:29). He isn't drawing their attention to the bread on the table. In using this, his favorite metaphor of the church as the body of Christ, Paul is reminding them that "just as the body has many members, and the members, though many, are one body, so it is with Christ" (1 Cor. 12:12). Paul is calling the Corinthian Christians to be aware of each other's needs, and take responsibility in caring for each other. He is saying a lot more than "Be nice to each other." He means that they should consider the mystery of their relationships in Christ, see what is going on, perceive the meaning of their actions, and catch the implications of their behavior. This is what discerning the body means.

Paul gives a practical suggestion to the early comers: "If you think you'll get too hungry, have a snack at home before you set out for the meeting. But then wait to begin the fellowship meal until all have arrived"

(1 Cor. 11:20-22). In a number of early Christian writings, this point appears – the character of the church is corporate. Being church means being gathered together. That is what their name for church meant: *ekklesia*, the assembly. This was a completely different thing from going to the baths or shopping in the market. All the members of the church must gather together, and then the worship could begin.

Contempt for the church and the humiliation of the poor shown by the richer Corinthian members – these described precisely the "unworthy manner" of partaking which Paul deplores in verse 27. Applying it simply to their own inward piety, many sensitive Christians have suffered guilty worries about whether or not to take communion.

While honoring the impulse to come to the table aware of our status as forgiven sinners, we must see that this particular passage has another focus. The unworthy manner is adverbial – that is, it points to the actions of eating and drinking at the Lord's table. It refers to the actions of the whole community celebrating the Lord's Supper. It is plural. Paul refers to the whole community's action. "Examine yourselves," "discern the body," says Paul. Celebrate the Lord's Supper in a manner worthy of the Lord. Honor each other, wait till you are all present, share your food and drink generously. The Lord is at the head of his table (1 Cor. 11:27-29).

If you, all of you together, don't "discern the body," if you refuse to celebrate the Lord's table in a worthy manner, says Paul, inherent consequences will unfold. You will "eat and drink judgment against" yourselves. And because of your injustice, "many of you are weak and ill, and some have died" (1 Cor. 11:30).

Hermas, a Christian prophet at Rome in the early second century, also perceived the connection between justice-making and the health of members of a Christian community. Refusing to share could have dire consequences for both the richer and the poorer members.

Some, he observed with dismay, "are inducing illness in their flesh and injuring their flesh from eating too much. And the flesh of others who do not have food is being injured because of insufficient food. Their body is being destroyed."[4]

Let us imagine. If Paul had had reason to commend the Corinthian church about their celebration of the Lord's Supper, what might he have said? What would have been good qualities of their fellowship with its memorial rituals? Surely the hallmark would have been above all that the presence of Jesus, the Just One, was honored. The generosity of their sharing would have reflected the mercy and kindness of God. In taking bread and wine at the Lord's table, they would have known his true presence. Central and celebrated would have been the God who shows favor to all alike, who never coerces, but invites. The discerning body of believers would have made right their relationships and shared gladly whatever resources they had, spiritual and material alike.

Paul could have rephrased his words in the previous chapter, in 1 Corinthians 10:16-17, to form a resounding conclusion to his compliment to the Corinthian community: "The cup of blessing which you bless is truly a sharing in the blood of Christ. The bread that you break is truly a sharing in the body of Christ. You are one, because you partake of the one bread. It is truly the Lord's Supper that you celebrate!"

Out of this powerful and cautionary story, we can draw positive values. Ensuring economic justice within the church and practicing generosity which is both spiritual and physical – these are ways in which we can truly honor Jesus' memory in our communion services. And they are ways in which we can draw on the ancient Hebrew memory of the Passover as a feast of justice and liberation.

We could summarize all of this in the New Testament Greek words which stand as names for the early Christians' common meals of breaking bread, remembering and celebrating their life in the Messiah Jesus. Several of these Greek words have given Christians the titles for the churches' communion meals.

Eucharistein: giving thanks – the eucharist.

Koinonia: sharing of life and goods – (Latin: *communio*) – communion.

Agape: God's love put into practical human loving – love feast.

Anamnesis: remembering Jesus – is the word for that part of the thanksgiving prayer at the eucharist in which the church recalls Jesus and his redemptive acts, not only in the past but as a reality brought alive in the present moment of celebration.

Lord's Table to Church's Table

How far we have come from the meal table services of the early communities! Is our "Lord's table" a contradiction or at least a misnomer? The church's table might be a more exact name. Who has access to this table? Who serves as host, and what does that role symbolize? Wrestling with these questions, early Christians' sharp focus on Jesus with his friends around a common table has gone fuzzy. Food has become minimal and its meaning spiritualized. Eyes are either spiritually turned inward or riveted on the stylized gestures of the one presiding. Specific words, particular patterns of doing things, and the proper credentials of the ministers have become the measures of what make a service valid. Our communion practice needs renewal.

Renewal of communion requires willingness to try new ways, to risk getting it wrong, to allow a variety of practice. But it doesn't necessarily mean throwing out older ways, even if they seem weak or worn thin. I hope the emphasis in this book will encourage communion practice which comes ever closer to the real meal and the common table of Christian community. The mystery which sets the Lord's table apart is that it is a common table of humanity, but transformed through acted memory by Christ's own presence and love.

If churches reclaim real meals as the setting for communion services, if they replace (or supplement) the ceremonial table with the dining table, surprising things might happen. The enormous symbolic power in the table, with its rituals of hospitality, conviviality, blessing, and shared food might once again enable congregations corporately and radically to imitate Christ and to be more attractively recognized as his very own people.

What might happen if churches tried to restore some of the ethos and spiritual qualities as well as economic practicalities of the early Christian communities? Communion services could be marked by joyful thanksgiving, by an unaffected simplicity of domestic relaxedness, by open and generous hospitality.

The underlying struggles of our churches are not so different from those of the early Christian communities. They also tended to ignore economic divisions. They also had to experiment with means of sharing. They also had to learn what it meant properly to remember Jesus, their Host at their common meals. Through our deepening experience of communion at the Lord's table we, both as individuals and as congregations, can increasingly become conformed to Jesus' own character, to become more and more like him in our corporate life. As we joyfully meet him at the table, we may find that we receive in the breaking of bread more than we even knew to hope for. Thanking, enjoying, confessing, praying, sharing – in all these qualities of life together, we will receive the hallmarks of the Lord's character upon us.

2

Jewish Blessings and Roman Banquets

EARLY CHRISTIANS forged unique forms and meanings for their worship through combining aspects of Jewish piety and religious forms with adaptations of Greco-Roman traditions. They worked creatively within the tensions and challenges of their missionary times to create distinctive and appropriate rituals. Christian communities today can in similar ways use inherited worship traditions creatively to develop within our common life joyous, vigorous, and flexible rituals appropriate to our own missionary times.

Jewish Blessing – the Background to Christian Eucharist

A great stream of praise flowed through the prayers of the early Christian memorial meals. That stream was Jewish thanksgiving, the habits and formulations of benediction that framed Jewish meals. When we remember that Christian fellowship meals had origins in Jewish meal rituals (especially the Passover meal), we can discover something about the ritual and the actual prayer forms employed. These prayers reflect a sense of deep dependence and thankfulness to God, who provided for all needs, physical and spiritual.

There was a Jewish benediction, a *berakah* (*berakot*, plural), for almost every moment and action of the day. A berakah, and a benediction called a *hodayah*, were important prayer forms in Jewish worship. A berakah included a call to praise, a declaration of motive for that praise, and an acknowledgment of God's benevolence. What God had done was expressed indirectly, as in "Blessed be God, who has delivered you ..." A hodayah was distinctive in its address to God, as in the doxology, "O Lord, my God, I will give thanks to you forever."

Other Jewish prayers did not address God, but simply launched into a recital of God's mighty deeds.[1] Everything Jewish people did called them to remember and thank God. They would not think of eating or drinking without first saying the appropriate grace or benediction. This was truly a discipline for thankfulness. Jewish prayer interweaves these various forms throughout Old Testament narratives and in the Psalms, for example in Psalm 31:21-24.

Blessed be the Lord,
>for he has wondrously shown his steadfast love to me
>when I was beset as a city under siege ...
You heard my supplications when I cried out to you for help.
Love the Lord, all you his saints ...

Be strong, and let your heart take courage,
>all you who wait for the Lord.

Jesus' words recorded in Luke 10:21-22 show the typical shape and tone of Jewish prayer, which uses direct address to God.

I thank you, Father, Lord of heaven and earth, because you have hidden these things from the wise and the intelligent and have revealed them to infants; yes, Father, for such was your gracious will.

Throughout the New Testament are many references to the impulse of the berakah and the hodayah. Jesus blessed the children (Mark 10:16). Though we don't know the precise words, we can imagine he might have prayed what we call the "Aaronic blessing."

>The Lord bless you and keep you;
>the Lord make his face to shine upon you,
>>and be gracious to you;
>the Lord lift up his countenance upon you,
>>and give you peace.

(Num. 6:24-26)

Jewish prayer piety shines through the New Testament epistles. "Whatever you do, ... do everything in the name of the Lord Jesus, giving thanks to God the Father through him" (Col. 3:17). The best-known Jewish thanksgiving of all is surely the Last Supper benediction of Jesus, "when he had given thanks" over the bread and the cup.

The Jewish tradition behind earliest Christian memorial fellowship meals was one which emphasized praise and thanksgiving. Every action, every moment of the day, was related to the gracious God who protected and provided for the dependent community.

How Jesus Said Grace at the Last Supper

It is possible that the command "Do this" had a more specific meaning than that the disciples should continue holding fellowship meals. One scholar argues[2] that Jesus' command refers to the Jewish rite of breaking bread, that is, the rite of grace at table. A characteristic grace or blessing ran like this: "Praised be thou, O Lord, our God, King of the world, who causes bread to come forth from the earth." But why would Jesus need to instruct the disciples to repeat the customary blessing?

He might have meant a special grace by which the table fellowship of the messianic community was established, which extolled the salvation of God and prayed for its consummation. Doesn't that sound like an echo of the Lord's Prayer? Such a grace at the breaking of bread, spoken by Jesus himself, would have burned into the disciples' memory. We're told that the Emmaus disciples recognized Jesus "in the breaking of bread," in his taking up and blessing the bread at the beginning of a meal. Isn't it possible, even likely, that Jesus had his own way of saying the table grace, unique and unmistakable?

The Gospel accounts of the Last Supper clearly describe Jesus' blessing actions with the bread at the beginning of the meal. There are three verbs: he took, he blessed, he broke. In the literature of the rabbis, these verbs are technical terms for the prayers of grace at table. At the Passover meal, this grace preceded the main course. Prior to the main course, there was the preliminary "appetizer" course with its symbolic foods and Passover liturgy.

Let us imagine the ritual at the Last Supper. Rising from his reclining position, Jesus, as host, sat to pick up the bread and recite the traditional blessing.

> Blessed be God, our Lord, King of the Universe,
> Who brings forth bread from the earth.

Perhaps this form, the one for daily use, had some special addition for the Passover feast. And it is probable, according to Jeremias,[3] that Jesus gave this blessing a special twist of his own. He may have had a distinctive way of holding the bread or of tilting his face. He may have used an additional phrase or a particularly characteristic emphasis.

As the host at the Last Supper, Jesus recited the blessing and everyone said, "Amen." Then, tearing off a piece at least the size of an olive for each participant, he distributed the bread. The fragments passed from hand to hand all the way to the ones most distant. When they had all received, he tore off a piece for himself, and they all ate at once. Normally this process of passing was done in silence, but we read that "he ... gave it to them and said, Take; this is my body" (Mark 14:22). How those words must have surprised the disciples! They were puzzling words, breaking into an accustomed silence.

After the supper (the main meal) came the traditional blessing of a ceremonial cup. Jesus, host at the Last Supper, sat up, took the cup of watered-down wine, and said,

Let us praise the Lord our God,
to whom belongs that of which we have partaken.

The disciples replied,

Praised be our God for the food we have eaten.

Then Jesus held the cup (the cup of blessing, 1 Cor. 10:16) a hand's breadth above the table and with his eyes on the cup spoke the formal grace for the Passover meal in the name of them all.

Blessed art thou, O Lord, our God, King of the Universe, who feedest the whole world with goodness, with grace and with mercy.
We thank thee that we have inherited a goodly and pleasant land.
Have mercy, O Lord, our God, on Israel, thy people, and on Jerusalem, thy city, and upon Zion, the dwelling place of thy glory, and upon thy altar and upon thy temple. Blessed art thou, O Lord, thou who buildest Jerusalem.[4]

After the disciples' "Amen," the cup went silently from hand to hand. "And all of them drank from it." Into the accustomed silence, Jesus spoke baffling words: "This is my blood of the new covenant, which is poured out for many" (Mark 14:23-24).

It Was Passover Time

Even though there was a sense of foreboding at Jesus' Last Supper, the underlying meaning of the meal was that of a Passover, one deeply ingrained in Jewish tradition. At its heart the Passover feast celebrated the covenant between God and his people.[5] God graciously, as a gift, liberated them from oppression. God fed them in the wilderness and gave them the law, Torah. God would be faithful to them, and they were to be faithful to God.

People were to observe the Passover feast not in honor of a remote event but as if they themselves had just been freed from slavery. The ceremonies and celebrations of the Passover feast (Seder) symbolized and dramatized events of God's gracious and miraculous deliverance from oppression. Every year the Jewish people appropriated anew, for themselves personally, the meaning of Passover.

In biblical times Psalms 113 to 118 (the Hallel Psalms) were closely associated with the Passover feast. Some were sung before and some after the meal itself. The verse "When they had sung the hymn, they went out to the Mount of Olives" (Mark 14:26) probably refers to the second part of the Hallel, Psalm 115-118.[6] According to its institution and as in all liturgical remembering, Passover celebration looks to the future.

This day shall be a day of remembrance for you. You shall celebrate it as a festival to the Lord; throughout your generations you shall observe it as a perpetual ordinance (Exod. 12:14).

Praise for God's deliverance from slavery in the past was joined to the prophetic yearning for messianic redemption and the establishing of God's reign. Jesus himself renewed Passover intent, because in him dawned the new age of Messiah. Later in this book we will look at themes of covenant, messianic age, and banquet of the kingdom.

Last Supper Was Rooted in Jewish Festival Traditions

So we see that the Lord's Supper roots firmly in Jewish piety, prayer forms, and festival tradition. Thanksgiving and praise for God's creation and continuing gracious intervention on behalf of his people are the keynotes. It is no surprise that the disciples' memorial meals took on a tone of thankful jubilation when, after Jesus' resurrection reunions, they continued to celebrate the true beginning of the new messianic age.

Through the Christian centuries, unfortunately, another mood eclipsed praise-filled thanksgiving. Somber focus on Christ's suffering and death replaced celebration for cosmic redemption. It is entirely right that we should pay close attention to the enigmatic bread and cup words of Jesus: "This is my body ... This is my blood." But nothing should obscure the overarching emphasis of truly thankful prayers that express joy in God's salvation, in the advent of God's reign.

Though the Christian fellowship meal first grew out of Jewish precedents, there is also another context for these meals – the conventions of festive and ceremonial banquets in the Roman culture.

Roman Festive Banquets

As the Christian faith spread out over the Roman Empire, it became less noticeably Jewish in its forms and manners. An important point of contact with Greco-Roman conventions was the Roman festive banquet. Just as we know the protocol for a ceremonial dinner in our own time – invitations, proper dress, formal settings of table, master of ceremonies, tasteless jokes, sequence of toasts – so first-century people knew what to expect at a formal banquet.

The festive banquet was a flexible form, eminently adaptable to all kinds of social groups. These might be celebratory family meals, funeral feasts, dinners of philosophical clubs or of trade guilds. Jewish and Christian assemblies organized their religious meals along similar lines, adjusting details as necessary.

What were these Roman meals like? How did the Christians adapt the pattern? A private home was the usual venue for a banquet, though a public building such as a temple complex also provided banqueting rooms. The dining room would be specially decorated and carefully furnished because this was the room where guests were received and the host's hospitality judged.

All banquets had common features. For example, invitations were sent out. Guests reclined in twos on couches (people were ranked around the room according to social status). Servants washed the feet of the guests before the meal. The meal itself consisted of two main sections or courses. The first course (*deipnon*) was the main meal, called the supper or banquet. After a linking ritual the second course (*symposion*), known as the drinking party, began.

Sometimes a preliminary course preceded the main meal. Special rituals marked off the end of the first course. Servants removed the tables and brought in a large bowl for mixing wine with water (one part wine to three, four, or five parts water).

Libations to the gods or other religious ceremonies marked the beginning of the second main section of the banquet. At festive Jewish meals, there was a ceremonial cup at this point (the cup of blessing), with its distinctive benediction.

The rest of the evening of a Roman banquet was for leisurely drinking of wine during discussion or entertainments. We can imagine a variety of Roman banquets, held by various clubs and societies. Sipping wine, philosophers carried on sophisticated conversation at their symposiums. Rich citizens showed off important guests to their business partners. Societies devoted to carnal pleasures reveled and drank according to the well-deserved stereotype of Roman excess. Family gossip and teasing banter was in order at wedding or birthday feasts.

Roman Banquet Tradition in New Testament Stories

In many New Testament accounts, we can easily recognize many features of this common meal tradition. Paul mentions that some Christians took meals at a temple (1 Cor. 8:10), obviously a local public building hired out for special occasions. The upper room where Jesus and his disciples held their last meal together was equipped with couches and vessels for washing feet.

We recall the convention of two courses at a banquet in the words "after supper [the first course] he took the cup" (1 Cor. 11:25). One of the disciples, the one sharing the two-person couch, "was lying close to the breast of Jesus" (John 13:23). Gospel stories of Jesus at festive meals indicate that he taught and discussed religious matters with host and guests (the symposium). Invitations to a great wedding banquet figured centrally in Jesus' parable (Matt. 22:1-14).

Social Codes, Etiquette, and Ranking

But we can go deeper than the externals of banquet practices. These meals revealed social codes and patterns of social relations. Shared meals created social ties and obligations. Common meals provided a place to display social rank. Jesus' advice to guests reminded them of the humiliation in store for anyone assuming too high a place at the table. It was much better to choose a lower-ranked couch and be invited by the host to a more honorable one.

For many societies and clubs, the chief and sometimes the only common activity was a shared meal. The banquet in a private home or hired room defined the boundary for the group. Friendship was especially associated with such occasions. Jesus was called "a friend" of tax collectors and sinners because he ate with them. To pious Jews, Jesus' behavior was scandalous; he defied proper social boundaries.

Social etiquette associated with the banquet was more than polite words and gestures. Etiquette was a category of social ethics, along with friendship, pleasure, and love. These were not just codes for individuals but indicated what would further the aims of the group as a whole. Harmony and good cheer were important. This puts Paul's concern for good order and peace in Christian assemblies into a social context. People should wait their turn to speak. They should behave in ways that edify the group (1 Cor. 11:17-34; 14:26-33).

Social ranking was ever-present in Greco-Roman times. It was especially evident at banquets, where positions on the couches went from high to low, right around the room. Reclining at a table was in itself a mark of high rank. Traditionally, banquets were only for free citizens (men) and excluded women, children, and slaves, although in late antiquity women began to be included as reclining guests at pagan Roman banquets.[7]

Social ranking was always in tension with social bonding, a strong feature of banquets. A shared meal tended to minimize social differences. However, even in the most ideologically equal groups, there remained vestiges of social ranking (such as paying special honor to an elderly person or a guest).

Christians Adapted the Roman Banquet for Agape Meals

Having looked at the forms and the social meanings of the festive meal for many kinds of associations and clubs, we should not be surprised that early Christians also had their own forms of banquets. Understanding the forms and ideology of the banquet, we can better understand New Testament Christian meal traditions. The fascinating question is, How did the Christians improvise upon and adapt the common meal tradition to express their faith and their common life?

The Christian communal meal served as a strong focus for the identity of the church. This was an arena in which the church had to tackle questions of inclusion (Gentiles, women, slaves). The communal meal was the event which kept alive the memory of Jesus. It was the area of life in which teaching, economic sharing, and discipline could be worked out.

There were Christian meals which did not refer primarily to the Last Supper and were not a commemoration of the death of Jesus. But great enrichment came where the Last Supper tradition was introduced with its theological themes and specific ritual words and blessings. The event to which the Last Supper referred (Passover feast) was itself a type of festive banquet, an event with its own great complexity and breadth of meaning.

Galatians 2:11-14 gives fascinating insight into a controversy of interpretation of communal meals between the parties of James and of Peter. James' Jewish Christians were proud to be fully Jews of the covenant as well as Christians. For them the Jewish scruples about eating with the uncircumcised continued valid. Paul was concerned that Gentile Christians who had not embraced all the practices of the Jewish community were considered second-class. Peter apparently had allowed some flexibility and had himself eaten with Gentile Christians. Paul felt compelled to bring into the open issues of community identity and solidarity enacted in their communal meals.

We have seen that Christian fellowship meals were based on a powerful social institution – the banquet tradition. As Christians adapted it to their particular ideals, they worked out questions and tensions within the forms and basic ideology of the banquet. Though their meal and worship practices varied, the early Christian communities held in common a sense of the function of the common meal to define boundaries and to bond the community together.[8] We might question whether they had lost sight of Jesus' radical practice of eating with stigmatized people and his teaching about inclusiveness at table as a mark of the great kingdom banquet to come. Such ideas might have stretched the Roman banquet ideology beyond its limits.

So what can we gain from watching the early Christians as they forge their worship forms from Roman and Jewish precedents? Our own cultural milieu is distinctly different, so we surely won't copy them exactly. But perhaps we could learn something from their ability to adapt the contemporary banquet form while infusing it with a unique ethos as well as enlarged social and theological meanings. In our own times, are there parallel contemporary social forms Christians could adapt to develop deeper expressions of worship or more effective communication to non-Christians?

Jewish Blessings and Jewish Passover Traditions

The Jewish piety of thankful prayer at every turn of the day comes directly to us through the Bible texts. We can explore this spirituality more fully, and perhaps integrate psalms into our communion prayers, just as the Jewish people used them in the Passover liturgy. Another rich source is the Passover liturgy itself. Can we grow in our understanding of its deeper story and its power in shaping both Hebrew and Christian consciousness?

If a community tells its story in the way the Jewish community recounts its Passover liberation, that group allows its history profoundly to shape its identity. With the multiple media of the Seder – symbolic foods, distinctive songs, probing questions, quotation of the tradition, prayers, and blessings – the community enters imaginatively into its own past. Doing this year after year, the stories of liberation and covenant shape their identity and reorient the Jewish people on their journey into the future.

This is a rich model for Christian communities. We can more fully allow the great story of God with Israel and the story of God in Jesus with his people shape our communities today. A community which neglects its memory is impoverished. And so we Christians in the eucharist employ symbolic foods, distinctive songs, questions, readings, prayers, and blessings to explore our identity as Jesus' people and to reorient our way to his.

By no means repudiating past tradition, there is great scope for creativity in celebrating eucharist. As we grasp more fully the range of meanings in it, we will become a freer and more innovative people. This is a call, in a sense, to play with the rite. We will find ways to clothe it with its proper range of stories, to interpret it visually, in gesture and music. We will ask it questions, learning how to express eucharist through the distinctive language of our own culture. The greater the care, craftsmanship, and love we pour into this rite, the greater will be Jesus' marks on us, on our way of relating to one another and to the world around us. Jesus' free spirit and creative love will be hallmarks of our common life.

3

Love Feasts

THE LOVE FEASTS (often called agape meals) of the early centuries were settings for Christian worship which continued the emphases of New Testament churches. Anticipation of Christ's return and the joyful banquet of God's kingdom revealed a wide and inclusive vision of God's purposes in history. Frequent love feasts gave opportunities for Spirit-inspired free worship and disciplined economic sharing.

Christian communities today might be very different if they were willing to experiment with frequent and informal agape meals. Doing this they would find practical expression for economic sharing and a willingness to worship freely and with vulnerability. They would deepen their missionary compassion and become a more winsomely hospitable people. Their entire community would be characterized by generosity, freedom in worship, hospitality to outsiders.

Joyous Messianic Banquets

However difficult it is definitively to determine New Testament patterns, certain things stand out. Jesus himself transformed a Jewish Passover meal tradition. He passed on a distinctive form of bread-blessing to his disciples. In his kingdom teaching, Jesus fused the Passover imagery of liberation with the messianic banquet imagery of God's salvation available to people of all nations.

The shared meal became a powerful symbol of God's kingdom. It was a foretaste of the messianic banquet. Throughout his ministry Jesus worked with this image of the banquet of the kingdom. He held table fellowship with outcasts and sinners. He showed that the banquet was already being celebrated – the kingdom was "at hand." Jesus' prophetic Word of Gentile inclusion at the table of Abraham, Isaac, and Jacob indicated his anticipation of the fulfillment of Isaiah 25:6-8: "On this mountain the Lord of hosts will make for all peoples a feast."[1]

Early Christian communities met at meal tables. They combined conviviality with serious teaching, prayers, and a ritual given them by Jesus himself. Their meals were patterned on the conventional festive banquet which they adapted to suit their developing social and congregational needs. These meals, called "breaking of bread," were continuations of the resurrection feasts which the disciples had celebrated with Jesus. They were joyous messianic banquets. The kingdom of God was truly at hand. Through the dynamic meal enactments that recalled Jesus' presence, a rich variety of theology emerged which we find in the New Testament and in subsequent documents.

New Testament Love Feasts

Agape was the name given to the Christians' common meal, as we see in Jude 12. It was meant to be a love feast, in which the Christians acted out the mutual, self-offering love their Master had given them as a hallmark. The Corinthian church also held a regular common meal, the one Paul seeks to correct in 1 Corinthians 11. Acts 2:42 also gives witness to Christian communities regularly gathering around tables. Scholars puzzle over the four phrases set out in this verse. Jeremias offers this reconstruction:[2]

they were devoting themselves

to the teaching of the apostles
and to the fellowship [*koinonia*]
to the breaking of bread
and to the prayers.

The four activities, listed in pairs, are dependent on "they were devoting themselves." It is possible this describes a two-part sequence in the service, first the teaching and the fellowship meal (agape), followed by the breaking of bread and the prayers. Acts 20:7ff. describes the place of teaching and conversation at the beginning of the Christian assembly. An apostolic letter could take the place of instruction. The five epistle references to it indicate that the holy kiss followed the reading of the apostolic letter.[3] This greeting could then introduce the fellowship meal. The Christian celebration concluded with psalms and prayers.

Not all scholars agree with this explanation. They argue over it, because they would like to know exactly how the early Christian common meal split apart the actual meal (the agape) on the one hand and the blessing of bread and cup (the eucharist) on the other. Some, such as Jeremias, have seen the separation already in New Testament practice. First Corinthians 11 made sense to him in this explanation, with the meal preceding the eucharistic ritual. Jeremias was concerned to draw together what others think to be a scattering of variant practices in the meal traditions.[4]

One scholar has posited Jerusalem-type meals which recalled Jesus' meals with disciples during his earthly ministry. He argues that these contrasted with Pauline community meals modeled on the Last Supper and emphasizing a memorial of Jesus' death. Other voices join the discussion. Was the Last Supper really a Passover meal? If so, how did Jesus alter the Jewish meanings? Perhaps there were differences in practice that reflected Galilean Christian communities.

What about those post-resurrection meals of Jesus with his disciples? Did they not leave an imprint on Christian meal-services? Maybe there were two major traditions – a celebratory bread-and-fish tradition and another more solemn bread-and-cup tradition. There are enough theories to make one's head swim.[5]

Whatever the differences, common to all these points of view and speculation is the central subject – the shared meal of the early Christian communities. In the frequent breaking of bread, these Christians remembered and met their Lord. This was the heart of their worship.

At some point, either in New Testament times or shortly afterward, two separate types of worship evolved – the agape meal with its distinctive patterns of informal worship and shared meal, and the eucharistic ritual with its specific ceremonies and words of blessed bread and shared cup of wine. Significantly, both types retained a strong emphasis on economic redistribution. The agape meal did this through table hospitality to the poorer members.

Similarly, in the eucharist, gifts-in-kind as well as money formed part of what came to be called the offertory. These provided help for the needy members as well as support for the clergy. But to begin with, these two types were just one, simply the fellowship meals of the Christian communities.

Agape Meals Around the Mediterranean

The agape meal, the love feast, we first see named in Jude 12. Reflecting the function of the meal in the associations and clubs of the time, these Christian agape meals defined the boundaries of fellowship. The church in Antioch witnessed the confrontation between Paul and Peter over whether Jewish Christians should eat with uncircumcised brothers. The conflict may have contributed to the break between Paul and Barnabas and to further estrangement between Paul and the church in Antioch (Gal. 2:11-14).[6]

In Corinth, some who were flagrantly immoral were excluded from church meetings. Members were cautioned: "Do not even eat with such a one" (1 Cor. 5:11). Participation at the Lord's table was meant to be consistent with a disciplined and moral life. The agape meals served as boundary markers for the community. People were visibly in or out of fellowship.

References to the agape meal continue through the early centuries of Christian history. In 112, because of pressure from the Roman governor Pliny of Bithynia, Christians in Asia Minor ceased their common evening meals. Such meetings were seen as potentially hostile political gatherings.

But no pressure could make them give up their early morning meetings for worship.[7] At about the same time, Ignatius described agape meals which were clearly important in the church's round of activities.[8]

According to Tertullian,[9] agape feasts in early third-century North African communities included more than shared food and drink. There was a ceremonial lighting of lamps. There were blessings and prayers at the beginning and end of the evening. There was time for "free worship." The purpose of the event was to help the needy members through sharing food, and to engage in informal worship with free prayer and edifying conversation.

Meanwhile, across the Mediterranean, other congregations were putting on agape meals, too. A bishops' handbook, the *Apostolic Tradition* calls it a communal supper, a common meal, or the Lord's Supper (chaps. 25-29). A church family hosted the meal, local ministers presided and blessed, while "the faithful and the catechumens" (church members and baptismal candidates) took part in an orderly manner.

These agape meals might have taken place on weekdays. But a communal meal held on a Sunday would have especially included Jesus' cup and bread sayings and thanksgiving prayers remembering his life, death, and resurrection. Sunday was a special day to Christians because it was the day of the Lord's resurrection, and it symbolized the first day of the new creation. But let's not forget that a Sunday was an ordinary working day. Unlike the Jews at this time, the Christians had no special concessions for worship. They had to fit in their worship as well as they could, either before or after a full day's work.

Changes in Agape and Eucharist

As the Christian movement spread out across the empire, changes were inevitable. Congregations grew in numbers. Christian worship and fellowship no longer centered on an actual meal table. The movement became less Jewish. Specialized patterns of ministry developed. Both agape and eucharist changed.

In some places, as we read in the case of governor Pliny of Bithynia, Roman legislation outlawed the meals of all fraternal societies. Perhaps the atmosphere and conventions of political or commercial clubs influenced behavior at Christian agape meals.[10] Christian writers of the third century warned about excesses of festivities at agape meals and the poor witness this was to non-Christian observers.

As numbers increased, the agapes could no longer serve as the focus of the entire community. Instead, they became special events put on by rich members for invited guests. The ministers said the blessings, to be sure, and provision was made for the poor. But the character of the agape was evolving. It was turning into a private event put on at the impulse of the richer members.

Love Feasts Degenerated

At times to gain legal status, Christians organized themselves as burial societies. This inclined their shared meals toward the character of funeral banquets. Such banquets could aid the hungry poor, celebrate the lives of the martyrs, and focus on the great banquet of the kingdom of God to come.

But unfortunately, according to Augustine in the fifth century, too often these meals had degenerated into "debaucheries and lavish banquets in cemeteries."[11] Fourth-century councils condemned abuses of the agape. Separated from the bread-and-cup ceremony of the eucharist, the agape apparently lost its rudder.

Eucharistic and agape meals coexisted in those earliest generations. The underlying meanings of the two types had been similar and clear: agape love, economic sharing, and thankful remembering of Jesus. But from the third century onward, there are fewer references to the agape and increasing criticism of abuses. Clement of Alexandria was concerned about merriment and lavish menus. Tertullian alleged sexual misconduct.[12]

In some places, at least, agape meals lacked sobriety and discipline. But as the agape meal faded away, the churches suffered irretrievable losses both in the intimacy of fellowship and in the free, informal worship characteristic of the love feasts.

What Can We Learn from the Ancient Love Feasts?

We have referred to a number of accounts of agape meals, most of them not in the New Testament. These reflect congregational practices, good or sometimes less good. They are not biblically authoritative for us. But they originate in times closer to Jesus and in cultures closer to his, so they have great value. Those people insisted the Lord's table was a table of economic justice. They developed mechanisms for ensuring generous sharing and redistribution, both within and outside their membership. Do we consider this a central meaning of communion services? If we do, how do we express it?

They celebrated their memorial and eucharistic love feasts weekly. Could we do the same? Churches that have moved to more frequent communion services testify to the beneficial effects. Early church agape meals combined both formal and free worship. Perhaps we could find creative ways to do that, too.

What difference would such changes in eucharistic practice make in the character of a church? A regular and frequent liturgical discipline of economic sharing at the table encourages generous responsibility for one another and for the needy outside our own group.

Early church agape meals provided both formal and free worship, so that those inspired to do so could speak prophetic words, pray, sing, or recite psalms. But these contributions were within a fairly regular pattern which had evolved. Even today such a deliberate combination of regular and spontaneous elements could be enlivening to an overly formalized service of communion.

Churches need worship which has formal and free aspects. Familiar, repeated aspects provide ease and space. People feel at home. Yet there needs to be room for expectancy and openness to Christ's presence perceived in different ways. A church with a strong yet flexible eucharistic pattern will nurture people who are poised and confident *and* open and ready to express their faith with freshness. They will not be severe, cautious, or bound by fossilized patterns and codes of language which cannot communicate.

4

Early Christian Eucharist

EITHER IN New Testament times or shortly afterward, agape and eucharist types of worship became distinct. Sunday morning was the time for eucharist worship. Its characteristic feature was the cup-and-bread ceremony which Jesus inaugurated at the Last Supper. Joyful thanksgiving was the dominant tone of the eucharists of the early centuries. That joyous tone should continue to be a hallmark of the overall life of a Christian community and particularly of our eucharist services.

We have imagined early Christian communities gathered around the tables of their agape meals, probably on evenings after work. Hosted by householders, these meals were occasions for social fellowship and economic equalization, as well as unfettered worship. Unlike early morning meetings which had time constraints because people had to get to work, evening agape meals could be more relaxed. But the morning gatherings persisted, especially on the Lord's Day. These developed distinctive patterns, too.

So we see that two separate types of worship settings evolved – the evening agape meals and the Lord's Day morning meetings[1] that came to be called the eucharist. The two types grew from the same root – the meal fellowship of the first generations of Christians – and retained common characteristics. They both included Scripture readings, prayers, homilies, and offerings for distribution to the needy. By the mid-second century, the agape retained a more informal ethos with its free worship and lesser time constraints. Eucharists were no longer meals but had the distinctive bread-and-cup ceremony inaugurated by Jesus at the Last Supper.

Confident Thankfulness

Tantalizing hints, fragments of prayers, and brief references survive as evidence of agape and eucharist services into the early second century. A distinction between the two types of service is not clear, for example, in the passage from the *Didache* (9), a second-century document from Syria. But the tone of the service is evident. These thanksgiving prayers over the cup and bread are filled with confident thankfulness.

We thank you (*eucharistoumen*), our Father, for the holy vine of David, your child, which you have revealed through Jesus, your child. To you be glory forever.

We thank you (*eucharistoumen*), our Father, for the life and knowledge which you have revealed through Jesus, your child. To you be glory forever.

Gratitude to God is the characteristic feature of their (early Christians') piety. "Like a warm breath it permeates the writings of the early period."[2] Clement of Alexandria says that whether a Christian is alone or with other believers, "always the mature Christian honors God by giving thanks for having come to know the right path in life." Christians don't offer God an external gift. Christians glorify God "who dedicated himself to us, by dedicating ourselves to him."[3]

Justin Martyr writes in second-century Rome: "We offer [God] in spirit solemn prayers and songs of praise for our creation and for all the means of prosperity, for the variety of all things, and for the changes of season."[4]

In the third century Bishop Origen sums it up: Christians are people with grateful hearts. Christians give thanks to God who "has bestowed upon us an abundance of benefits ... We fear being ungrateful. The sign of our gratitude toward God is the bread called eucharist."[5]

Christians were convinced that in Jesus the Messiah, God had inaugurated his kingdom, cosmic in its scope, and that they were to have their place within it. What grounds for joy and amazement! In their own time, God was bringing fulfillment of prophecies of the Old Testament. They were called to be God's people of peace and reconciliation. "Swords into plowshares, spears into pruning hooks" – Isaiah's and Micah's vision of humanity putting war away forever, had come true in their common life. Were they not with the implements of peace "farming piety, cultivating justice, brotherly charity, faith, and hope?"[6]

Even though they were persecuted and killed, many of these Christians knew a joy and hope beyond bounds. They were unafraid of death. No longer tyrannized by the fears and compulsions of their former life, these Christians worshiped God with verve and energy. They called their worship eucharist. An apt name it was, which caught both the spirit of their lives and the content of their prayers.

And so we can see that though description is scanty, something of the scope and tone of the prayers comes through. It is no wonder the service came to be called "eucharist" because thanksgiving, *eucharistein*, the sign of their gratitude to God, shines out.

Justin Martyr related in detail a Lord's Day morning worship service in Rome. This is the earliest precise description of the order and content of a Christian eucharist.

Christian Worship – in Rome, A.D. 150

On that day which is called after the sun, all who are in the towns and in the country gather together for a *communal celebration*. Then the *memoirs of the apostle*s or the writings of the *prophets* are read, as long as time permits. After the reader has finished, the one presiding gives an *address*, urgently admonishes his hearers to practice these beautiful teachings in their lives. Then all stand up together and recite *prayers*. After the end of the prayers, the bread and wine-mixed-with-water are brought and the one presiding sends up *prayers* and *thanksgivings* to the best of his ability. The people chime in with AMEN. Then takes place the *distribution*, to all attending, of the things over which the thanksgiving has been spoken, and the deacons bring a *portion to the absent*.

Those who prosper, and who so wish, *contribute*, each one as much as he chooses to. What is collected is deposited with the one presiding, and he takes care of the orphans and widows, and those who are in want on account of sickness or any other cause, and those who are in bonds and the strangers who are sojourners among us. He is, in short, the *protector of all those in need*.

(Justin, *Apology* 1.67)

Earlier themes of Christian worship still shine through. This is a community gathered together every Lord's Day, now in Rome called Sunday, to hear Scripture applied to their lives, to pray, to give thanks over the shared bread and cup, and to care for the needy among them. The service includes freedom within an accepted pattern. Undoubtedly this Roman church would have held agape meals on weekday evenings or Sundays as well as early morning prayers before work. That would have been typical of the round of weekly gatherings in early Christian communities.

Wide-ranging Prayers of Thanksgiving

It is both instructive and inspiring to observe the range and particularity of the table prayers of the early Christians. The *Didache* prayers that follow the ones quoted above, yield a harvest of thanksgivings, as shown by the added emphasis:

We give thanks to you, holy Father, for your *holy name* which you have enshrined in our hearts, and for the *knowledge* and *faith* and *immortality* which you made known to us through your child Jesus; glory to you for evermore.

You, Lord Almighty, *created all things* for the sake of your name and gave *food and drink* to people for their enjoyment that they might give you thanks; but to us you have granted *spiritual food and drink for eternal life* through your child Jesus.

Above all, we give you thanks because *you are mighty*, glory to you for evermore. Amen.[7]

Justin Martyr mentions Christian eucharistic prayers which give thanks to God

both for *creating the world* with all things that are in it ... and for *freeing us from the evil* in which we were born, and for accomplishing a complete *destruction of the principalities and powers* through him who suffered ...[8]

Justin Martyr also describes eucharistic prayers in his Roman community:

Then bread and a cup of water and of mixed wine are brought to him who presides ... and he takes them and *offers praise and glory* to the Father of all in the name of the Son and of the Holy Spirit, and gives thanks at some length that we have been *deemed worthy* of these things from him. When he has finished the prayers and the thanksgiving, all the people present sing out their assent by saying "Amen."[9]

As early as 215, in the *Apostolic Tradition*[10] the thanksgiving prayers at the eucharistic service assumed the shape of a credal story with an outline of the salient points of redemption history. The one presiding was not expected to say the prayers word-for-word, but the content of his improvised prayer should generally follow the given outline. Different members could offer prayers to augment the leader's prayer. Notice the sequence of thanks for all the events of the story of redemption through Christ's incarnation, suffering, death, and vindication. Following the words of institution comes the thankful offering by the people, who do not grovel in self-denigration but stand forgiven and "worthy" before God. The prayer for unity in the Holy Spirit culminates in doxology, the exalted purpose of the entire service.

We render thanks to you, O God, through your beloved child Jesus Christ, whom in the last times you sent to us as savior and redeemer and angel of your will;
    who is your inseparable Word, through whom you made all things, and in whom you were well pleased.
    You sent him from heaven into the Virgin's womb; and, conceived in the womb, he was made flesh and was manifested as your Son, being born of the Holy Spirit and the Virgin.
    Fulfilling your will and gaining for you a holy people, he

stretched out his hands when he should suffer, that he might release from suffering those who have believed in you.

And when he was betrayed to voluntary suffering that he might destroy death, and break the bonds of the devil, and tread down hell, and shine upon the righteous, and fix the limit, and manifest the resurrection, he took bread and gave thanks to you, saying, "Take, eat; this is my body, which shall be broken for you." Likewise also the cup, saying, "This is my blood, which is shed for you; when you do this, you make my remembrance."

Remembering therefore his death and resurrection, we offer to you the bread and the cup, giving you thanks because you have held us worthy to stand before you and minister to you.

And we ask that you would send your Holy Spirit upon the offering of your holy church; that gathering them into one, you would grant to all who partake of the holy things (to partake) for the fullness of the Holy Spirit for the confirmation of faith in truth;

that we may praise and glorify you through your child Jesus Christ, through whom be glory and honor to you, to the Father and the Son with the Holy Spirit, in your holy church, both now and to the ages of ages. (Amen.)[11]

Gratitude to God was "the characteristic feature of [early Christian] piety." Clement of Alexandria [third century] says that "what [we] owe to God is lifelong thanksgiving; always and everywhere, not only on certain feast days and in holy places, but throughout the whole of life ... [we] honor God by giving him thanks."[12] Justin explains Christian thanksgiving in detail. We thank God:

for having founded the world with all that is in it ... for freeing us from wickedness ... for having totally weakened the powers and principalities through [Christ]. We offer God in spirit solemn prayers and songs of praise for our creation and for all the means of prosperity, for the variety of all things and for the changes of season.[13]

Notice Justin's wide range of thanksgivings, typical of early Christian eucharists – thanks for creation, redemption, victory of Christ over evil, for nature. Even in days of persecution, Christians' reflex in worship and prayer was to be thankful. Calling their worship by that name – "giving thanks" – undoubtedly reminded the Christians of its inner meaning.

Do these descriptions of early Christian eucharists give any hints for today's communion services? In looking at agape meals, we considered the value of regular and frequent celebrations of the Lord's Supper. In both types of services, agape and eucharist, the economic factor was important. Re-equalization and generous sharing were featured within the services themselves. Outstanding features of these early eucharists which could be provocative for us are the balance of clear forms with spontaneous or flexible expression, and the repeated rooting of worship in the story of Jesus and his teachings. But most important of all is the overall tone of thanksgiving.

Parents carefully insist that their children "say thank you to Aunt Sue" and also teach them "thank you" prayers. Parents responsibly shape the character of their children so that they develop habits and reflexes of gratitude and the ability to express it easily. In the same way, churches need reminders and opportunities to say thank you to God. Christian communities, like children, thrive on learning to be thankful. They, too, will develop habits and reflexes of gratitude. They will learn to express it easily. The whole service of eucharist centers around God's gracious gift to his people, and our receiving that grace with joy. All the forms and freedoms of expression will resound with thankful words and songs.

An important way to develop the spirit of thankfulness is to incorporate hymns and psalms full of praise and thanks. There are examples from many different places and times. You can read the hymns as poems if suitable music is not available. Here is a very old text by Johann Franck, from the seventeenth century, full of wondering joy:

> Deck thyself my soul with gladness
> leave the gloomy haunts of sadness.
> Come into the daylight's splendor,
> there with joy thy praises render
> unto him whose grace unbounded
> hath this wondrous banquet founded.
> High o'er all the heav'ns he reigneth,
> yet to dwell with thee he deigneth.[14]

5

Medieval Mass and Divine Liturgy

THE MIDDLE AGES brought changes to the joyful, thankful, generous-spirited quality of early Christian eucharists. Many delight in this period's Christian aesthetic expressions of piety – cathedrals, stained glass, music. Yet disputes over creeds, power struggles, clergy-laity divisions, development of awe-inspiring rites, and the tight grip of the penitential system – these all contributed to an immense loss of the sense of a worshiping community.

The earlier corporate character of Christianity gave way to another model. Christians were now an aggregate of individuals within a huge hierarchical structure which dispensed benefits according to tightly controlled means. The character of individuals within that system reflected uncertainty of their worthiness and fear of a terrible Judge. Significant distinctions, moreover, continued to characterize Eastern and Western Christian traditions.

Though the worship of the earliest period was full of joy and thanksgiving, by the fourth century there were strong indications of a substantial shift of tone. The youthful, clean-shaven Good Shepherd Jesus of earliest depictions had given way to the haloed Christ of glittering mosaics which depicted him as emperor and judge. Severe disputes over the human and divine natures of Christ had resulted in an overemphasis on the majestic Christ enthroned in the heavens. This was no longer the Jesus of the New Testament – Master, Pastor, Intercessor, and Advocate.

The Sunday service of eucharist, celebrated in massive buildings and attended by large crowds, had become remote, splendid, and mysterious. Overawed and afraid, people increasingly shied away from the communion Table. Bishop John Chrysostom, calling the eucharist "the shuddering hour," complained, "In vain do we stand before the altar; there is no one to partake."[1] Afraid of death, people were terrified to contemplate standing before the celestial judgment throne, depicted in massive size overhead. And wasn't that the same Christ whose body and blood were revered at the altar before them? They felt almost grotesquely unworthy.

The altar, now the focus for a rite both terrible and awesome, was fenced off in a clergy-only space. The once movable table, a practical piece of furniture, had now become this altar surrounded by careful attendants intent on creating and preserving its mysterious and holy purpose. This altar and the awesome service of the sacrament together came to be called the *mysterium tremendum*.[2]

A theology of ordination developed which set the ordinary people (*laos*) apart from the class of priests. Secular privileges such as exemption from taxes and military service combined with biblical misunderstandings to make the clerical order attractive to increasing numbers. Elaborate rites of induction, special clothing, and a complex hierarchical structure characterized clerical life and made it more and more distinct from that of the laity.

An elaborate penitential system had shifted the focus from a continuously reconciling community to an emphasis on the status of individuals before God. Priests and people alike asked the dreaded question, "Am I worthy?" Church assemblies had lost the atmosphere of a joyful redeemed community celebrating their living hope in communion with the risen and returning Lord Jesus.

A Christian Eucharist in Syria, A.D. 385

Something of the contrast to the ethos of early eucharists shows in the *Apostolic Constitutions*, a bishops' handbook of church order which originated in Syria around 385. The author's choice of similes, comparing churchgoers to passengers on a ship or to sheep and goats in their pens, reveals the psychological and literal distance between what are now called clergy and laity, two divisions in the church. Deacons kept busy, walking around during the service with a long rod to discipline sleepers, gigglers, and whisperers. One can almost hear the echo in the vast building, here likened to a ship (nave) for the first time. Just a few years later, Bishop John Chrysostom in Constantinople complained about people no longer coming to the communion table.

> When you call an assembly of the church, as one that is the *commander of a great ship*, charge the *deacons as mariners* to prepare place for the *people as for passengers*. Let the building be long, with its head to the east, with its vestries on both sides at the east end, and so it will be like a ship. In the middle let the bishop's throne be placed, and on each side of him let the presbytery sit down; and let the deacons stand near at hand, in close and small-girt garments, for they are like the mariners and the managers of the ship. Let the laity sit on the other side [of the fence] with all quietness and good order. And let the women sit by themselves, they also keeping silence. If anyone be found sitting out of place, let him be rebuked by the deacon, as a manager of the ship, and be removed into the place proper for him. For the church is not only like a ship, but also like *a sheepfold*. For as the shepherds place all the *brute creatures*

distinctly, I mean goats and sheep, according to their kind and age, so it is to be in the church. Let the deacon oversee the people, that *nobody may whisper, slumber, laugh, or nod.* All ought to stand wisely and soberly and attentively ... After the prayer is over, let some of them attend upon [the altar], and let others of them watch the multitude, and *keep them silent.*

(Apostolic Constitutions 2.7)

Sin and the Penitential System

In the early centuries, what to do about sin committed after baptism stirred great debates among church leaders. Some were reluctant to allow that Christians could be forgiven for sin after they had been baptized. Others made provision for Christians who repented of the three major sins – denying the faith, adultery, and murder. Such people could admit their sin to the bishop and accept a discipline of repentance, or "do penance." Penance could last a long time, perhaps a lifetime.

Gradually a catalog of lesser sins with specified periods and acts of penance developed. Penance often entailed public humiliation, such as standing outside the door of the church in sackcloth and ashes, asking for prayers, or lying stretched out on the floor of the church before dismissal in the middle of the service. Even short periods of penance made the lives of ordinary Christians difficult.

And so the severe reality of the penitential system directly touched ordinary people's lives. In apostolic times the text "Examine yourselves, and only then eat of the bread and drink of the cup" (1 Cor. 11:28) required an "unrestricted manner" of application to all communicants. After a time discipline was strengthened by the requirement for sacramental confession of criminal sins before taking communion. And by the tenth century, sacramental confession was obligatory before each and every reception of communion.[3]

In addition, applications of various Old Testament purity laws made increasing cases for exclusion. Sexual activity, menstruation, and childbirth, as well as dietary restrictions made it more and more difficult for people to take part. Eventually, in the twelfth century, theologian Peter of Blois tried to put a holy gloss upon the situation: "From infrequent celebration has grown reverence for the sacrament."[4]

Awe-inspiring Rites Inspire Fear

In the late fourth century, we see Christianity universalized by act of state, a religion full of people afraid of the table, dreading hell. The pagans used to be afraid of God; now the Christians were terrified of God's condemnation. They quailed before Christ the Judge depicted in his purple and gold, no longer dressed in the tunic and boots of a farmer. The Good Shepherd with a lamb over his shoulders now represented not

Christ, but St. Peter! Awe-inspiring rites did more than inspire awe. They frightened people to the core. Judgment, no longer upon pagans who defied God, was upon themselves. What could they do to atone for their sins? How could they gain favor with God again? The elaborate penitential system provided the only way.

How could things have come to such a low state? "And how could it continue even through a period we are accustomed to regard as the flowering of ecclesiastical life, the central Middle Ages?" asks the venerable Roman Catholic liturgical scholar, Josef Jungmann.[5] Jungmann can't believe it revealed lukewarmness in faith, otherwise how to explain the enthusiasm for monasticism during this period? Missionizing of the Germanic tribes was undoubtedly superficial, he asserts, and the sacramental understanding of people on the fringes of the empire "unfolded very slowly." But the heart of the problem, he says, is that in the struggle against Arianism, the divinity of Christ was overstressed. "The humanity in Christ, Christ's mediatorship, which draws us to Him, receded into the shadows." People's religious imagination separated them from God and drew them instead to the saints, in spite of traditional teaching.[6]

From the twelfth century onward, a great wave of sacramental awe passed over the medieval Western church. People thought gazing at the elements could replace receiving the sacrament. When the "Sanctus bell" rang, they were to look up in adoration as the priest raised the consecrated bread. But by the sixteenth century, people fell down on their knees during the consecration of the bread and wine precisely so they could not look at the holy and mysterious elements. This became a kind of spiritual communion, explained to be as valuable and efficacious as taking the sacrament itself. A further development was the teaching that the priest ate and drank as the representative of the entire community.

Private Masses

The phenomenon of a daily private mass further eroded eucharistic theology. Because of increasing numbers of monks who were ordained priests, daily celebrations of mass characterized monastic communities. Priests were obliged by their vows to celebrate mass, so any given day saw a number of masses in the monastic churches. In spite of protests from some theologians, this practice spilled over into parish churches. There they came to be known as "low masses." Celebrated at side altars, these were spoken inaudibly, with no congregational responses or singing. In fact, nobody besides the priest needed to be present. Low mass came to be understood almost as a priest's private and personal devotional exercise.

Mass as a Work of Grace

Attached to the distortion of a private mass was an even more insidious notion – that saying mass could be in itself a work of effective grace, bringing benefit in this world as well as the next. In many monasteries and churches, wealthy people or groups of craftsmen endowed daily masses to assure their salvation from eternal damnation.

We see then that across fifteen centuries, the Western church has traveled a great distance from its original eucharistic understandings. A baptized Christian who should regard the bread of heaven as "daily bread" now felt enormous reserve and timidity. Even a pious person "looked more to human weakness than to the grace-made dignity of the Christian."

Significant as well is the medieval emphasis on the status of the individual communicant, rather than on the eucharistic celebration of the community of Christians as a body. Required to confess and take communion at least once a year, medieval European Christians were no longer active participants but watchers. The mass was a priestly act. Ordinary people participated by looking on.

Canon of the Mass

The eucharistic prayer, also known as the consecration prayer, of the Roman mass is a cluster of short prayers called the canon. The name derives from an early time when elements of eucharistic worship were more fluid, but this central section was marked in manuscripts, "Here begins the fixed text (*canon*)." Canon, meaning "rule" or "measure," became the name for the prescribed series of prayers.[7]

The canon – an outline of the prayers
1. Introductory dialogue – the *Sursum corda*: "Lift up your hearts ..."
2. Prefatory prayer, culminating in *Sanctus*: "Holy, holy, holy ... blessed is he who comes in the name of the Lord"
3. A plea for acceptance of the offerings of bread and wine
4. Prayer for the living and the departed
5. Prayer of offering of bread and wine
6. Narrative of the institution of the Lord's Supper
7. Anamnesis – oblation (commemoration, remembrance)
8. Prayer for acceptance and fruitful reception
9. Prayer for the living and departed
10. Two doxologies

Sacrificial Emphasis in the Mass

A significant difference in emphasis arose between the Eastern (Orthodox) and the Western (Catholic) liturgies. Sacrificial formulas such as these dominated the Western eucharistic prayer:

these offerings, these holy and unblemished sacrifices

(Canon 2)

accept this offering made by us (Canon 4)
we offer a pure victim, a holy victim, an unspotted victim
(Canon 6)
accept these offerings as the offerings of Abel and Melchizadek
(Canon 7)

In the Eastern Orthodox tradition, on the other hand, a number of other motifs besides sacrifice and offering appear more important in the eucharistic prayer. These include the kingdom of God, salvation history, prayer for the Spirit to descend, intercessions. The Western church continued to develop sacrificial language and emphasis in private masses and expanded offertory prayers. By the time of the Reformation, the sacrificial motif truly dominated the mass. In the words of Josef Jungmann,

> The later Middle Ages did so much to emphasize the sacrificial aspect, and stressed in so many forms and fashions the value of the Mass for gaining God's grace and favor for the living and the dead, that not only did the Reformation find a subject for immoderate indictment, but even the Church authorities, both before and after the storm, found reasons for making certain corrections.[8]

In its clarification of sacrificial theology, the Council of Trent stressed that the mass was not a mere meal, nor just a memorial service to recall a sacrifice made long ago. The mass was in fact, itself "a sacrifice, and possessed its own power of atonement and petition. The Mass was to be understood as simultaneously the sacrifice of Christ and the sacrifice of the Church."[9]

The Formative Power of the Mass

Did the liturgy of the Catholic Church in the early Middle Ages contribute to the Christian formation of the pagan peoples of Europe? Was it effective, from a pastoral point of view, in imprinting Christian values and virtues upon them? Taking a strongly positive view of the necessary enculturation of the Christian faith, Jungmann says, "The answer is unequivocal. The formative power of the liturgy was both profound and vast. A tremendous process of transformation … was taking place: the transformation of society from paganism to Christianity." This is an optimistic opinion. It refers to the taking over of local cultural forms, keeping only an Oriental essential at the core, the "divine institution" together with forms from the primitive church.[10]

The downside is not difficult to find. What had happened to the joyful, thankful character of early eucharists? Where was the free participation of the congregation and the economic sharing of the early love feasts? After centuries of emphasis on the need for private forgiveness, there was no legacy of learning to be communities of forgiveness. In spite of its fixation upon the cross and sacrifice of Jesus, the church did not emphasize Jesus' challenge that his followers should forge cross-shaped lives of discipleship, following in the Master's steps. The church, wedded to state in structure, power, and interest, used exclusion from mass as threat and sanction. Most devastating of all, the central liturgical fact of this period, according to William Willimon, was the virtual "dissolution of the worshiping community."[11] Reflecting on the shape and emphasis of eucharistic worship in the medieval Catholic Church, there seems more loss than gain.

Not All Loss, But Some Gain

But we cannot deny the grandeur of cathedrals, churches, and private chapels built in this period. The artistic beauty of countless paintings and musical masterpieces is breathtaking. They speak of deep religious devotion and commitment. There have been individuals and communities of mercy and holiness, expressing God's love, whose piety has been rooted in the Latin mass. The Holy Spirit of God is active.

The simple fact is that this mixed story of faith and unfaithfulness is our own history. This is the story of Western Christianity, of which we Protestants are heirs as surely as the Roman Catholics. It is unrealistic and irresponsible to think we can ignore "the Christian centuries" in order to reclaim some kind of biblical purity in worship. So what good can we make out of our heritage, the story of Western Christianity?

In the first place, Western Christians of many hues are on a common search. We are returning together to biblical and early church roots. This is not a revisitation with the purpose of point-scoring and putdowns. It is a search for revaluation and purification. This task is greatly enhanced by the fact that involved are people from a spectrum of emphases within the larger tradition. God has preserved in each of our histories certain values, understandings, and practices. These insights are not simply for each group's own pleasure. There is a purpose in this. We can remind and enrich each other in the renewal of worship.

As we shall see later, scholars of many traditions have been studying the early church. They have with one voice described the problems arising in the intervening centuries – the lack of corporate participation, the dominance of the clergy, the fixation on death and sacrifice, a prevailing tone of dourness. As a result of the work of theologians, historians, and leaders of worship, the services may once again legitimately be called eucharists.

Early church study has become a meeting ground for many churches today and has profoundly affected the theologies and practices of initiation, of nurture, and of evangelism. It has helped to draw Christians together toward unity in the Spirit. This is a corporate task. In doing it together, we often discover a surprising gift of recognition: we belong to each other in Christ!

Second, this is a serious process of historical revaluation. In doing it we must acknowledge the distortions in order to regain the ideals. For example, though the medieval abuses of the penitential system can never be justified, the ancient tradition nevertheless carried on the memory of the importance of confession and forgiveness.

Some Protestant reaction has been to pitch out liturgical confession, private or corporate. But we must be more subtle than that. We can retrace the steps of the Reforming traditions, each one of which maintained important features of this theme. Lutherans remember God's grace and the impossibility of doing anything to earn God's forgiveness. Calvinists took seriously the necessity for preparation to approach the communion table. They found that special congregational meetings and the use of psalmody were especially helpful. Anabaptists emphasized corporate purity, and used the kiss of peace, love feasts, and the foot-washing ceremony as liturgical means to deepen the vitality of the gathered church.

Catholics and Protestants together can gain depth in our current practices of confession and forgiveness by listening closely and sympathetically to each other. We can name the unfaithfulness not only in the Catholic medieval past but in subsequent distortions of grace and forgiveness in all our traditions. Together we can return to our common origins, to the early church, and to Christ himself, who showed us what God's grace, mercy, and forgiveness are like. Christ calls us to be mature, grown-up people, like God in our gracious mercifulness. We can best get to these insights through seriously dealing with our separate histories as well as our common Western Catholic history.

Third, we need to embrace the whole long story of the church as our own. If we push bits of it away, blaming and condemning others, we will not grow up in our own faith. God is infinitely able to deal with humanity, continually recalling us to his love. Varieties of sinfulness are immense, but so are varieties of faithfulness to God's true ways. At the table we need to recount the stories of God's faithfulness across time and across geography. This will help us increasingly to grasp how this "old, old story of Jesus and his love" transforms the broken world around us. Christians are a global people of God, and our experiences resound across time and eternity. If we deeply grasp that large sense of solidarity, it will mark us and make us people of wide vision.

East and West – Distinctives and Disputes

We have traced eucharistic practice in the Western European church, and now we will look at least briefly at what happened in the Eastern church. The description of a fourth-century Sunday communion service in a large church in Syria comes, in fact, from the Eastern church (see page 47). But in those days people didn't mentally separate East from West. The church was "catholic," meaning universal or general. It was more than simply a local congregation. All Christians believed they belonged to one common body. But though they had so much in common (orthodoxy), Christians developed various interpretations and worship practices within their faith.

One important difference was the use of Greek in the Eastern empire and Latin in the Western empire. Inherent differences between the languages imprinted the formulation of faith and worship. But there were further psychological tendencies which distinguished Eastern and Western Christianity. Westerners were precise and terse with their liturgical language. With a more literal turn of mind, they became more concerned with the material elements of bread and wine and what actually happened to them in the consecration. Easterners delighted in symbolism, in visual and allegorical approaches to theology and prayer. As time went on, their liturgical prayers became more and more florid. They interpreted the entire liturgy in symbolic fashion to represent the life and ministry of Christ.

Joining of empire and church made religious disputes into political struggles; temperamental and theological differences were mixed with power plays among bishops, emperors, and monks. By the time Eastern and Western Christians considered themselves distinct from each other (tenth and eleventh centuries), the precise differences had become almost inconsequential. They differed on the type of bread for communion, on which version of the Nicene Creed to use, on how to regard statues in churches, and on particular rituals and wordings. The Eastern Church regarded certain teachings of the Western Church as contradicting the basic truth of Christianity, such as the immaculate conception of the Virgin Mary and papal "infallibility."

The best-known dispute of Eastern Orthodoxy with Rome is over the wording of one small phrase in the Creed, the "filioque clause." The Greek Fathers teach that "the Holy Spirit proceeded from the Father *through* the Son," while the Western Church teaches that "the Holy Spirit proceeded from the Father *and* the Son (filioque)."

The Orthodox Churches have a great deal in common with the Roman Catholic Churches, but today have more contact with Protestants and Anglicans. The East sees the splintering of the Western Church at the sixteenth-century Reformation as a domestic problem of the West. If the Western Christians could just get themselves together, in the view from the East, then perhaps church unity could become a serious option. East and West might once again unite. Church leaders on both sides are concerned about this. In fact, Pope John Paul II has said that he will consider his papacy to have failed if, by the year 2000, the Eastern and Western churches remain divided.[12]

Learning from the Eastern Church

We in the West are in a period of "rediscovery of our Eastern Christian relatives, fellow members of the Body of Christ, who at first may impress us as living relics."[13] We may find some springs for renewal within these ancient forms and manners of piety. Orthodox icons are serving Western Christians not as decorative and primitive paintings but as vehicles to deeper prayer and meditation. The sense of "at-homeness" among the participants in the Eastern liturgy strikes any Westerner who attends. People move around freely, some kneel, some stand, children come and go. This is in contrast to the rigid manners in many Protestant services, where people sit poker-faced on pews or on fixed chairs as though in a lecture room.

In looking closely at the text of the Divine Liturgy, unchanged for fifteen centuries, we find fascinating surprises. These three examples can serve to remind us of themes retained from ancient Christianity which could be relevant for us today.

The first is the striking way in which the liturgy begins. The opening words are: "Blessed is the Kingdom ..." The eminent Orthodox scholar Alexander Schmemann presents the eucharistic liturgy as a journey, the journey of the church into the dimension of the kingdom of God. This dimension is a kind of fourth reality, where ultimate values and the presence of Christ come to us in vivid color. This is not escape. Instead, it is a vantage point from which Christians can deeply perceive the reality of our world. From the beginning of the eucharistic journey, the destination is clear: the fully realized reign of God. Schmemann reminds us that to bless the kingdom is more than mere words. It means that we declare it to be the goal "of all our desires and interests, of our whole life ..."[14]

What Schmemann says simply reminds us of Jesus' words in Mark's account of the inauguration of his ministry. "The time is fulfilled, and the kingdom of God has come near" (Mark 1:15). Might the words which articulate the purpose of Jesus' ministry and the goal of his life journey be good ones to open communion services in other Christian traditions, too?

A second point to observe is the repetition of the Beatitudes in every service. These succinct verses are the palette of colors with which Jesus paints his vision of the kingdom which is near and into which he invites all who will come. They distill the heart of Jesus' life and teachings. In the Orthodox liturgy, the Beatitudes stand as a doorway into the service. They are heard just before the Gospel reading. It seems only right that Christians who profess to follow the Rabbi Jesus should regularly and at length, sing and repeat his sayings.

A third observation about the Eastern liturgy is its emphasis on the resurrection of Christ. In the extracts below are prayers which reveal the joy and thanksgiving for the vindication of Christ, his resurrection and ascension. "Death by death he has destroyed!" Protestant churches often reflect the piety of the medieval Western Catholic tradition in its fixation on the crucifixion and the death of Christ. We would do well to be aware of the roots of this piety and be willing to correct its imbalance with more joyful attention in our communion prayers to the resurrection of Christ and the coming of the kingdom.

The Divine Liturgy (Eastern Orthodox Liturgy of John Chrysostom)

(beginning)
Blessed is the *kingdom* of the Father, the Son, and Holy Ghost; Now and forever, world without end. AMEN.

(after the people have taken the bread and wine)
We have seen the *resurrection* of Christ, wherefore let us worship the Lord Jesus for he is holy, he only is without sin. Your cross, O Christ, we worship, and your holy *resurrection* we laud and glorify.

O come, all you faithful, let us bow down and worship Christ's holy resurrection. For by the cross has joy come into all the world. Evermore blessing the Lord, let us sing his *resurrection*: for in that he endured the cross, *death by death has he destroyed*!

Shine, shine, O new Jerusalem, for the glory of the Lord is risen upon you. Rejoice now and be glad, O Zion. O Christ! O great and most sacred Passover! O Wisdom and Word of God and Power! Grant that we may more and more truly have communion with you in the Day of your Kingdom which knows no night.[15]

6

Reformation: A Communion Revolution

THE UPHEAVAL of the Reformation issued in both positive and negative results for communion services. Common concerns of all the Protestant Reformers were for broader participation by the people, the use of local languages, simplified orders of service more closely modeled on Scripture, strong preaching, and more frequent communion. Clerical power, however, remained largely unchallenged, and a heavily penitential tone persisted in Reformation communion services.

The Ancient Heritage: Pattern of Eucharistic Worship

As we consider what happened to the mass in the sixteenth-century Reformation, we should first recall the basic pattern of the ancient Christian eucharist. The overall shape of the mass of the Western church was the same as that of the eucharist in the Eastern Orthodox churches, called the Divine Liturgy. There are two main parts, the first of which contains Scripture readings, prayers, and sermon, and the second which is the sacramental service of bread and wine.

Service of the Word (from Jewish background)
  Readings
  Sermon
  Prayers
Service of Bread and Cup (distinctively Christian)
  Prayer of Thanksgiving
  Institution narrative
  Breaking bread, sharing cup

In the Eastern Orthodox tradition, the first part is the Prayer of the Catechumens. This part of the service includes candidates for baptism. The second part, the Prayer of the Faithful, is only for the baptized.

The Roman Catholics call the first part Liturgy of the Word and the second part Liturgy of the Sacrament.

The Heritage Distorted, Both Pattern and Participation

As the chart shows, the roots of the Christian eucharist are two. First is the Jewish tradition of readings, sermon, and prayers which comprised synagogue meetings. Second is the distinctively Christian service of bread and cup at the Lord's table.

Both Western and Eastern eucharists conform to this simple overall pattern. By the Middle Ages the mass focused primary attention upon a particular way of presenting and understanding the second of the two sources – the service of the eucharist. Elements of the first part, the Service of the Word, were still present. However, except for churches where there was preaching, everything was said or sung in Latin, not known by the people. The Psalms and Bible readings were totally unintelligible. People could hear but not listen to the Word.

The language of the entire mass – Latin – was alien to most people, sermons were inconsequential, and congregational participation consisted mostly of being bodily present. People were required to take communion once a year. This entailed confessing their sins to the priest beforehand, performing necessary penance, and receiving absolution. At mass they were offered only the bread. The priest alone took the cup in behalf of everybody.

Mass came to be regarded as a commodity in the marketplace for gaining God's grace and forgiveness, on behalf of the dead as of the living. Sacrificial theology pervaded, gaunt crucifixes loomed, and some unscrupulous priests peddled antidotes to the terrors of hell – masses and more masses. It is no wonder that the storm of the Reformation blew and uprooted with such vehemence.

Common Concerns of the Reformers

The sixteenth-century Reformers' zeal was to restore biblical worship. This meant putting renewed emphasis on Scripture, both its public reading and exposition. They swept out ceremonial actions and many "superstitious" elements such as pictures, statues, gestures, vestments, and verbal formulations.

The Reformers wanted to counteract the routinized worship of the mass and its control by the clerical hierarchy. They wanted to restore the eucharist to the people, and encourage them to participate through faith. In spite of significant conflicts, the Reformers agreed on a number of things about the Lord's Supper.

1. Their stated principle was to reform by biblical precedents and to discard abusive accretions of church tradition.[1]

2. They saw the value of frequent communion services.

3. They wished all participants to receive both bread and wine.

4. They wanted a fuller participation of the people through vernacular language, hymns, responses, psalms, and Spirit-inspired contributions.

5. They used fuller Bible readings and extensive sermons in eucharistic services.

In spite of these common goals, there remained contentious issues as well as unexamined areas of theology and practice of the Lord's Supper. They argued passionately, both with Catholics and among themselves, about how Christ was present in the eucharist. Some, the early heralds of the Reformed tradition in Switzerland and South Germany, tended toward a more symbolic view. They emphasized Christ's presence in the hearts of those partaking, those who took bread and wine with faith.

Huldrich Zwingli, for one, said that "the true body of Christ is present by the contemplation of faith."[2] Some Anabaptists spoke of Christ's presence through the Spirit in the community of faithful disciples gathered around the Lord's Table. Martin Luther held that Christ was really present in the bread and wine but explained this in a different way. He likened it to the union of fire and iron when the iron bar is heated white-hot: "Every part is both iron and fire." John Calvin taught that since the ascension, Christ's humanity has been translated to heaven, but in the eucharist the Spirit "transfuses life into us from the flesh of Christ."[3]

How Did the Reformers Reform?

The Reformers' stated aim was to reform only on the basis of Scripture. *Sola scriptura!* The Protestant slogan meant that all doctrine and faith are based on Scripture only, not church traditions. But what could that mean for worship patterns? The New Testament simply does not give distinct models or instructions. The Reformers did the best they could but often on the basis of reaction or accommodation.

Luther, Both Conservative and Radical

In 1520 Luther published *The Babylonian Captivity of the Church,* a searing denunciation of the entire medieval sacramental system. He declared it to be insidious and false to the Word of God. The *Babylonian Captivity* was "an intellectual revolution," a foundational document not only for Lutheran but for all subsequent Protestant worship. It marks the first major division in Western Christian worship, "creating two distinct inheritors of the Western tradition: Protestants and Roman Catholics."[4]

Not all of Luther's reactions and ideals could be realized. Medieval Christians were not used to taking communion frequently. People resisted change. Luther adapted to them by giving them the initiative: they were to inform the pastor if on that Sunday they wished to partake. If no one asked, the pastor was to proceed with a service of the Word. Because few asked, this shortened service soon became the norm. Such reform was not specifically by the principle *sola scriptura* but by adaptation to what the people were willing to bear.

Luther's methods of worship reform were both conservative and radical.

59

Whenever he could, he preserved the forms of the old worship. If the Scriptures did not specifically forbid something, the church should keep the practice. So Luther retained, for example, the elevation of the host as well as much of the old ceremonial.

But in some respects he performed radical surgery. The Canon, the cluster of short prayers at the heart of the mass (see page 50), he eliminated in his German Mass of 1526. He replaced it with the Words of Institution only, from Scripture. And so Luther purged the Canon, what he called "that abominable concoction drawn from everyone's sewer and cesspool," so no mention of sacrifice remained. In the German Mass Luther also eliminated major sections of the Roman mass, such as the Gloria in Excelsis and the Nicene Creed. At the same time, the Word, especially in the sermon, became the focal point of the service.

Luther's services, now in the language of the people, featured congregational participation in service music and newly written hymns. This created a kind of "folk mass to educate the unlearned."[5] By drastically shortening the great eucharistic prayer, eliminating other traditional parts, and making the sermon central, Luther seemed to marginalize the Lord's Supper.

Zwingli and Calvin

Huldrich Zwingli, the Swiss Reformer and contemporary of Luther, held more radical views on worship and the sacraments. He taught that on the basis of sola scriptura, baptism and Lord's Supper must be observed, but they are "signs" or "pledges" of God's redemptive actions on our behalf. This language opened him to severe criticism. Many have said that the implication of his statements on eucharist is that the Lord's Supper becomes "a kind of visual aid, a helpful reminder of God's grace and forgiveness," but does not in itself convey grace and forgiveness.[6]

Zwingli strongly countered the ideas prevalent in his time that Christ was present in some manner in the bread and the wine of the Lord's Supper. Because of this, Zwingli was accused of "emptying the sacraments" and of demoting eucharistic bread and wine to simple reminders of salvation achieved long ago at Calvary.[7]

Zwingli was considered excessively rationalist. His eucharistic doctrine was often dismissed as "mere memorialism." In Zwingli, according to Louis Bouyer, the sacraments are "no more than vivid images that speak to the simple and remind us of what we know already by means of the word: the love that God has shown us in Jesus Christ."[8] C. W. Dugmore described Zwingli's sacramental views not as real presence, but as real absence.[9]

Wayne Pipkin, on the other hand, contends that these are not fair representations of Zwingli's views. "If bare memorialism and what it implies are Zwinglian, then Zwingli was not a Zwinglian."[10] Pipkin has shown Zwingli as a pastoral Reformer whose eucharistic spirituality was of a highly developed nature. For him commemoration was not so much looking back as an encounter with Christ in the present. The emphasis is on the relational dimension of the believer with Christ within the circle of other believers. Zwingli believed that Christ's presence could be known among the participants at the table.

Zwingli's services were in the language of the people, so they could hear and understand. But because he eliminated congregational responses and forbade music, participation was restricted mainly to listening. In the spare surroundings of church buildings cleared of everything visual and ceremonial, people had only to be taught, exhorted, and edified. Zwingli established for an entire sector of Protestantism, the churches of the Reformed tradition, an austere and didactic form of worship. But we do well to return to his own writings, where we find a fervor and beauty of prayer language and a strong pastoral heart. If present-day churches in the Reformed stream show "mere memorialism" in their eucharistic worship, they will profit by reexamining and perhaps finding more than they expect in their Zwinglian roots.

John Calvin of Geneva, a second-generation Protestant Reformer, stressed church government and doctrine more than matters to do with worship. Holding a "high" sacramental view, he believed the Lord's Supper was genuinely a means of grace. Christ is fully present in the Supper by means of the Holy Spirit, but this is something to be experienced and not explained. Christ's presence is real, a spiritual reality. Calvin hoped that the Lord's Supper would become the normal Sunday worship, but he met strong resistance and had to be content with a monthly communion service in Geneva.

Luther, Zwingli, and Calvin, the magisterial Reformers, worked at reform of worship on the basis of understandings of state-enforced civil order and uniformity of church practice within a particular jurisdiction and geographical region. They desired to reform by Scripture alone but, despite periodic struggles with local state authorities, they fundamentally accepted the constraints of traditional Christendom views of power and ecclesiology.

Anabaptist Understandings of the Lord's Supper

At the same time, all over Europe many small groups, often called Anabaptists, were also observing the Lord's Supper. These were the first "free churches." They rejected control by civil or ecclesiastical authorities outside their local groups. They recast their worship on the basis of their perceptions of scriptural precedent. They advocated heartfelt spontaneous prayer and forms of worship marked by "Spirit leading." Most of them rejected external forms and ceremonials, whether Catholic, Lutheran, or Reformed. These groups devised the simplest ritual forms possible and accompanied them with appropriate Scripture readings and extemporaneous prayers.

In a fascinating parenthesis in the German Mass, Luther himself yearned for such a "truly evangelical order" in which Christians would not need prescribed outward forms and structures. They would meet in small groups and devise patterns which they found most helpful.[11]

The Anabaptists, as John Rempel has recently demonstrated,[12] held distinctive strands of eucharistic theology. Rempel examines the writings of three Anabaptists: Pilgram Marpeck, a water engineer by profession; Dirk Philips, prolific codifier and apologist of Anabaptist views; and Balthasar Hubmaier, an academic theologian and preacher.

These men differed on some points. But what they held in common shows an Anabaptist theology and practice of the Lord's Supper creatively distinct in their own time. The believing community gathered around the table of the Lord, sharing the bread and wine, genuinely knows Christ's presence. The Spirit shapes the community's life in conformity to the cross of Christ and to his sacrificial life of love.

Marpeck's and Dirk's understandings help to correct what many have seen as a reductionism in some Reformation groups which limited the Lord's Supper simply to a human act of remembrance. In Hubmaier's theology comes a profound synthesis of the themes of faith, reconciliation, community, and mission.

Agreeing with Zwingli and Bucer, these three Anabaptists argued that, because of Christ's ascension, he cannot be bodily present on earth and thus not literally present in the bread and wine of eucharist. Strongly drawn to the Gospel of John, they tended to conflate Christ in his divinity with the Spirit. Because of their understanding of a limitation upon the possible earthly activity of the ascended Christ, their emphasis fell on the action of the Spirit in the Lord's Supper. The faithful community would demonstrate in all of its relationships, with brother, neighbor, and enemy, the incarnated love of Christ. They strongly believed that the faith which is expressed ethically is the Spirit's gift, and not a humanly generated response.

The Anabaptists held in common with magisterial Reformers the concerns for establishing worship forms on the basis of Scripture alone, using the vernacular language, singing of hymns, extensive reading and expounding of Scripture. However, these "free church" folk introduced distinctive emphases in their Lord's Supper observances.

Anabaptist Practices of the Lord's Supper

Anabaptists called for a "pure" church made up of a community of voluntary believers living holy lives in the way of Jesus. Descriptions of Anabaptist observances of the Lord's Supper reflect their concerns for fostering disciplined and accountable relationships, for developing rites which reflected and built communal reconciliation and unity, and for encouraging one another in faithful and costly following (*Nachfolge*) of Christ. The following three excerpts of Anabaptist writings on the Lord's Supper illustrate these concerns which focus especially on the manner and the outcomes of sharing the bread and the wine.

> The Lord's Supper shall be held, as often as the brothers and sisters are together, thereby proclaiming the death of the Lord, and thereby warning each one to commemorate, how Christ gave his life for us, and shed his blood for us, that we might also be willing to give our body and life for Christ's sake, which means for the sake of all the brothers and sisters.[13]

Most Anabaptist groups departed from this early desire for frequent communion. Yet this passage from the Swiss Anabaptist Congregational Order of the late 1520s illustrates several typical Anabaptist themes. One is the convention of referring to the "brothers" of the church, with a face-to-face, familial ethos, in contrast to the society-encompassing church of the Catholics and the Reformers alike.

Another is the language of commemoration, echoing a Zwinglian tendency toward regarding the Lord's Supper as a memorial. But this is not a mere memorial, as the final phrases indicate. The commemoration of Christ's suffering means the brothers declare their willingness to lay down body and life for the sake of Christ, which means their willingness to do so for each other. Such a memorial is more than a pious mental process. Living out this memory may cost their lives. Anabaptist eucharistic spirituality was communal, a direct challenge to the individualistic and subjective piety of the established churches.

> Whoever does not share the calling of the one God to one faith, to one baptism, to one spirit, to one body together with all the children of God, may not be made one loaf together with them, as must be true if one wishes truly to break bread according to the command of Christ.[14]

This paragraph from the *Schleitheim Confession* of 1527 contains a radical understanding of the meaning of Jesus' words, "This is my body." Christ makes one loaf of all the children of God, all those who are called into unity of faith, baptism, and spirit. Christ is truly present among his own, creating through their communion a reconciled and reconciling community.

The Pledge of Love is a unique rite found within Balthasar Hubmaier's *Form for the Supper of Christ.*

Whoever now desires to eat this bread and drink this drink of the Lord's Supper, let us rise and respond with heart and mouth in the Pledge of Love.

Brothers and sisters, if you desire to love God before, in, and above all things, in the power of his holy and living Word; if you desire to serve, honor, and adore God, and to sanctify his name; and to subject your sinful will to God's divine will which he has worked in you by the living Word, then let each say individually, "I desire it." **I desire it.**

If you desire to love and serve your neighbor with deeds of love, to lay down for him or her your life; if you desire to be obedient to father, mother, and all authorities according to the will of God, and this in the power of our Lord Jesus Christ, who laid down his flesh and blood for us, then let each say individually, "I desire it." **I desire it.**

If you will practice admonition toward your brothers and sisters, make peace and unity among them, and reconcile yourselves with all those whom you have offended; if you desire to abandon all envy, hate, and evil will toward others, and willingly cease all action and behavior which causes harm, disadvantage, or offense to your neighbor; if you will love your enemies and do good to them, then let each say individually, "I desire it." **I desire it.**

If you desire publicly to confirm before the church this pledge of love which you have now made, through the Lord's Supper, by eating bread and drinking of the cup, and to testify to it in the power of the living memorial of the suffering and death of Jesus Christ our Lord, then let each say individually, "I desire it in the power of God." **I desire it in the power of God.**

So eat and drink with one another in the name of God the Father, the Son, and the Holy Spirit. May God accord to all of us the power and the strength that we may worthily carry out this pledge and bring it to its saving conclusion. May the Lord Jesus impart to us his grace. AMEN.[15]

The entire service, prepared for and used in Hubmaier's parish in Nikolsburg, Moravia, expresses important Anabaptist emphases. The Pledge of Love, used liturgically as the community's preparation for taking the bread and wine of communion, focuses these concerns upon the practical meaning of love in the life of the individual believers and in the community. For Hubmaier the meaning of the Supper was to be proved in practical ways in which Christ's love was expressed. Plain words or inward feelings would not be enough. The meaning of the Supper was love. The call to each participant was to become conformed to Christ's own way of sacrificial love. Following Christ in life – this is a characteristic

Anabaptist emphasis, and an appropriate challenge at the conclusion of ⁷⁄ this communion order.

Clerical Power Unchallenged

On the whole, the Protestant Reformers continued to emphasize the role of the clergy; they perpetuated a hierarchical distinction between laity and the clerics. In this Reformed formulation of 1678, it is clear that the ministers are in charge of preaching the Word, administering the sacrament, and governing the church.

> Where the Word of God is rightly preached, and the sacraments truly administered, according to Christ's institution, and the practice of the primitive church: having discipline and government duly executed, by ministers or pastors of God's appointing and the church's election, that is a true constituted church.[16]

Look at the implication of this statement. What is the true church? It is that church subject to those few people within it – the clergy – who have the power over Word, sacrament, and discipline. In this formulation we see that even the independents, much less the magisterial Reformers, didn't reform the power understandings of the medieval church. They didn't touch that most sensitive nerve of all, the power of the clergy.

What Did the Reformers Accomplish?

The Reformers were people of their time. In some respects they did not break out of a medieval mind-set into the pure scriptural worship they yearned for. They continued to put great stress on the sinfulness of individuals and the necessity for personal forgiveness before coming to the Lord's table. A penitential tone surrounded their communion services. The entire Western Christian tradition was focused on the cross and sacrifice of Christ as well as on the sorrow and unworthy sinfulness of those approaching the Lord's table.

Yet the reforming groups accomplished much in their sacramental worship. They simplified their rites, used the ordinary language of the people, increased participation of the congregation, developed congregational singing, and fostered new emphasis on preaching. But ordinary people resisted attempts in all the reforming traditions to establish more frequent communion. It was simply too much to ask. A ⁊ tragic and unintended effect of the Reformation upheaval was to drive the ⁊ Lord's Supper to the very edges of congregational worship life.

Isn't it amazing! People took the question of communion so seriously. They piously tortured, drowned, and exiled each other over what was said to happen at the words of institution. Reformation debates surrounding the Lord's Supper were literally burning issues. All the Reformers agreed on the importance of communion. Yet after all the terror and tragedy, where had they arrived? In all the traditions, despite beneficial innovations, communion was marginalized. Within the Catholic Church, despite daily masses, ordinary people partook only once a year. And in the churches of the Reformation, the same tendency held true. In some cases communion was considered so important that it could be held only a few times a year. Sometimes the ceremonies of preparation were dauntingly rigorous and exhausting. Eucharist had no chance to serve as a lively focus at the center of a congregation's worship life.

Was this an "anorectic" approach to the Lord's table? Thoughts of food may be an inward obsessive focus, yet it seems impossible to eat. Was the excitement at hearing the Bible read and taught so great that the table paled in comparison? For whatever reasons, the table of the Lord became unapproachable, inaccessible.

Outside of the marginalized Anabaptist or free churches, there was little sense that communion shaped the worshiping community. Community was a given; it was shaped by the sociology of the parish. To paraphrase the words of John, the medieval communities of Christendom existed by blood and by the will of the flesh. These Christendom communities did not need communion to create and nurture their kind of community.

7

Modern Developments: Innovation and Recovery

THE FIRST SIX chapters addressed aspects of the Western heritage of Lord's Supper beliefs and practice through the sixteenth century. In this chapter we examine the power of the Enlightenment in shaping communion piety. We look at several Christian denominational communities, children of the sixteenth-century Reformation, now challenged by modernity, a second revolution. How did they respond to the prevailing rationalist Enlightenment piety?

Would Martin Luther feel at home in a modern German church's communion? What would John Calvin preach about in Geneva today? And Thomas Cranmer – could he comfortably use one of the modern prayer books of the Anglican communion? How would sixteenth-century Anabaptists respond to a twentieth-century Mennonite communion service in Amsterdam or Winnipeg? Perhaps the Reformers would recognize and joyfully embrace their descendants' piety. But it is possible they would have some difficulties doing so.

Protestants recognize the Reformation as a good thing, the great watershed. In many ways it was good. There was now intelligible worship in the local language, fuller participation of the congregation, and improved teaching of Bible and credal truths. But the Reformation, I believe, was incomplete and partial at critical points.

For example, Luther's reformation of the liturgy was reactive. He removed everything from the German mass (1526), his order for communion, except the narrative of institution. Why did he save that? Because he was a medieval Western Christian for whom those words still produced a sacramental "moment." Luther's revision reflected a tradition emanating from the fourth century on, one which highlighted the words *Hoc est corpus meum*, "This is my body" (Matt. 26:26). If Luther could have gone further back for his reforming source, he might have made a more thorough and more satisfying revision.

Baptismal initiation is another area in which Reformers, though they jettisoned what they considered superstitious and ceremonial accretions, continued a Christendom pattern of infant baptism, separated by a number of years from confirmation. This was most likely not a genuinely early church practice, though the Reformers may not have realized it. They developed theological explanations to undergird what was, historically speaking, probably a "defective" practice.

In such respects the Reformation was incomplete and reactive. But it was undeniably a powerful engine for irreversible changes in the four traditions (Lutheran, Reformed, Anabaptist, Anglican) which in the sixteenth century developed out of the breakaway from Rome.

A Second Revolution

An even bigger change was in store, however. A major shift took place, a movement which created a "rupture with the past." James White calls it an "unbridgeable gap" between Reformation times and ours. This "second revolution" profoundly desacralized worship.[1]

During the eighteenth century, in the period known in the West as the Enlightenment, Christian worship changed. Whereas the Reformers sought early sources for renewal of sacramental worship, in the Enlightenment church leaders looked for ways to accommodate or adapt eucharistic worship to the prevailing worldview.

At this time people tried to understand their faith and piety in exclusively rationalist and moralist terms. Some thought of God as a metaphorical watchmaker who observed his creation from outside. God did not intervene but expected people to do their best to improve what they could.

German churches, for example, continued (infrequently) to observe communion, but they did so because it was a biblical command. As emphasis on the sacrament declined, services became more simple in form and more centered around the Word. Church buildings were transformed into preaching halls, with balconies and raised pulpits. All worship aimed toward the improvement of human behavior. "Be good" was the message. K. R. Lang suggested these admonitions to accompany the distribution of communion bread and wine.

> Enjoy this bread. May the Spirit of devotion rest upon you with its full blessing. Enjoy a little wine. The power of virtue does not lie in this wine but in yourselves, in religious instruction, and in God.[2]

Suitable sermon themes for Advent, advised William Nagel, included "On the stealing of wood" (Matt. 21:1-11, "and others cut branches from the trees") or "On the value of human expressions of good wishes (Hosanna!)." On Christmas Day one might preach on "the hardiness of shepherds and a warning against the use of fur caps" (Luke 2:1-10). After Easter, the Emmaus story might inspire a homily "on going for walks."[3]

This extreme rationalist mentality, applied to all aspects of faith and piety, surely blasted a gap between the Reformers' religious sensibilities and ours. To consider eucharist in a symbolic way often brings the familiar accusation: Zwinglian! But Zwingli's worldview and his confidence in God's active presence in a worshiping congregation is far from mere memorialism. Moralistic admonitions at anti-sacramental communions, so common in our own time, derive not from Zwingli but from the legacy of that second revolution known as Enlightenment rationalism.

We will now consider the witness of five denominational groups, to see how their communion piety and practices were affected by the prevailing Enlightenment worldview.

1. The Church of England

At the end of the seventeenth century, Christians in England found themselves in two distinct sectors – the people of the "church" and the people of the "chapel." Each group, the Church of England on the one hand and the Dissenting Churches on the other, worshiped distinctly from the other. The Dissenters included those called Congregationalists, Baptists, and Presbyterians. The Dissenters, like their Calvinist antecedents, looked only to Scripture for the shape and content of worship.

The bishops of the Church of England respected not only the authority of Scripture but also the worship traditions of the ancient church. The mark of the Reformation upon Anglicanism is a unique blending, in fact, a "compromise between Calvinism and its *bete noire*, Roman Catholicism."[4] In Reformation times, Archbishop Cranmer drew richly from both sources in preparing the Book of Common Prayer, which, remarkably, has admirably served all groupings within the church from Anglo-Catholics to Evangelicals.

Chapel and church have much in common. The first revolution, the Reformation, impressed its mark upon both streams. But the terms *chapel* and *church* provide shorthand designations for differing concepts of the nature of the church and its relation to the state. They also imply a difference in architecture, in use of music, and in the relative emphasis upon Word and sacrament. The second revolution, Enlightenment rationalism, especially marked the church.

In the eighteenth century, observance of the eucharist fell to a low ebb, in an intellectual atmosphere which rejected any sense of personal providence and repudiated belief in divine intervention. Bishop Benjamin Hoadly (d. 1761) referred to Christ as "He, who was once present with his disciples, is now absent."[5] Other bishops, perceiving the dangers of scientific rationalism, warned their clergy against "reducing revelation to reason, faith to philosophy, and Christian ethics to prudential morality."[6]

But the tide of modernity flowed strongly. Eucharist, required by law in all parishes three times a year, now held purely memorial, didactic, and moralistic value. Its purpose seemed solely to enhance social harmony. Understandably, great attention centered on the pulpit, the source for good advice and prudent admonition. Sermons became oral essays, discourses on morality and charity. There was no room for mystery or miracle, for revelation or prophecy. Inspiration and emotion were laughed at. They had no place in a rational scheme of things.

Reaction was inevitable. The eighteenth century gave birth to several revival movements which in varying ways attempted to bring together the traditional and the charismatic, the formal and the spontaneous elements of early Christianity. One of these was Methodism.

2. Methodism, a Counter-Cultural Movement

Out of the cold crucible of eighteenth-century Enlightenment Anglican-ism, the brothers Wesley emerged: John the evangelist and organizer, and Charles the hymn writer. They never intended to lead a schismatic move-ment; they simply wished to renew and revitalize the Church of England, in which they were both clergymen. John and Charles were branded as "enthusiasts," the worst epithet in eighteenth-century English church circles. One critic dubbed Methodism as a type of "spiritual influenza."[7]

The kind of Spirit-filled enthusiasm the Wesleys practiced took them to the poor. It took John on tireless missionary tours, crisscrossing the country on horseback in all seasons. Enthusiasm turned him to the resources of early Christianity. John introduced watch-night services, prayer vigils, and hymn singing. He emphasized the value of daily prayers and of frequent communion.

Drawn to early Christian piety through the influence of German Lutheran Pietists called Moravians, John Wesley rediscovered the love feast.[8] He introduced this ancient communal rite into his religious method for new Christians. In the prevailing religious atmosphere which did no more than instruct individuals to try to be good, the love feast was a rad-ical innovation. It was not the sacrament of eucharist. But it was a form of worship with life-giving potential. Here was the old but now new idea of sharing – sharing actual food, sharing with the poor, sharing confession, sharing testimonies and thanksgivings. In the love feast people once again celebrated their common life and exercised their mutual care. God was vitally active and present to them in this old-new form of worship.

The Wesleys wrote special hymns for love feasts. One of these, called "Grace Before Meat," is still a favorite table grace:

> Be present at our table, Lord.
> Be here and everywhere adored.
> Thy creatures bless and grant that we
> May feast in Paradise with Thee.

The normal order of service for a love feast in Wesley's time was thus: hymn, prayer, sung grace, distribution of bread, collections for poor, circulation of the loving-cup, sermon, testimonies and verses of hymns, closing exhortation by minister, hymn, benediction. The bread was either semisweet biscuits or seed-bread shaped as a loaf and cut into slices. The water, or occasionally tea, passed from hand to hand in a two-handled mug.

One of the delights of worship at the love feast was its freedom for testimony and thanksgiving. Testimony, in turn, drew attenders into deeper faith. One young man, William Clover, "borrowed" his sister's ticket and entered a love feast on false pretenses. He was just curious. William aped what everyone else did. When they stood, he stood. When they knelt, he knelt. Mouthing words he didn't know, he pretended to sing the hymns. He was nonplussed to be offered bread and water – the elements of the love feast. How could he refuse? William was sure he, an unbeliever, was damned to all eternity for falsely receiving the sacrament. But the testimonies gripped his heart and his imagination. This love feast was the first step to William's conversion.[9]

Adapting and incorporating the love feast into a disciplined round of religious meetings, John Wesley reclaimed two ancient and authentic qualities of Christian table practice: *koinonia* (sharing or communion) and *agape* (love). And so we see that John and Charles Wesley, with their many pastoral and missionary assistants, developed a unique "method" for individual and corporate Christian life. They led a dynamic religious renewal, truly countercultural. God was not an absconded watchmaker! God's Spirit set fire to Scripture and powerfully blew through the everyday experience of the "Methodists." Call them enthusiasts. Call them daft or mad. These folk were not subject to the rule of rationalism.

3. Restoration Groups

The rule of rationalism, along with attendant individualism and liberalism, did not deter God's creative Spirit from working even within the prevalent European worldview. In this period there seemed no doubt that people should approach the Bible directly and find there the resource to challenge any assumed authority. Creeds, beliefs, synods – all should be scrutinized.

Within the ferment of scrutiny and reevaluation of traditions, new groupings of Christians formed. Christian Churches (Disciples of Christ) and (Plymouth) Brethren were a vigorous movement, both in Britain and in North America, to restore Christianity through reclaiming its New Testament roots.

Disciples and Christians

First, we encounter the story[10] of three earnest Presbyterian ministers who, through independent and rigorous application to New Testament church practice, found their communion piety and observances set alight. Through a Glasgow missionary training school set up by the brothers

Haldane,[11] two of them caught a vision of a "Second Reformation" for the church. This is the story of three ideals of Restoration worship which, accomplished in the nineteenth century, made eucharistic history:

1. The Lord's table is open to all Christians.
2. Weekly Sunday communion is the norm.
3. Lay members preside at the Lord's table.

By their disciplined study and reflection, these three nineteenth-century Presbyterian ministers[12] were fired with a dream of Christian unity based on New Testament faith, practice, and patterns. "Division among Christians is a horrid evil," said one of them, Thomas Campbell.

Thomas and his son Alexander, weary of divisive and sterile Scottish Reformed church life, became leaders of a movement in Scotland and Ireland for restoration of early Christianity. They wished to pursue Reformation in ways which the sixteenth-century Reformers were unable or unwilling to do. They believed that as Christians continued to search, they would find the Scriptures an unfailing source for more truth. But Calvinists "stick fast where they were left by that great man of God, who yet saw not all things."[13]

Later, as missionaries in North America, the Campbells traveled widely and preached their convictions, bringing together believers calling themselves "Disciples." The Campbell brothers joined with another former Presbyterian minister, Barton Stone, who had similar ideals. Stone and his followers had called themselves simply "Christian."

In 1832, convinced that denominationalism was wrong and that creeds were not necessary, the Disciples and the Christians joined forces. Their form of biblical restorationism became the basis for the Christian Church. Applied to their forms of worship, this biblicism indicated that "nothing ought to be [received into the] worship of the church, or to be made a term of communion, which is not as old as the New Testament."[14] Love was always to be the basis of unity among Christians. Participation in the Lord's Supper was always to be according to individual conscience.

Observing New Testament evidence for such a practice, the Restorationists reintroduced a weekly Sunday eucharist. To them it was brilliantly clear: if regular Sunday Lord's table was right for the earliest Christians, it was right for Christians in every age! So they just did it; they celebrated the Lord's Supper every Sunday.

One reason the Christian Church could do this was that, unlike practice in other Christian traditions, lay persons presided at the table. Was that style not obvious to any close reader of the New Testament? Nowhere was there a stipulation for a particular class of ministry to lead the community in breaking bread. The Christian Church never had to postpone communion because some specially "ordained" person wasn't available to preside. The one who led the service had no set text but simply prayed and led as well as he could. It was only reasonable for Christians to worship in a manner as closely modeled on New Testament practices as possible. It was eminently sensible to sweep away irrational accretions of tradition and misplaced power, aspects of Christian history which had brought only trouble and strife.

These Restorationist congregations found new life in old roots, just as the Methodists had done. In both cases, eucharistic renewal was more than dusting off ancient texts or rites. A Spirit-led dynamic provided both the vision and the practical ways of working the vision out.

Brethren

In the 1830s a group called by outsiders "Plymouth Brethren," but who preferred the simple name Brethren, addressed the same questions that engaged the Disciples and the "Christians" of America. What does unity in Christ mean? Can we have the eucharist? Who may partake? Must ordained clergy preside? They came to answers quite different from those of early Puritan separatists who had pulled away from Anglicanism but nevertheless required clerical leaders for valid and proper communion.

One of the earliest leaders of the movement was Anthony Groves. Hampshire-born in 1795, he was well educated and practiced dentistry in Plymouth and Exeter. Particularly in Plymouth, his friends were educated and pious men. Under their spiritual influence, Groves recognized his call to missionary service, and he developed an increasingly radical vision of Christian life. He came to regard the accumulation of possessions as a hindrance to simple faith and piety. As they awaited the fruition of their missionary vocation, Groves and his wife, Mary, opened their hearts and their entire lives in generous service to others. During this time Groves was drawn more and more to convictions about the depth of true Christian unity.

Although he was a strict Anglican churchman, Groves had friends among nonconformist groups. They were involved together in Bible study and discussion groups meeting in homes, which minimized denominational barriers. Through his biblical studies, Groves observed and greatly admired the apparent freedom and generous fellowship of New Testament churches. He saw that early believers who met together as disciples of their Lord freely broke bread, as he had taught them. It seemed clear that, if the Scriptures were to be a guide, Christ's disciples should set every Lord's Day apart to remember him in that way. Groves proposed, for common participation, the simple principle of union, the love of Jesus, instead of a unity achieved by judgment in minor things.[15]

Gradually, through his devotion to biblical study, Groves was loosened from conventional establishment views on violence, economics, and clericalism. In the end, he could not go forward for ordination in the Church of England, a requirement for missionary service abroad.

True to his intuitive sense and his thorough biblical study, Groves continued in his search to express Christian unity. He wrote to a friend, an Anglican clergyman,

> I do not exclusively join [your communion because I feel] this spirit of exclusiveness to be of the very essence of schism, which the apostle so strongly reproves ... I am ready to break the bread and drink the cup of holy joy with all who love the Lord and will not lightly speak evil of His name. [A person is holy] because Christ dwells in him, and manifests Himself where he worships. [I will] with my Lord, join him as a member of the mystical body, and hold communion and fellowship with him in any work of the Lord in which he is engaged ... Oh! when will the day come, when the love of Christ will have more power to unite than our foolish regulations have to divide the family of God (16 December 1828).[16]

Groves and his friends intuitively moved toward Christian unity, but John Nelson Darby addressed that unity head-on. He was the dynamic and charismatic early leader of the Brethren. Darby clearly articulated the question and its biblical rationale, but he was ultimately unable to inspire practical application to his insights.

Darby was born in 1800 of wealthy Anglican Irish parents and received a fine education in law. But in 1825 he abandoned his career and took orders in the Anglican Church. Darby's first assignment was as a curate in a wild area of the Wicklow Mountains. A tireless missionary, Darby made a memorable impression on any who met him.

> Every evening [Darby] sallied forth to teach in the cabins, and roving far and wide over mountain and amid bogs, was seldom home before midnight ... [Darby] only wanted [people] to submit their understandings to God, that is, to the Bible, that is, to [Darby's] interpretation![17]

An exegete of clarity and persistence, Darby wrestled with the theological meaning of unity in Christ. He asserted that Christians' unity is in Christ and Christ alone. Scripture states it clearly: Christ, in his death, will draw all [people] to himself (John 12:32-33). The death of Christ is surely the center of communion "until he comes" again (1 Cor. 11:26). And is not the Lord's Supper the outward symbol and the means of effecting the unity of Christ's body? For "we who are many are one body, for we all partake of the one bread" (1 Cor 10:17). Is not unity a gift of redemption in Christ, a gift which Christians have perversely refused to accept?

Darby exposed the heart of the question and gave a biblical and theological answer. But tragically, Darby's teaching engendered harshness of spirit and a movement which became increasingly conflict-ridden. Others in the burgeoning Brethren movement argued and struggled with practical implications of his answer. Was a disciplined church possible? Did "indiscriminate admission" to the Table destroy the church's witness? Even today, these questions to some extent shape the way the assemblies break bread together.

To recognize unity within the body of Christ – this is what lies behind the manner in which the Lord's Supper is announced in a Brethren (Open) assembly today. "The table is open to all who are in right relationship within a Christian congregation." But the recognition requires more than an individual's spontaneous desire, as a visitor, to break the bread and drink the cup with the host assembly. Strongly implied is the necessity for accountable membership in a local body of the church. When they travel, Brethren may carry letters of recommendation from their home assembly, ensuring that they may break bread with other Christians wherever they go.

In their attempt to follow scriptural patterns, the Brethren have developed informal, Spirit-led worship at the breaking of bread. This is usually in the form of quiet worship in which the gifts of the members shape the proceedings. Scripture verses, prayers, and songs may follow one another as members are inspired to lead. When it is time, a member takes up the bread, gives thanks, and breaks it. (There are only members, no clergy.) Then the stewards serve the seated members. Giving thanks and sharing the cup follow an intervening period of silence, Scripture, or song. The ideal for this service is that it should be open, unstructured, and free. The only criterion is whether the Spirit of the Lord, through the breaking of bread, is active, recognized, and received by the worshipers.

By rigorous application to biblical norms, the Brethren, in their service of the Lord's Supper, evoke the character of early Christian worship. As we saw earlier in this book, Christians maintained through the first several centuries a significant measure of freedom of form, words, and manner. They made space for prophetic and spontaneous expression. The Brethren have tried to recapture this quality in their free worship at the table, an ideal for other Christian groups to emulate.

So we see the fruit of rigorous, persistent Bible study – a renewal of depth and vitality in the communion services. These Restoration groups, though not always able to live up to their ideals, have nevertheless given witness to the power of certain qualities of early Christian worship at the Lord's table. They have wrestled with the sometimes conflicting desires for a disciplined church and the open recognition of Christian unity, freely expressed in communion. They have maintained an insistence upon the simplicity and naturalness of a Christian fellowship without hierarchical classes. Many have held on to an ideal of spontaneous worship animated by the Spirit and led by the many-gifted members of the local church.

Churches within this tradition both express and develop the ideals which underlie their origins. Members take seriously each one's responsibility to study the Scripture. They seek unity in the Spirit. They expect to contribute to open worship at the Lord's table. Responsible, face-to-face relationships can flourish in a church in which all are peers and all are ministers one to another.

4. The Anglo-Catholic Movement

Out of the crucible of the early nineteenth-century rationalistic worldview emerged a powerful movement for revival in the Church of England. It has been dubbed the Tractarian Revival or the Oxford Movement. Insisting on an "apostolic succession" of ordination, this movement stressed the authority and tradition of the church of the first four centuries.

Often viewed as a Catholic antithesis to an evangelical position, it may more creatively be considered as a supplementary force. Evangelical movements had revived personal religion in England and continued to emphasize both Word and sacrament. The Oxford Movement reclaimed almost-forgotten elements of thought and practice from the ancient church.[18] For example, there was a renewed sense of the corporate holiness of the universal church and willingness to seek faithfulness within the historic traditions. Worship was worthy itself, not merely as a prelude to good ethical activities.

Major lasting influence from this movement has flowed in the areas of worship ethos and spirituality. A quiet reserved piety restored a sense of reverence in public worship. A deepened spirituality for many people has been fostered through establishing monastic communities, offering retreats, organizing pilgrimages, promoting devotional reading, and encouraging regular participation in communion.

Closely aligned with their reverent sacramental piety was the social vision of the Anglican inheritors of the Oxford Movement, later called Anglo-Catholics. For example, religious communities worked out their vocation to relieve distressed people. They visited the sick and poor in homes, hospitals, workhouses, and prisons. They taught children. They gave shelter to the homeless and buried the dead. Such works of charity connected directly with the piety of their sacramental life.

As in every revival, music played a significant part. The Methodist revival had its Wesleys. The Oxford Movement had its great hymn crafters, superb translators of ancient Christian texts, J. M. Neale and Edward Caswall. These hymns powerfully conveyed and fostered the ethos of reverent piety characteristic of their movement.

5. Pentecostals

Even though many date the origins of the Pentecostal Movement from the early twentieth century, it could just as well be considered the great-grandchild of Wesley. The line of the Holiness Movement runs right through the nineteenth century, surfacing at various points. It emphasized a personal experience of the work of the Spirit, the "second blessing" of sanctification. In their worship God is present and active through the Spirit. Healings, prophecies, tongues – all are manifestations of the living God who hears and answers prayer. What could be further from eighteenth-century rationalism?

Pentecostals in a sense are "the first post-Enlightenment tradition."[19] It doesn't surprise them that God directly answers and intervenes in their meetings. They ask and expect God to heal them, touch them, and baptize them with the fire of the Spirit. Pentecostal worship emphasizes praise and testimony to God's actions of salvation and healing. Every action is expressive and personal. "Do we allow the Spirit to have his way?" is the question that serves as the sole criterion for worship.

How do Pentecostal communion services reflect this theology? Jesus commanded it, so they obey. They observe the Lord's Supper as one among many ways of worship. But because of Pentecostals' expectation and experience of the Spirit's presence in a variety of manifestations, the Lord's Supper is not a supreme focus. Foot washing, healing, and baptism stand together with the Lord's Supper as scriptural ordinances which edify the community.

Twentieth-Century Renewal

By now we are two and a half centuries from the original blaze of the Enlightenment. As we have observed, Christians reacted in various ways to the pressures of rationalism upon their faith and piety. Positive effects came about from closely reasoned study of Scripture and tradition. Negative effects such as a didactic, moralistic view of communion became deeply embedded in the piety of many denominations.

This problem is still with us. All too common is a view of communion which is individualistic, narrow, and small. The question stands: how can we reclaim the piety of early Christianity which in the presence of the risen Lord, at his table, engaged the whole of the community's life – individual, social, and material?

In our own century this question has gripped people across the whole range of Christian denominations. Ours is a period of energetic worship renewal. Many groups have found clues to the way forward, and through cross-fertilization of resources on many levels, Christians are finding new balance, new energy, and new life in their Sunday worship.

The Liturgical Movement

The liturgical movement is not something people of all denominations are drawn to, and some would not give it a second glance. But perhaps it affects even those who do not actively embrace the idea that liturgical renewal might make a difference to them.

All renewal movements have historical roots. The work of nineteenth-century church historians underlay a surge of twentieth-century scholarship on worship documents of the early Christian centuries. Those efforts were marked by cooperation between representatives of differing traditions. Christians have come more and more to recognize their common roots and to rejoice in learning together what kind of plant should be growing out of them.

In our century Catholics and Protestants – pastors and priests as well as scholars and teachers – eagerly searched early Christian materials which served as sources for renewal. This could properly be called a movement of the Holy Spirit, since "its effect has been to increase the holiness, charity, social witness, and ecumenicity among Christians in our tragically divided world."[20] The vitality of Protestant theological enterprise has joined the pioneering spirit of the Catholic liturgical renewal. Each has affected the other although they were formerly opposing traditions.

One of the most important effects is that Protestant denominations have recognized and reinstated the Lord's table as integral to regular Sunday worship. The interplay and balance of the ancient two-part form of worship (Word and table) has been restored. At the same time, Catholic liturgical reform has insisted upon renewed space and importance for the Word read and preached.

Many changes the Reformers insisted on, which have been common among Protestants, now are incorporated into Catholic eucharistic theology. These include replacement of Latin by local languages, taking both wine and bread at communion, the full and active participation of the community in the actions of worship, and the assertion that it is the entire community which celebrates the Lord's Supper, not just the priest who says the words.

Obviously, not all Christians belong to the great liturgical traditions: Anglican, Catholic, Lutheran. What about their communion practices? How have they been touched by the renewal of liturgical worship? Vigorous discussion goes on in free church papers, quarterlies, and manuals for ministers. Leaders in Presbyterian, Methodist, and Baptist churches have encountered new challenges to their traditions' interplay of traditional forms and inspired spontaneity in worship.

The most thoughtful among them have not thrown out the flexibility of their denominational patterns, but have undergirded them with stronger theological and biblical rationale. A good example of this type of work was *Orders and Prayers for Church Worship* (an excerpt of which is in "A Baptist

Pattern" in Appendix A). The authors' concern was to strengthen the essential content of the service but retain spontaneous openings to the Spirit-inspired, prophetic elements of worship. What we see is major groupings of Christians who, through examining the resources of their history – those shared with others as well as distinctively their own – are finding ways of renewal.

In Reformation times, within the space of a half century, five distinct traditions quickly evolved, each one holding the particular concerns of their own constituency: Lutheran, Reformed, Anglican, Anabaptist, and Puritan. In the manner of the Big Bang, each successive century saw a new worship tradition evolve into Quakers, Methodists, Revivalists, and Pentecostals.

Each of the traditions, old and newer, has continued to change, adapting to the needs and conditions of the times. But all these traditions are still distinctive. Learning and borrowing from each other has not meant they meld together. The various traditions retain the emphases and manners which are uniquely their own. This is good. Healthy interaction, willingness to learn from one another, and wholesome borrowing happen among groups who have a strong sense of their own identity.

But there are many Christian groups and networks outside these denominational designations. They know only their own manners and experience. Pride may hold them from Christian interaction. Domineering leaders sometimes grasp at a theology which reserves power to themselves. There is no room for wider Christian critique upon their internal structures of authority. Groups who have weak origins and are unsure of their identity resist learning from others. Often born in isolation, they hold onto it for protection. Where are their resources for renewal?

All Christian traditions, including especially the weak and the twisted ones, can flourish anew if they enrich their sacramental life, particularly an enlarged practice of communion. We all have the Bible as sourcebook. We have the risen Christ inviting us to his table. We have the Spirit, who unfailingly renews and heals. But we ourselves have a part to play. We have to make room for the renewal. What greater gift do we have than the Lord's table, from Christ himself. We don't have to rely on words alone, nor on elusive experience. We can all learn from each other.

With the Anglo-Catholics, all can approach the table with reverent expectancy. With the free traditions, the Reformed can make space for Spirit-led spontaneity in prayer and praise. With the Reformed, the Pentecostals can sing psalms and pay disciplined attention to the Word expounded. With the Anabaptists groups, the Anglicans can honor the John 13 tradition of servanthood and humility in the foot-washing service. With Anglicans and Lutherans, the Baptists can pray the lucid and fervent collects of the ancient church. Hymns – Anglo-Catholic, Methodist, and contemporary – enable us all to sing praise to Christ with the church universal. Each tradition has so much to give, so much to learn.

The Convergence Movement

"The convergence movement" is a phrase coined by Robert Webber to refer to a new celebrative style of worship emerging among many Christian denominations and traditions. Advocates of liturgical renewal draw on liturgical, sacramental, charismatic, and evangelical aspects of the Christian faith. Out of these resources a type of Sunday worship is evolving that is rooted in Scripture, aware of Christian history, and committed to relevance.[21]

Running in contemporary lines with the liturgical movement has been the neo-Pentecostal movement (1950s) and then the charismatic movement (1960s onward). These have had effects upon virtually every denomination and have given birth to many independent fellowships and networks. The impact has been primarily through music. Instrumental groups with gifted leaders, new types of choruses and songs, dance and gesture – all have contributed toward a new freedom and a joyful, uninhibited spirit in worship. People may speak prophetic words, sing, or pray spontaneously.

This charismatic tendency influenced and infiltrated the worship of all the liturgical traditions. It brought energy, vitality, intensity, and fervor – spontaneous elements which infused the patterned structures of the older liturgies.

The influence is flowing in the other direction, too. The leaders of many charismatic fellowships, after several decades of "free worship," are reporting exhaustion and even boredom with a spontaneity which inevitably becomes routinized. The pursuit of continuous novelty, the search for freshness, the need for music ever new – these have proved to be demanding and all too often force their worship through the filter of a single leader. The multi-voiced praise of the early days has given way to the leadership of highly skilled music groups which mold and control the direction of worship. Even the temptation to entertain has sometimes been too strong to resist.

Many charismatic fellowships are now turning to older traditions in search of depth in worship theology. They are tending to use some fixed forms, such as the traditional Apostles' Creed, psalms with responses, or ancient litanies. They are also turning to more frequent and fervent observance of the Lord's Supper. In this service they are finding a place to offer their strengths of joyful praise and music, along with the rich traditions of biblical materials and historical Christian worship forms.

Since the 1980s leaders in a wide variety of churches have found recognizable elements in each other's journeys – evangelicals with liturgicals, charismatics with evangelicals, liturgicals with charismatics.

Shapers of this tendency toward creative borrowing and convergence include people as diverse as Anglican Archbishop George Carey and Pentecostal leader Earl Paulk, who calls Pentecostals "to merge form with power." Paulk advocates that Christians rediscover "the supernatural power of God's presence and grace"[22] in the sacraments of the church.

Robert Webber has written a number of books explaining ways in which evangelicals are drawn to liturgical worship. The evangelicals bring with them the high regard and warmth of scriptural faith. Webber details these common elements among the convergence movement:

1. A restored commitment to the sacraments, especially the Lord's table
2. An increased motivation to know more about the early church
3. A love for the whole church and a desire to see the church as one
4. A blending of practice [of evangelical, liturgical, and charismatic] yet [maintaining] unique points of view
5. An interest in integrating structure with spontaneity in worship
6. A greater involvement of sign and symbol in worship
7. A continuing commitment to personal salvation, biblical teaching, and the work and ministry of the Holy Spirit[23]

Webber believes that the former walls between denominations and separate traditions are becoming veils which can be drawn back, giving all the chance to recognize one another's faith and to sense an underlying unity in Christ. In the century ahead, may Christians of many traditions find increasingly creative ways to bear witness together, in harmony, to God's kingdom coming. May the Lord's table be a place of focus for such a witness.

A Liturgical Church with a Special Charism of Prayer

Listen to a little story of someone who needed prayer. Louise was a pious Christian, but not a member of her local Anglican parish community. Her own church was faithful to its traditional worship practices. The people were friendly but reserved. Louise felt her own church wasn't the place to go with her concern for the safety and survival of her troubled friend. From previous visits to the parish church, she had sensed there an unusual commitment and depth in the intercessory prayers. So, burdened for her friend, Louise went to an evening communion service. She hoped there would be a way to ask others to join her in praying for her friend. What Louise encountered in that service was a powerfully attractive incarnation of convergence worship.

The vicar led a prayer book service. It included Scripture readings and set prayers. A variety of singing and instrumental music comprised of traditional hymns and contemporary songs-hymns intertwined with the wordy elements of the service. In his sermon the vicar explained a biblical approach to healing prayers and encouraged people to open themselves to it. There was time for quiet reflection, then several people came forward to give personal faith experiences of the week.

The peace greeting linked the first part of the service into the communion prayers, thanksgivings, and songs. A simple litany of intercessions reminded people that Christ's gifts of forgiveness, peace, and communion were not only for themselves but for many. Christ's arms on the cross were opened wide to welcome all who turn to him. After the communion there was a fervent stillness in the congregation.

The vicar said, "You don't have to go home. You can stay here and continue praying. If you want special prayer for yourself or for someone else, you may come forward and we will kneel with you to pray." That was exactly what Louise was hoping for. She went up and was joined with two others who asked one question – the first name of her friend. Then together they surrounded with love and prayer both Louise and her friend. Only the Spirit knows whether such prayer was "effective."

Louise was not interested in evaluating that communion service. It was enough for her that through joining the congregation's communion service, she found in the worship a combination of words, gestures, songs, silence, and prayers which was more than a simple sum of its parts. She was able to fulfill her desire to help her friend.

This was not merely liturgical worship. It was worship in which fixed forms of word and sacrament joined with silences and open spaces for free prayer and response. This was a fully recognizable Anglican communion service but one which achieved its fervor and depth through the convergence of a variety of impulses: liturgical, contemplative, and charismatic.

It is possible that Louise's experience in the parish church will cross-fertilize with her own congregation's communion practices. This is how Christians continue to learn from each other and how worship may be continually renewed.

Coming Home

Finally we look at a small movement of contemporary worship renewal which illustrates another face of convergence. It's called the home church movement, a new tendency which in form and spirit is as old as the Christian movement itself. Here is a member's description of a home church meeting, abridged and recast:

At around 9:30 on a Sunday you will see a few cars turn into a steep tree-lined driveway and go down to a large, two-story house. People get out. Children arrive on bikes. All head for the kitchen and living room of the Whitings, our regular Sunday morning meetinghouse. Naomi and John are tidying the kitchen. There is greeting, conversation, and lots of laughter, with people putting their food contributions on the countertop. By 9:45 people drift into the living room, and the musicians are playing to encourage them in. Children hand around the music books. We sing from six to twelve songs, until everyone has arrived. We stop for a reading from the Bible story book, or the children act parts of the story or ask questions. Sometimes there are drawings and maps.

Then we start the prayer time. The format varies. We often talk together about points for prayer, but then we go into smaller groups to pray, some to the kitchen, some to another room or outside to the courtyard. The groups are usually split arbitrarily, with children and adults in each group. After the prayers we gravitate toward the kitchen for morning tea. The table is set up, food laid out on it, and the drinks made ready. There is lots of chatter. If the weather is good, the children run around to work off excess energy. When all is ready, we gather around the table, but before the tea is poured, we have communion. Various people take turns in leading it. Some read from the Bible, or perhaps talk about something significant, and pray briefly. After this, bread and the drink may be passed around as a more formal communion, or we may do it more informally.

When communion is finished, the tea is poured and the plates are passed. We don't hurry morning tea. But sometime between 11 and 11:30, one or two adults call the children and lead them in an activity, either outdoors or in another room. Older children may play board games. Adults reassemble in the living room for the morning's study, or we may pray about something which was not appropriate to bring up in the earlier prayers with the children. At noon we get ready to leave, but some linger on to converse.[24]

The form of assembly of the home church is believed by its proponents to be similar to that of the New Testament churches which met in homes. These churches were familial in ethos and full-orbed in character. That is, they engaged the members' whole lives, spiritual, social, and economic. The churches were participatory, always open to the unexpected, and giving scope for a wide variety of spiritual gifts. They were missionary in impulse and were places of conflict. Paul honed his theology of the gospel of reconciliation out of a crucible of cultural, social, and personal tensions within home churches.

Some aspects of New Testament churches reflected their unique cultural settings. For example, households held extended relationships and were not made up of single people or of small nuclear families. Traditional lines of authority transferred from households to the churches meeting in the homes. The shared meals of Christian meetings were the ordinary meals of the household, but given special meanings. The time of meetings was probably variable, either before or after work on workdays. But Christians worshiped on other days as well. Some of these qualities have little to do with contemporary Christian household life.

But in fact, the modern home churches have many things in common with those earliest Christian assemblies. Each home church is a whole church. It is not a stepping-stone to a "regular" church which will eventually meet in a special building when there are "enough" members. The home church is not just for fellowship or just for evangelism. It is a whole church. The home church is not an added extra for Christians deeply involved in other Christian activities. It is a whole church, a basic unit of Christian nurture, worship, mission, fellowship, and support.

The life of the home church in all respects depends on the gifts that the Spirit gives to it. Leadership in various areas is recognized, but the primary gift in establishing a home church is the gift of hospitality. Two or three people, specially gifted for doing this, provide a hearth, a welcoming and safe place for others to gather. That is the only setting in which a home church can thrive.

The home church is intergenerational and does not give way to ageism for either the young or the old. Children and adults learn and worship together, though they separate for some activities. The home church is a face-to-face community, with all the tensions as well as securities that provides. It is a type of small community which many people in our fragmented and lonely societies are longing for. It is a human place to grow up in faith, a place where one knows and is known.

The home church is eucharistic. Its primary symbol of meeting is the Lord's table which is the community's table. They break the daily bread, they pass the cup of their shared discipleship. The Lord is present with and in his people gathered in his name. "This is my body," he says. "This is the cup of the new covenant."

Earliest Christians would recognize familiar qualities of such an assembly. It's all there: the family ethos, old and young together, the gifts of the Spirit freely offered, song and praise to God, prayers for the world, hospitality, fun, and food – all shared at the communion table of the risen Lord. In the ethos of a home church, the church comes home!

Conclusion

We have observed the five-hundred-year journey of Western churches from Reformation times to our own. What do we now make of the examples of patterns of piety and practice that have evolved?

It seems clear the Restorationists were right in seeing the continuing source for renewal in Scripture. Each generation finds fresh insights from the New Testament communities. The Moravians, Brethren, Methodists, and Anglo-Catholics found life in the early Christian roots of eucharistic worship. The Spirit continues in each generation to bring forgiveness, healing, and hope at the Lord's table. Christians of many backgrounds are finding joy in discovering their unity in study and in prayer. Out of these conjoint efforts has come a fruitful cross-fertilization in communion insights and ways of praying and sharing at the table.

Expectant openness to the Spirit and humility in listening – these are essential qualities in communities that will continue to experience vitality in their eucharistic worship.

COMMUNION: VARIATIONS ON THE THEME

Introduction to the Variations

WHEN WE COME to the communion table, do we think about what we are doing? How do we understand the actions and words? What do we hope may be the outcomes of the service? Do we allow our religious imagination to play a role in connecting the service to our daily lives – in visualizing cross, banquet, journey, city, towel and basin, cup and loaf? These connections will deeply affect our emotions and our inner volition.

Is it possible that such connections could make a noticeable difference in our everyday lives? Can we imagine ourselves – the people of our congregations – changing, becoming more merciful, more thankful, more passionate for justice? This might happen as we deepen our understanding, more fully engage our feelings and energize our practice of communion.

This part of the book may help to expand the theological and biblical resources we draw on in our communion services. As our understandings are enriched, and as we employ a wider range of biblical texts and images at the table we will notice the effects. Our churches will change. They will more and more become communities marked by God's person and gift, mediated to us through Christ who is host at his table.

We will consider a range of communion themes. Some are central to all Christian traditions. Others are more strongly associated with particular groups. Running through all these meanings is the Christian assertion that God who is Spirit reaches out to communicate with us through this eucharistic service of bread and wine. As we partake in these material gifts which sustain physical life, we discover that we receive much more than we expect. We receive gracious forgiveness, joy, healing, and reconciliation. These are the fruit of our dependent and loving relationship with God. They are the mysterious gifts we receive at the table of the risen Christ, truly present in his body, the church. But there is more.

That "more" is the mystery of the transformation of our minds, emotions, and lives. More and more we will be recognized as Jesus' own people, marked by his manners and lifestyle. And others will be drawn to Jesus, into the vibrant and compassionate communities living in his way.

8

Historic Themes
Come Alive

Giving Thanks

THIS THEME is the first and most important one for all communion
services. Jesus' people are full of thanksgiving: we are a "eucharistic"
people. Now, at the end of the twentieth century, the term eucharist has
come into broad use among Christians of many traditions. This new name
is, in fact, one of the oldest names of all. Eucharist, a term used
historically by the Orthodox churches, now serves as a focus for a deeper
potential unity among Christians at the Lord's table. These days Roman
Catholics frequently say "Eucharist" instead of mass, which came from
Missa est, the dismissal phrase at the end of the Latin service: "Go. It's
over." All Christians can claim strong biblical precedent for using the
name eucharist, which reminds us of the joyful spirit of the shared
fellowship meals of the earliest Christian communities.

To give thanks or to be grateful are the simple meanings of the Greek
eucharistein. In the New Testament it appears interchangeably with its
synonym, *eulogein*. English versions sometimes translate it as "give thanks"
and other times as "bless."

There are four New Testament passages recounting the institution of
the Lord's Supper – in Matthew 26, Mark 14, Luke 22, and 1 Corinthians
11. *Eucharistein* is the word behind "giving thanks" in all except the bread
words in Mark. To point out this variation, some versions translate, "He
took a loaf of bread, and after blessing [*eulogein*] it, he broke it" (Mark
14:22). Because *eucharistein* is consistently associated with the institution of
the Lord's Supper, that word became the name for the bread-and-cup
service. It has always been primarily a service of thankful blessing.

Praise and thanksgiving filled the first Christians' prayer at their
community meals. They expressed the breadth and length of holy history,
in which God acted sovereignly to bring salvation and life. Their worship
was a part of that great story. We can say exactly the same about present-
day eucharist services. The tone of joyful praise and thanksgiving, either
quiet or extroverted, is always the order of the day.

One way to establish genuine eucharist is to call the service by this
name. The name of an activity helps to shape people's attitudes toward it.

It makes a psychological difference to me, for example, if I am faced with a test, an evaluation, an indicator, a quiz, or a profile. The name matters. And so, if substituting eucharist for Lord's Supper seems strange to some congregations, it would at least be a useful discipline always to refer to the Lord's Supper as "a service of thanksgiving."

In chapter 20, "Praying at the Table", are samples of thanksgiving prayers. It is helpful to look closely at these, either to adapt them for use or to find a broad and strong outline for our own prayers. We can heighten our sense of thanksgiving with suitable music and visual surroundings. These practical applications are addressed in the next part.

Remembering Jesus

Many Christians think of communion as primarily a memorial meal. The theme of remembering Jesus' redemptive action is vital, particularly if Christians bring that memory to life both individually and as a faith community. Jesus' people are people of vigorous, truthful memory-keeping. Remember Jesus! Remember what he did for us! Remember that we belong to him! Knowing our identity makes all the difference in how we live.

Luke 22:19 records Jesus saying, after he broke the bread, "Do this in remembrance of me." The phrase does not recur after the cup. In 1 Corinthians 11:24 and 25, the words "do this in remembrance of me" follow both the bread and the cup. In addition, the phrase "whenever you drink it" (11:25) accompanies the cup. This "whenever" of 1 Corinthians 11 is the only word in any of the institution narratives which indicates that Jesus intended a continuing practice. The other Gospel descriptions tell what happened on that particular night but do not include words to serve as warrants for a repeating practice.

In 1 Corinthians 11:26, Paul adds his editorial comment: "For whenever you eat this bread and drink this cup ..." He reflects an ongoing tradition of a repeated cup-and-bread ceremony. Paul interprets it theologically and assumes this will serve as the basis for continuing practice of the ceremony. So we see that a specific command by Jesus to repeat the ceremony is not universally in the Gospel accounts. Yet from the earliest generation, this practice was securely established, at least in some communities. The community of the Gospel of John apparently practiced it differently, with its memory tradition of the foot-washing ceremony within Jesus' final discourse.

Yet whatever the variations from one community to another, all the believers were concerned with perpetuating the memory of Jesus. As we saw in chapter 1, "Last Supper to Church Supper," they remembered Jesus at many tables, and they remembered his teachings about the great banquet of the kingdom to come. They remembered his friendship, his compassion, his mannerisms, his prayers, his parables, and his teachings.

How could they forget him? Jesus, they knew, was deeply concerned that his disciples might forget the integration of piety and lifestyle which he taught and modeled. They might go on saying, "Lord, Lord," and not do the will of the Father (Matt. 7:21; 25:11-12).

The remembering of the communion service must include the full story of Jesus' life – not only the events of his suffering and death. It must include reference to God's whole plan for redemption – to the incarnation and to Jesus' entire ministry. It is a remembering of his betrayal, arrest, trial, crucifixion, burial, resurrection, his appearances after the resurrection, and his ascension. It must be the whole story, not just a part of it. Unlike the classic creeds, which skip from the Virgin's womb to Christ's suffering under Pontius Pilate, we must remember and retell what went on between. And we must reflect on the meaning of this great story – God's love for the world and God's great plot to set the world free for life.

Let us follow the early disciples in this kind of full-bodied remembering. Yes, it has to do with the events at the Last Supper. But the memory we perpetuate is full of incidents, stories, and sayings of Jesus' ministry. So we continually develop and pray through our theological reflections upon them. Our faith is rooted in a real person who spoke and acted in a real world. We do more than tell stories; we see their significance in revealing God to us and in showing us how to live today.

To remember Jesus in eucharist requires much more of us than a mental process of recalling things about him and repeating stories of things he did. When Jesus' people gather in the Spirit at his table, we believe he is vitally present in uniting us with himself and with each other. We will ponder this mystery more fully later in this book.

However, part of what we do in the eucharist is to keep Jesus alive in our community's memory. This is what good memory-making is about: We tell the story. We reflect on it. We "do" the memory – we act it out. We live it out in our work and our relationships. "Doing" his memory requires us to follow in Jesus' way, depending fully upon God, yearning for God's kingdom to come, living out God's merciful love in our everyday lives. In these ways history becomes living memory.

The communion service helps us to do all of these things. It is a powerful ritual (see "The Language of Ritual" in the next part) in which we employ material, use significant words, commit ourselves to an inner vision and understanding of ourselves as God's own loved children, and determine to follow the path of Jesus. People who "do the memory" of Jesus will be changed people, becoming more and more like Jesus.

Feasting in the Kingdom

Christians always had their feet in two worlds at once. They believed that Jesus was Messiah and that in his coming, future time had begun. Yet they lived in ordinary time. This is the subtle balance we also must keep. We have a foretaste of God's reign and a longing for God's justice and shalom to be established. Yet we live in that in-between time of groaning and longing of which Paul speaks in Romans 8:22. The whole creation is in labor, eagerly waiting its redemption. Living in this tension, we become people of expectant hope. Taking part in the communion service we dramatically express this present confidence and future hope. We go out into our everyday responsibilities with renewed energy. We are recognized as people eager to work and pray for change, for the coming of God's reign.

Praying the Lord's Prayer, we repeat Jesus' longing and confident expectancy for God's name to be hallowed, for God's will to be done and God's reign to be established in the present and in the future, throughout the earth and the entire cosmos. From the earliest times, this kingdom prayer has been associated with the church's table and has ensured that the themes of God's reign *now* and *to come* shall remain central. The memorial meal of the church is a foreshadowing of the great celestial banquet in which all nations will eat and drink with joy in the presence of God.

At the Last Supper, Jesus didn't invent a ritual with new meanings. He crystallized it out of his rich Jewish tradition and from the insights of his messianic ministry. From the foundational covenant-making story of Sinai, Jesus remembered Moses and Aaron and the elders of Israel going up the mountain. There they "saw God and ate and drank" (Exod. 24:9-11). Immediately before this joyous meal in the presence of God, Moses had taken blood and thrown half of it against the altar and half of it over the people. This was the blood of the covenant, the vivid background to Jesus' cup-words at the Last Supper, when he speaks of the new covenant in his own blood.[1]

The Old Testament tells many stories of sacred meals. Deuteronomy is especially rich in references.[2] Psalm 23 uses the metaphor of a festive meal to celebrate God's generous care, even in the very face of danger: "You prepare a table before me in the presence of my enemies; you anoint my head with oil; my cup overflows" (Ps. 23:5). Prophets comfort an exiled people with a vision of feeding and feasting when they would be homeward bound and eventually restored to their own land (Isa. 49:9ff.; Ezek. 34:13ff.).

The prophet Isaiah declares an even bigger vision. This vision includes not only Israel but all peoples who will share in the blessings of the everlasting covenant (Isa. 55:5).

> Ho, everyone who thirsts, come to the waters;
>   and you that have no money, come, buy, and eat!
> Come, buy wine and milk

without money and without price.
Why do you spend your money for that which is not bread,
    and your labor for that which does not satisfy?
Listen carefully to me, and eat what is good,
    and delight yourselves in rich food.
Incline your ear, and come to me;
    listen, so that you may live.
I will make with you an everlasting covenant.

(Isa. 55:1-3)

Isaiah prophesied the day when the Lord:

will make for all peoples a feast of rich food,
    a feast of well-aged wines,
of rich food filled with marrow,
    of well-aged wines strained clear.
And he will destroy on this mountain
    the shroud that is cast over all peoples,
    the sheet that is spread over all nations;
he will swallow up death forever.
Then the Lord God will wipe away the tears from all faces.

(Isa. 25:6-8)

Isaiah's words undoubtedly shaped an inner vision of God's reign for which Jesus prayed: "Your kingdom come, your will be done on earth as in heaven."

Jesus' big-visioned prayer matched his meal actions and his meal stories. He antagonized people with his assertion that many foreigners, non-Jews, will "come from east and west and will eat with Abraham and Isaac and Jacob in the kingdom of heaven" (Matt. 8:11). Jesus ate in the most surprising company – with collaborators, sinners, and unclean people, as well as with the rich and influential. But it was especially among the socially marginal that Jesus was already celebrating the kingdom banquet.

The eucharist has its origins in the festival meal of the Passover. The accompanying liturgy expressed longing for the Messiah to come, for God's liberating reign to be established. Jesus incorporated his own integrating vision with this powerful Passover imagery. He told his disciples to continue feasting in his memory, but that he himself would not join them again until God's kingdom would be established (Mark 14:25). After the resurrection the early Christians, in their joyous common meals, especially because Jesus appeared among them again, considered that the kingdom was indeed being established among them.

The Aramaic phrase, an ancient invocation of Christ, *Maranatha!* (1 Cor. 16:22), means "Oh, our Lord, come!" It is an equivalent of

94

"Amen, come, Lord Jesus!" (Rev. 22:20) and may well have been a part of early eucharistic worship. It appears at the end of the meal prayers in the early-second-century *Didache*, a handbook for a Syrian Christian community.[3] Another poignant phrase appears in the same meal prayers. "Let Grace [a title for Christ] come, and let this world pass away!" It gives evidence of a deep-seated and joyous expectation. These expressions may come from the Jewish habit of saying, after the benediction, words of joyful hope for Israel's coming redemption.

Paul closes his recitation of the tradition handed down to him with an exhortation: "Proclaim the death of the Lord until he comes." This does not mean just preaching about a past event. The proclamation is the eschatological declaration of this meal as the beginning, the inauguration sign of the new covenant. Time is overlapping, the time of now and the time to come when God's reign is fully realized.[4]

Early Christians eagerly looked for Christ's appearing in glory. But they expressed his coming in two dimensions. Christ was truly present at the meal of the eucharist, yet he was also awaited.[5] The eucharist is always celebrated in the time of hope for the second coming, of which Christ's first coming was a promise. The church yearns for the fulfillment of that promise. At every eucharist the prayer for the *parousia* (Christ's return) is "partially fulfilled as the church is given a taste of the future."[6]

Perhaps such intensity of joy and expectation of Christ's return seems distant from our experience. But the themes of the banquet of the kingdom and the return of the Lord are potent ones we cannot bypass. What more energizing picture might there be than the one Jesus gave of peoples from east, west, north, and south coming to his table! His table is a large one indeed, and there is room for all.

Sharing in the Lord

At the table, Jesus blessed, broke, and shared the bread among his disciples and in doing so laid the foundation for the strongest veins of memory for Christians. Jesus willingly "laid down his life." He shared his bread, his life, his teachings. In following that generous model, we too learn to lay our lives down and share generously. This is the lesson of koinonia, one of the most profound themes of the Lord's table. By sharing in the Lord's loaf and in his life, we become able to share with each other and the world in need around us. Our church communities will be known as generous, life-giving communities. This dynamic is what lay behind the tradition which Paul passed on to the Corinthian Christians.

"The bread that we break, is it not a sharing [koinonia] in the body of Christ? Because there is one bread, we who are many are one body, for we all partake of the one bread" (1 Cor. 10:16b-17).

Here Paul uses his favorite picture of the church as the body of Christ. Eating together of the nourishing bread, we are made members of one living, breathing body. Jesus is the head of the body, and we are all animated by his Spirit. Through sharing the one bread, we find a mysterious unity with each other.

Notice that Paul equates the bread and the sharing (1 Cor. 10:16b). The emphasis falls not so much on the physical bread itself as on the acts of breaking and sharing. The word *this* refers to the act of blessing and breaking the bread. The act signifies the whole idea: my body broken for you. It points both to Christ's death on the cross, as well as to his sharing or self-giving.[7]

The same is true of the ceremony with the cup. The emphasis is on the action of sharing the cup of destiny. "The cup of blessing that we bless, is it not a sharing [koinonia] in the blood of Christ?" (1 Cor. 10:16a). Here, as with the bread, the weight falls not on the cup or its contents, but on the koinonia, the participation in the blood of Christ. The cup does not equal Christ's blood. It signifies the new covenant possible because of Christ's blood.[8]

For Jewish Christians, the symbol of a shared cup was potent. The cup which was passed around the table at the conclusion of a festive meal signified the bond between host and guests, a sacred relationship in that culture. At Jesus' last Passover meal with his disciples, the bond was even stronger – that of a rabbi with his devoted followers. Disciples literally followed their rabbi, intellectually, spiritually, physically. They went wherever their rabbi led them.

Jesus asked his disciples, "Are you able to drink the cup that I drink?" (Mark 10:38). "They replied, 'We are able.'" What Jesus really asked them was, "Are you able to share my destiny? Are you able to share the cost of my calling?" To share the cup of Jesus would signify commitment to a common path, whatever the consequences might be. Jesus picked up their blithe answer. In their easy "We are able" they didn't know the implications of what they were saying. They were saying more than they knew. Imagine Jesus looking intently at each one as he anticipated the dark events to come. He nodded his head. "The cup that I drink you will drink" (10:39). Jesus spoke of the cup of shared destiny, of the inevitable suffering to come.

Paul develops the theme of koinonia in the suffering of our Lord, of participating in his death so that we can become truly alive in his life. "If we have died with Christ, we believe that we will also live with him" (Rom. 6:8). New creation comes about when we are "in Christ" (2 Cor. 5:17). When the love of Christ, which called him to his death, controls us, we too die and live with him (2 Cor. 5:15). What closer union could we imagine than that described by Paul?

> For I through the law I died to the law, so that I might live to God. I have been crucified with Christ; and it is no longer I who live, but

it is Christ who lives in me. And the life I now live in the flesh I
live by faith in the Son of God, who loved me and gave himself for
me (Gal. 2:19-20).

Although this meaning – sharing Christ's path of suffering – may well
have been in the background, it probably wasn't primary in Jesus'
reference to the cup of blessing. Jesus probably connected the shared cup
with the disciples' shared reception of the benefits of what that cup
signified – the atoning power of his own death.

We can see what Paul thought the shared cup meant. He reminds the
Corinthian Christians that the cup of blessing at their fellowship meals
signified more than the memory of a committed bond between rabbi Jesus
and his disciples. Paul recalls Jesus' words: "This cup is the new covenant
in my blood" (1 Cor. 11:25b).

Even though the phrases aren't precisely the same, all the Gospel
accounts of the cup words agree that Jesus compares the wine in the cup
with his blood. The reference is clearly to the inauguration of the
covenant at Sinai. Now, by the blood of Jesus, the new covenant comes
into being. We will consider the theme of covenant later.

Reconciling and Making Peace

A people of peace! That is how early Christians saw themselves. From
earliest times a major theme of the eucharist was the miracle of unity
among believers of divergent classes, languages, and cultures. Christ who
is our peace has made unity by breaking down the dividing wall of
hostility. Christ makes a new humanity possible, bringing people into
reconciliation within himself and with each other. This is the great
affirmation of Ephesians 2:11-22.

Reconciliation is at the heart of the gospel. When gospel and peace are
pulled apart, terrible things can happen, as we have seen in countries
where Christians have preached a personalized salvation and have not
emphasized that the gospel has everything to do with how to live out
national or clan identity.

New Testament Christians expressed the miracle and the delight of their
Spirit-inspired unity in a unique gesture – the holy kiss,[9] also called the
kiss of love (1 Pet. 5:14). It isn't clear whether this kiss was a part of an
"order of service" with well-developed theological understandings. But it
does seem significant that the theme of peace is closely associated with the
kiss in three of the five mentions in the New Testament letters. Churches
were intensely concerned for fostering reconciled relationships. Love and
unity were primary foundations for their life together.

In early Christian written liturgies, the kiss appears just after the readings
and prayers, at the beginning of the bread-and-cup ceremony. The
explanation for this position was Jesus' admonition to leave one's gift at

the altar, if relationships are bad, and make things right before resuming worship (Matt. 5:23-24). The kiss was called "the kiss of peace" or simply "the peace" and functioned in several ways. It was a hinge in the service, between the prayers and the eucharist proper. It was an expression of unity and love among the people. And it was provided an opportunity, on the spot, to make things right.

Eventually the peace became stylized and clericalized. In some places its essential meaning was abused. In medieval England the peace was passed in a thoroughly hierarchical sequence, from the priest through the nobility, gentry, and eventually to the common folk. The poorest woman was the last to receive.[10]

The good news is that the ancient kiss of peace has reappeared in twentieth-century eucharistic worship. Why not! The peace greeting is one of the genuinely "primitive" elements of Christian worship. Just because it's early doesn't mean it's good or necessary. But the kiss (greeting) of peace is important because it reminds us and dramatizes for us a central truth about the Christian faith, about Jesus' work of *shalom*, peace. Jesus is the Lord of peace. We are to be his people of peace.

The communion service with its prayers, its kiss of peace, and its symbolic memorial feast comprises what we refer to as "unitive rites" of the church. This simply means that the service is altogether about reconciliation and unity, both with God and with one another. The purpose, the process, and the effects are unitive.

Our communion services may offer a time and space for making things right, through receiving forgiveness and passing it on. There are no dikes to hold in God's mercy. If God's own people receive it, that gracious forgiveness will spill out, flooding the plains with the kindness of the kingdom. God's love is for the whole world, and we who recognize and receive that love will spill it out, pipe it out, ship it, give it, send it wherever we go. The liturgy of the table can be like the stone well at an artesian spring, with the Spirit-water gushing out, splashing over our handheld bottles and mugs. This water is to satisfy the thirst for reconciliation among all the peoples of the world. Our task is to be *pani-wallahs*, "waterboys," purveyors of living water to the parched and thirsty world.

9

Christ Is Present, the Mystery Is Revealed

Mystery of the Faith

FOR TWO THOUSAND years, Eastern Christians have referred to the eucharist as "mystery" or as "the mysteries." In the earliest days of Christianity, the faith was a mystery in the sense of a secret kept safe from intruders or persecutors. A couple of centuries later, when whole populations were incorporated into Christianity, now a state religion, the meaning of mystery changed. It became necessary for the liturgy as a whole to function as a dramatic revelation of Christian faith. It was like a complex "mystery play" which was meant precisely to communicate the mystery of the faith. It did this through action, color, words, music – all the senses – to people coming to Christianity from pagan backgrounds.

In the early period the liturgy was a common action of the whole people; in the Middle Ages, the clergy and people were increasingly separated in order precisely to protect the mysteries. The implicit message was that the mysteries, known and handled by the clergy, were awesome, fearful things. Communion spoons ladled the precious sacraments directly into the mouths of communicants, avoiding possible desecration by their hands. Elaborate screens and panels of religious icons (pictures) separated the area reserved to priests. The awesome and mysterious character of the sacraments was enhanced by "appearances and disappearances of the priests [going behind and coming out from the icon screen], veiling and unveiling of the elements, opening and closing of the doors [in the icon screen], and various gestures connected with the sacraments."[1]

The great twentieth-century Orthodox theologian, Alexander Schmemann, taught that the great mystery of the kingdom of God is the bringing together in "mystical and existential, rather than rational synthesis," God's complete otherness and God's mysterious presence.[2] The liturgy is the event in which God's transcendence and immanence are supremely known. In the joy and peace of the Holy Spirit, the church experiences in the present what can only be known fully in the fulfillment of the kingdom. This, according to Schmemann, is the mystery of the faith.

Eastern Orthodox liturgical theology made connections with Roman Catholic liturgical renewal, especially in Maria Laach and other

Benedictine monasteries in nineteenth-century Germany. Through this, what is known as mystery theology came to the West. That in turn had a strong impact on the *Constitution of the Sacred Liturgy* (1963), the liturgical document of the Second Vatican Council in Rome.[3]

Jesus Is Present!

Great debates have centered around the idea of the presence of Christ in the eucharist. We will begin our investigation with New Testament passages which shape the background to the whole mysterious reality of Christians' universal assertion that when we gather in his name and at his table, the Lord Jesus is truly present with us.

Christians retell the stories of Jesus' post-resurrection appearances with a breathless joy. In the first instances, we remember, the disciples were huddled in dejection and fear, and then dumbfounded at hearing Jesus' "Shalom!" and awe-struck at the sight of his broken hands and side. But they must have started to anticipate seeing him again. Acts 1:1-5 reports that Jesus "presented himself alive to them ... during forty days and speaking about the kingdom of God. While staying with them, he ordered them ... to wait there for the promise of the Father."

These experiences imprinted the earliest Christian memory of Jesus' fidelity to his promise, "I will be with you." He said he would be with them, and he was truly with them! How this was possible, they couldn't grasp. They saw him die; they laid him in the tomb. Yet he was truly with them again in resurrection reality. He talked with them, he stayed with them, he ate with them. But in the ascension accounts, the disciples face the beginning of a new phase. They are to receive "what my Father promised" (Luke 24:49). They anticipate seeing him "come in the same way as [they] ... saw him go into heaven" (Acts 1:11).

For fifty days after the resurrection, they waited and wondered, reminding each other of Jesus' command and promise. At Pentecost they had their first grasp of what this promise would be like – the Spirit of strange empowerment and holy fire. It was in the presence and energy of this Spirit that they learned to live, the Spirit whom they associated with the living presence of their Lord Jesus. In their shared meals, they remembered Jesus, his teachings, his life with them. Now they realized he was truly but mysteriously present with them, even though they could not see him in his flesh.

The marvelous imagery of vine and branches in John 15 uncovers the distinctive theme of "abiding" in Christ. We encounter a favorite eucharistic symbol in the allegorical story of the Father as farmer with his vine. The vine is Jesus, and the branches are believers. Just as in John 6 Jesus is the bread from heaven and the fountain for life-giving water, here Jesus the vine is the source of true life. But to be nourished by love which is the sap of the vine, believers must remain on the vine. They must keep connected to the vine. Partaking of the heavenly bread and the living water was symbolic of vital belief in Jesus. In the picture of vine and branches, believers are intimately united with the source of life – God's love.

Even though wine is not specifically mentioned, there is no doubt that this passage and its vine image were associated with the eucharist in the community of the Gospel of John. All the early Christians knew about the Last Supper with its words of institution. The association of the cup of the Supper with the image of the vine can be assumed from the designation "the fruit of the vine" in both Mark and Matthew.

Raymond Brown points out the eucharistic overtones of John 15. Instruction on bearing fruit appears five times in the first eight verses but is mentioned in only one other place in the Gospel of John. The grain of wheat which falls into the earth and dies "bears much fruit" (12:24). This motif of Jesus' death is intrinsic to all the accounts of the Last Supper and its eucharistic institution. In addition, there are echoes in style and structure between chapters 6 and 15 of John. "I am the living bread" (6:51) and "I am the true vine" (15:1) parallel "This is my body" and "This is my blood." Brown suggests that the vine allegory emphasizes that believers who are united to Christ in the eucharist must bear fruit in their lives and deepen the bonds of love among themselves and their Lord.[4]

Paul develops his own expression to convey the intimate union and connection between Christ and the believer. He calls it "being in Christ." Paul means that the believer's identity is derived from an intimate spiritual union with Christ. This relationship is nurtured and expressed within the life of the body of Christ, the church, and in the memorial fellowship meals of the church. The cup of blessing and the bread that the church shares makes them all "one body" (1 Cor. 10:16-17).

These are three examples of teaching and experiences of early Christians which witness to an awareness of an intimate presence of Christ when they met in his name. In the early years believers didn't try to explain exactly how this could be true; they just knew Christ was there with them.

In the fourth century believers began speculating about *when* Christ became present: was it at a "moment" of consecration? In the ninth century, debates arose about *how* Christ was present: was it by a miraculous change in the elements? As attention centered more and more on the bread itself (no longer ordinary everyday bread, but a pure white, holy wafer), people adored Christ's presence in the sacrament. This was an activity which "was personal, private, subjective, and individualized rather than a corporate activity related to the words and actions of the service itself." Performing the mass came to be "a way to produce the real presence of Christ so that Christ's people might adore him rather than commune with him."[5]

If we can bear to experience and accept a reality which we can't fully explain, and which we don't need to speculate about, then we can join with our early Christian brothers and sisters in rejoicing in Christ's presence at his table. It might make for some baffling testimonies ("I saw Jesus' face reflected in the wine"), unusual sights and sounds (tongues of fire and sounds of wind), or evidence of healing prayers ("It was Jesus' touch, I know it!"). But we can join those earliest disciples, after the resurrection, in our yearning and expectation that Jesus truly communes with us at his table. And we can join countless generations of Christians since then who know that the Lord Jesus is present in his body, the church, by his Spirit, and in the love of God.

Symbol and Sacrament

There is a mysterious quality to abiding in Christ or communion with Christ. Christians have tried to explain it in different ways. The most highly developed way is in the language of sacrament. Speaking of sacrament involves related ideas – of signs, symbols, and rituals. These are closely intertwined. It is helpful to try to explain and separate the meanings of these words.

Catch phrases you might hear include these: "Signs point to something beyond themselves." "We use symbols when we need to say something beyond words." "Rituals are habitual actions, often helpful." "Sacraments operate through human faith." "A sacrament is a visible sign of an invisible grace."

What we do and say in worship always moves beyond what we can completely express in a rational way. We need to open ourselves up to the allusive, to our religious imagination. The way we do this is through metaphor, through symbol, sacrament, and ritual. If we try to rule out this dimension, we may become stuck either in a rigid rationalism or a limp sentimentality.[6]

For some theologians, Christ himself is the only sacrament. He, entering our human existence, communicated God to us. God, who is Spirit, reached out to us who are human, both body and spirit. Others emphasize the church as the great sacrament. In a parallel to the incarnation in Christ, God's love and mercy continue to be made visible through the church. In the earliest centuries Christians, on mention of the "great sacrament," would immediately have assumed baptism was the subject under discussion, so momentous was its impact upon their lives.[7] But through the intervening centuries, sacramental discussion and dispute have centered more and more on the supposed material changes in the bread and wine at the Lord's table. We Christians are burdened with a terrible history of searing arguments and divisions over these questions.

Sacrament talk, about relationship with God

Whatever tradition we come from, we know by experience that God is in vital communication with us at the communion table. But how is this possible? What makes this table, this assembly, this bread, this cup, able in such a special way to convey God's love and grace? How do ordinary bread and wine become more than what they appear? In other words, how do they become sacramental?

Sometimes something ordinary can be taken up into a completely new context of meaning. It then comes to mean something quite different from its obvious meaning. The liturgical term for this is process is trans-signification. It is an attempt to describe what happens to the meaning of bread and wine in the service of eucharist.

Another part of the explanation is that when we take the bread and wine, we do it with our inner imagination fixed on our relationship with God. God is Spirit, but we humans are both body and spirit. So when God who is Spirit reaches out to us, we can only respond according to our nature, the nature God has given to us. We take the bread which we call the bread of heaven, the bread of life, bread for the journey, the body of Christ. Inwardly and by faith, we receive this bread which brings us life. God touches us through our whole being, which is both spirit and matter, body and soul.

However, God only does this if we open ourselves to receive. If we refuse to acknowledge that we apprehend and respond to God through both the material and the spiritual, we limit both God and ourselves in our relationship of communion. We don't do wrong to limit ourselves to words. But it is as though we only ever speak to God on the telephone. Limited forms of communication limit a relationship. God is personal and we are personal. Our communication is personal. Our communion at the table is personal, sacramental communion. So it necessarily reflects the manners and means of the personal communication between us mortals and our God who is Spirit. Those means are primarily God's gift to us, a complex of material, of imagination, of our faith and our commitment.

Symbols

In human relations, we use our whole selves to convey personal (spiritual) communication. Gestures, frowns, hugs, a pat on the head – through any of these we "say" something specifically personal to the other. All of these, as well as the words that might go along with them, are symbols. All humans "talk symbol." We give gifts to express appreciation and present memorial objects to honor or value someone's work. We acclaim political figures with ceremonial banquets, publish Festschrifts to beloved professors, lay wreaths and wear armbands on solemn funeral days. We humans are skilled at these visible words, powerful communication through the material stuff of our life. We meet each other with our whole selves, body and spirit.

Words are important in a relationship, but somehow words aren't enough. If I tell my husband I love him, does he reply, "I already know that. You told me before"? No, he throws his arms around me, declares his love anew, and promises he will always stick by me. Then surprise! He produces from his briefcase a little "pressie" he picked up for me on his way home. His personal, loving response is a complex of words, gesture, gift, and promise. In marriage and in friendships, we communicate on many levels, expressing our spiritual relationships in the physicality of our bodies and with the material of creation.

Some symbols are more potent than others. A traffic notice posted along a country lane with a black cross of equal arms conveys its message bluntly: an intersection is coming up. The traffic sign gives vital information.

A similar sign is on the front wall of my home congregation. But there the cross marks convey a different message. This sign of a cross is not to convey information. It is a reminder of a person, of an event in his life. It is about suffering and about victory. This cross is the rallying place for all of humanity, a place of healing, forgiveness, and hope. The layers of associations and meanings go on and on. The cross on the front wall of my home congregation is much more than a sign to give information. But purely as an object, it isn't worth much. It isn't strictly necessary.

In fact, one could say that "symbols serve no useful purpose. We don't eat a birthday cake for its nutritional value, nor do we put candles on it for the light they shed."[8] Flowers watered with our tears are not placed to make a tombstone look pretty. To make an ordinary object or gesture speak beyond itself, we deliberately take it out of its ordinary context. We give it a spiritual or relational meaning. The blue ribbon I buy from the market stall can become either a first prize at the school sports day or, pinned on my lapel, a badge of political affiliation. In a similar way, whether at a picnic lunch or at a communion table, the ordinary gesture of breaking apart a loaf of bread carries different symbolic meaning.

Any gesture or object is empty until we fill it up with meaning. That meaning may speak of relationships or of shared experiences. Every friendship has its unique symbols – the whistled tune, a hand gesture, pet name, or secret joke. We humans are endlessly creative in filling up empty things and making them symbols which enrich relationships. We are good at "talking symbol."

So it is in our relationship with God. We respond with our whole selves, our bodies, our words, our feelings, with gifts and gestures, tears and songs. All are symbols which express a deep relationship of dependence and love. We talk to God in symbol language, with our words and with meanings beyond words. "We need the Word," said Augustine, "but also visible words."

Christians who use the language of sacraments deal with symbolic signs and point to the mysterious quality in the meeting place of the physical and the spiritual. God who is Spirit meets and communicates with us in the wholeness of our life – life which is both physical and spiritual. For the church, our communication with God comes into sharpest focus when we gather together for corporate worship. Here is the interface between ourselves and God. We express our relationship in multiple ways. We express it in songs, in words, in gestures, in gifts, in promises. We express our relationship to God through our memory, our imagination, our tears, our shouts, our dances, and our arts.

It may be easier to grasp how we express ourselves in symbolic ways toward God than to consider that God expresses love and relationship toward us through symbols. But this is exactly what sacramental language is about. Donald Baillie gives an illustration of a little boy in the nursery with his new governess. The child is afraid and hides his face. The governess knows it is up to her. She calls his name, she comes closer to him, she offers to read a book with him. She uses gestures, words, and objects to convey her heart to the child. Only then can he respond. God works faith and friendship in us, just as the governess gained response from the little boy.

God woos us in many ways, through inarticulate inner longings, through the words and gestures of other people of faith, through the endlessly creative Spirit, to bring us into relationship. God uses symbolic gifts, sacraments, what some call "means of grace." These are all "employed by the graciousness of God to express and develop a gracious relationship between us and himself."[9] This kind of grace is not a commodity, it is personal. Grace is the nature of the relationship between us and God.

Through the symbolic (sacramental) bread and wine of communion, we can lay hold of the promises of God. We can reach out to grasp in faith what God offers to us as pure gift. We can drink the draught of undeserved forgiveness. We can chew the assurance that we are God's chosen, loved children. The whole work of redemption lies behind this bread and wine made sacrament – God's promise, gracious gifts, and our receiving of it.

The word sacrament is not a biblical term. Of its several equivalents in theological language, the most important one is mystery. This doesn't mean a sacrament is incomprehensible, but in the biblical sense, it relates to a divine plan shown in Jesus Christ (Rom. 16:25ff.). The classic way to express this is that what was visible in Christ is again visible in the sacraments.

10

Communion Themes for Life in the Congregation

Forgiving and Restoring

AT THE LAST SUPPER, as recorded in Matthew 26:28, Jesus links the shared cup with forgiveness. Jesus' blood is poured out "for many for the forgiveness of sins."

Christians have always come to the Lord's table to receive that unmerited forgiveness. We must not forget that during his ministry, Jesus repeatedly challenged his hearers to pass forgiveness to others, to be merciful as God is merciful. At the Lord's table we receive forgiveness. Can we rise to Jesus' challenge to become a forgiving people, passing that mercy onward?

At the Last Supper, Jesus referred to his blood as poured out "for the forgiveness of sins" (Matt. 26:28b). From this statement it is easy to jump to the familiar line of thought: guilt, confession, forgiveness. The phrase "guilt offering" springs to mind. Is this what Jesus had in mind in the image of his blood poured out for forgiveness? Does the Old Testament help us to understand Jesus?

It is important to notice that sacrifice in the Old Testament was not primarily concerned with guilt. Ritual praise or ritual cleanness were the primary intentions of ritual sacrifice. "Guilt offerings" are dealt with in Leviticus 5, where restitution was spelled out (5:16). Leviticus 4 speaks of "sin offerings" required "when anyone sins unintentionally in any of the Lord's commandments" (4:2). "Forgiveness, in the Old Testament as in the New, is a gift of God's grace, not something which can be earned by sacrifice."[1]

The cup of blessing (1 Cor. 10:16) is truly a cup of forgiveness as well as a cup of fellowship (koinonia) because one of its many facets of meaning is the matchless gift of gracious liberation we receive. The new age of Jesus the Messiah is the new age of forgiveness. Forgiven people are empowered to live as forgiving people, passing on good news of freedom from the compulsions and domination of sin. The cup of blessing joins the themes of fellowship and liberation in communion (koinonia).

Early Christianity was a religion of forgiven, redeemed, confident believers. Christians were not worried about going to hell. The pagans, not they, had to worry about that. They praised God whose "judgments have been revealed" and whose "judgments are true and just!" (Rev. 15:4; 16:7). They looked with anticipation for God's vindication of the righteous. Their God had taken power and had begun to reign. God's judgment would be reward for the faithful, for "all who fear your name, both small and great," but it would be destruction for those "who destroy the earth" (Rev. 11:18).

Pastorally, the themes of repentance, forgiveness, and restoration are vital to the life of the church. Although a penitential tone does not dominate, the communion service is a natural place for the themes of restoration to be spelled out. Space can be provided for people to enter into them through both private and corporate prayer.

Examining the life of individuals and of the congregation in relation to the love and mercy of God is a sure route to honest appraisal and humility. Only when we glimpse God's character do we see ourselves with clarity. We confess who God is, then we confess ourselves in relation to God. Only through this process do we grasp our need for forgiveness through God's mercy. Only then are we able to receive God's forgiveness and allow it to become an energizing force for forgiving others.

The liturgical traditions have profound yet simple confession prayers in their eucharistic services. Here is one form of penitential prayer at the Catholic mass. It is cast in "I" language and the confession is spoken individually. Together, the personal confessions form a corporate prayer.

> **ALL**: I confess to almighty God and to you, my brothers and sisters, that I have sinned through my own fault in my thoughts and in my words, in what I have done, and in what I have failed to do; and I ask ... [that] you, my brothers and sisters, pray for me to the Lord our God.[2]

An Anglican form is plural and corporate. The priest's words of absolution are full.

> **ALL**: Almighty God, our heavenly Father, we have sinned against you, through our own fault, in thought, and word, and deed, and in what we have left undone. We are heartily sorry, and repent of all our sins. For your Son our Lord Jesus Christ's sake, forgive us all that is past; and grant that we may serve you in newness of life, to the glory of your name. AMEN.

> **Priest**: Almighty God, who forgives all who truly repent, have mercy upon you, pardon and deliver you from all your sins, confirm and strengthen you in all goodness, and keep you in life eternal; through Jesus Christ our Lord. AMEN.[3]

Confession prayers would be strengthened by conforming them to Jesus' concern for us to show mercy and forgiveness to one another, a response which flows freely from receiving God's forgiveness ourselves. Free-church Christians often move too quickly, too lightly, to appropriate God's forgiving mercy. Sensitivity to our sin and regular confession of it are necessary components of mature Christian faith. Communion services can help to shape a healthy and realistic awareness of sin, both corporate and personal, and also to provide a setting in which we receive and rejoice in God's gracious forgiveness.

Healing

Jesus was a Healer and calls his people into healing work and healing presence. Can we learn from him the compassion and the sources of effective praying which will help us to discern special gifts of healing prayer as well as to offer many types of merciful support for those who suffer in all kinds of ways? The communion service can become the locus for prayers that build up the faith of the community and reach out in compassion to those who suffer outside as well as within it.

It may seem strange to isolate healing as a theme separate from forgiveness or from reconciliation. In Jesus' ministry the three are closely related. We might expect them to appear together in the earliest services. But though the meanings of forgiveness and reconciliation are historically integral with the eucharist, healing seems to have another history.

In the early centuries prayers for healing, invoking God's miraculous power, were one form of evangelistic contact with pagans. God's power to heal still draws many to him. But in our own time, highly publicized evangelistic campaigns with spectacular healing services are often a focus for pagan scorn. One result is that some skeptical Christians, reacting against abuses, steer clear of healing prayers altogether.

However, many churches, aware of a great longing and need for this kind of ministry, are beginning to include within their eucharist services specific prayers for healing: intercessions, prayers with whole family groups, anointing with oil, and prayers for physical and psychological healing.

The origins of people's troubles are often a mixture of mental, physical, emotional, and relational factors. It's an outdated dichotomy to say that we go to the doctor for help with physical problems and to church for relief from spiritual ones. These sufferings are intricately bound together. Many stories of Jesus' healing ministry can form the basis for loving and discerning prayers for healing. If these prayers accompany the regular, ordinary worship life of the church, so much the better. When we wait until a person is at death's door to call the elders for anointing, we withhold a blessing for all concerned.

If we are wary of praying for the sick, let's apply ourselves to the model of our Master and learn from the experience of many holy, praying Christians across the ages and today. Our reputation will become known – we will be recognized as compassionate people who pray for the sick. And just as happened long ago, this mark of Jesus' ministry upon his people will be experienced as good news.

Christ's Sacrifice and Ours

It isn't easy to become life-bringers. It is much easier to be selfish and fully absorbed with our own concerns. The communion theme of sacrifice challenges us to a deeper grasp of Jesus' self-offering, which in turn can shape our lives to reflect his life of generous selflessness.

Over the centuries Christians have diverged widely in their use of sacrificial language and imagery in relation to the Lord's table. Catholics point to 1 Corinthians 10:14-22 to establish that the table of the Lord from the start was understood as a sacrificial meal, distinguished from the tables to heathen gods, where unclean meat was offered.

Certainly the language of Old Testament sacrifice appears in early church discussions of the eucharist. Frequently cited is the prophecy of Malachi in which a "pure offering" would be made in all places (Mal. 1:11). This metaphor appears in virtually all the early texts about eucharistic celebration. In reference to the Lord's Supper, remembrance of Jesus' Passion blended with ideas of offering and sacrifice.

We saw in chapter 5, "Medieval Mass and Divine Liturgy," that sacrificial imagery and language dominated the medieval Catholic mass. In its crystallization of sacrificial theology, the mid-sixteenth century Council of Trent had stressed that the mass was not a mere meal, nor a memorial service to recall a sacrifice made long ago. The mass was itself a sacrifice and possessed its own power of atonement and petition. The mass was to be understood as simultaneously the sacrifice of Christ and the sacrifice of the church.

The Reformers drastically reduced or else cast out of their revised eucharistic services altogether any prayers implying that the eucharist was itself a sacrifice. There was one sacrifice alone – that of Christ himself on the cross. The only sense of human offering they could retain was that of worshipers offering themselves in the service.

So we recognize that the term *sacrifice* has a hot history in discussions about the Lord's Supper. Objections to using sacrificial language focus on the fear that it might undermine the all-sufficiency of the cross of Christ. Sacrificial language implies a specialized priestly class that creates a hierarchical split within the church. Arguments about the language of priesthood, sacrifice, and offering deal with the exercise of power, with the accessibility of "holy things" to all, and particularly with questions about the self-regard of Christians. Do we humans have anything to offer to God?

It would be a great loss to abandon the language of sacrifice in relation to the Lord's Supper. Without entering into disputations, we can consider some biblical and early Christian reflections on sacrifice and sharing and on motives which lie behind them. These reflections can enrich our understanding and careful appropriation of sacrificial language in relation to the Lord's Supper.

"I appeal to you therefore, brothers and sisters, by the mercies of God, to present your bodies as a living sacrifice, holy and acceptable to God, which is your spiritual worship" (Rom. 12:1). Paul here refers to self-offering as a holocaust, that is, something fully given up. The offering is the best we have to give. When the sacrifice is made, there is nothing held back. Nothing is held in reserve. There is no hidden benefit for ourselves.

The motive for our offering is that God has given in that way to us – "by the mercies of God." We have received God's immeasurable gift of forgiveness and freedom through Christ. God has given us ourselves back. We are therefore free to "spend" ourselves (2 Cor. 12:15) through the "renewed mind" of Romans 12:2. We are free to sacrifice ourselves to God and in service to others, in the Spirit of our Lord.

This kind of self-offering is to be a distinctive characteristic of the church. All that we have – time, money, energy, love, material possessions – all this flows freely among us. There are to be no poor among us. This is possible only because of the sacrifice of Christ for us, who "though he was rich, yet for [our] ... sakes he became poor, so that by his poverty [we] ... might become rich" (2 Cor. 8:9). We know this kind of equalization expresses God's way because of the manna stories of the Exodus journey. There is to be a "fair balance," and everyone will have enough (2 Cor. 8:14-15).

Early Christians struggled with this, just as we do today. But they had another problem. Early Christians were often accused of atheism. They performed no overt public acts which could be seen to benefit the public order. There was no visible cult, and there were no sacrifices. Christians held secret meetings and seemed to manipulate spiritual, magical, powers for private purposes. Early Christians had to answer these serious charges. Many of them alluded to the Old Testament tradition that "obedience is better than sacrifice," and they made an equivalence of prayer with sacrifice. Their "sacrifice of thanksgiving" (Ps. 50:14, 23) counteracted any ideas of sacrifices necessary to dispel the anger of God.

Christians defended their worship with the argument that sacrifices of prayer and thanksgiving and the virtuous life of Christians served to benefit the state. Pressed about the apparent absence of visible sacrifice, Christian apologists developed explanations of their fellowship meals which might be comprehensible to a pagan inquirer. In the mid-second century, Justin explained that bread and wine were offered ritually as a memorial and a thanksgiving (*Apology* 1.65-67). This was done to remember the suffering of Christ. All Christian thanksgiving was because of Christ's saving death. Thus Justin had a spiritual understanding of sacrifice and a sacrificial rite.[4]

Ultimately, we gain the best perspective on sacrifice by looking at Jesus, who gave his life as a gift – a sacrifice – to his Father. This gift ultimately meant total loss in his humiliating death. Jesus was a Man "consumed in the fire of Spirit, consumed by the Father's will for mercy, grace, reconciliation, because the cost of these in a sinful world is death."[5] As we are drawn into communion with Christ and his people, we are sustained by the priceless gift, the sacrifice of his life. We ourselves can give only because we have received. As we individually and as communities continue to grasp in our communion services the significance of Jesus' gift, we mysteriously become sacrificial people, truly sustained by Christ's priceless gift.

Making Covenant

The covenant theme reminds us that we are a chosen people, a people with a character and a mission. We are to be a distinctive people, made holy in the likeness of God's holiness. As a people infused with God's character of love and justice-making, we will be noticeable, if not always praised by the world around us. God makes the new covenant with us, at the table of our Lord.

Covenant, though theologically central, isn't easy to understand, so let's explore some of its biblical references – first the new, then the old covenant. Then we will consider blood sacrifices and finally the celebrative feast.

"This is my blood of the covenant, which is poured out for many for the forgiveness of sins" (Matt. 26:28). The text seems to underwrite an authoritative tradition which will endure. In Matthew's Gospel the disciples appear as bearing authority, almost larger than life. The Last Supper words in Matthew are similar to Mark's, but a different atmosphere surrounds them. Jesus commands the disciples to eat; he commands them to drink. Emphasis seems less on discipleship and martyrdom and instead is on links to Old Testament sacrificial references (Exod. 24:6-8; Isa. 53:12; Jer. 31:34).

The words of institution recorded in Luke and in 1 Corinthians refer to the new covenant which Jesus is establishing in his cup. "This cup that is poured out for you is the new covenant in my blood" (Luke 22:20). "This cup is the new covenant in my blood" (1 Cor. 11:25).

Through the pouring out of Jesus' blood, the new covenant would be established. How do we understand this? What did Jesus mean by "in my blood"? How can this "cup of blessing," which we Christians share at the Lord's table, be "the new covenant"? Talk of a new covenant implies a preexisting covenant.

111

Old Testament texts throw light on the theme of covenant, old or yet to come. In Exodus 24 Moses "told the people all the words of the Lord and all the ordinances" of the Torah. The people answered together, with one voice, "All that the Lord has spoken we will do" (24:3). Moses then took the blood of the sacrificial animals and threw it over the people, saying, "See the blood of the covenant that the Lord has made with you in accordance with all these words" (24:8). The gesture may seem bizarre to us, even though the words promising obedience and commitment make sense. It is tempting to write off this sacrificial ritual as primitive and crudely obsolete. But there are useful points here, ones which explain the foundation of the old covenant.

Three themes of the covenant

First, this old covenant is between God and a people, a chosen community. It is not a description of an individual contract. It signifies a two-way relationship. God, their Liberator, gives the people the gift of Torah, the wise indicator for their communal life. The people receive the Torah and pledge their obedience. Second, this covenant required sacrificial blood for its ritual. An animal was killed, its blood was sprinkled on the people, and some parts of the animal's body were burned as an offering to God. Third, this covenant called for a celebratory feast of the people before their God. They joyfully remembered how their God had delivered them out of slavery, and led them to freedom. "They beheld God, and they ate and drank" (Exod. 24:11b).

These themes of the covenant – the identity of God's people, the necessity of sacrificial blood, and the celebratory feast – lay behind Jesus' reference. Each one has its significant place in our theology of communion.

Of the three, sacrificial blood is most problematic for us moderns. Killing animals and tossing blood around in the name of religion seems remote and revolting. But we have to talk about blood because the Bible does. "Without the shedding of blood there is no forgiveness" (Heb. 9:22). We unthinkingly put together a disjointed theology based on the assumption that blood equates with death. Prevalent theologies of atonement emphasize the necessary death of Jesus. His blood signifies his death. The wine in the cup of blessing at the Last Supper surely meant Jesus' death-blood poured out "for you" (Luke 22:20b), "for many" (Mark 14:24), "for the forgiveness of sins" (Matt. 26:28b). The blood of Jesus' death was necessary.

However, to deepen our theology of the communion cup, let us start with what blood meant in Old Testament ceremony. "For the life of the flesh is in the blood; and I have given it to you for making atonement for your lives on the altar; for, as life, it is the blood that makes atonement" (Lev. 17:11). "For the life of every creature – its blood is its life" (17:14a).

In Old Testament sacrifice, the *life* of the animal – its blood – is given. It is not the death of the animal which is given to God. The Torah does not call for sacrifice which requires suffering and loss. The meaning is not that life is destroyed. Life is given.

It is true that an animal's death happened to facilitate the blood rituals, the renewing of the covenant, and the celebratory meal. Precisely because of respect for blood (life), the death of sacrificial animals was surrounded with ritual care. But the focus was not on death itself. Think of it like this: we wouldn't say that Christmas dinner is about the death of turkeys. Yet obviously many turkeys die at Christmas-time. In a more profound way, of course, the meaning of the Old Testament sacrificial meals was about the lifeblood and not the death-blood of sacrificial animals.

> The meaning of the sacrifice is that the livingness, the vitality of the animal, is put up before God to represent the vitality and the livingness of the offering. To give is to be alive to God ... It is precisely the life of the animal, the blood of the animal, that goes to God, representing the life of the person who will henceforth live for God.[6]

Old Testament law emphasized the purity and the perfection of a sacrificial animal. It had to be the best, the first, the most valuable. The purity and perfection of life, a gift from God, was to be given back to God. A person would identify with the quality of the animal. The life of the animal represented the life of the giver, the supreme gift to God.

This may well be the image in Paul's mind, when he urged Roman Christians to offer their very selves to God as "a living sacrifice, holy and acceptable to God, which is your spiritual worship" (Rom. 12:1). We are to offer our best, our purest gift to God – worship welling up from our whole selves.

God's chosen community celebrating at a festive meal – this is the practical picture of the theology of the new covenant. In Jeremiah the term "new covenant" appears for the first time. The context is of despair and hopelessness, but the prophetic word blazed out:

> The days are surely coming, says the Lord, when I will make a new covenant with the house of Israel and the house of Judah ... I will put my law within them and I will write it on their hearts; and I will be their God, and they shall be my people ... They shall all know me ... for I will forgive their iniquity and remember their sin no more (Jer. 31:31, 33b, 34).

God gives another chance to these people who, in spite of God's own faithfulness to them, were dismally faithless in response. The accent here is on the close relationship between God and the people. God's way will be within them; from the least to the greatest, they will all know God. God will liberate them again, free them from their iniquities. God will restore, heal, and lead the people into a new relationship – committed, free, and life-giving. The new covenant will newly constitute the people, bound to one another and to God in love and allegiance.

As Jesus looked around his Last Supper table, he thought of this prophetic dream for a covenanted and faithful people. He picked up the ceremonial cup, pronounced the blessing, and then added the powerful words: "This cup is the new covenant in my blood, poured out." Jesus' blood, his life of pure devotion and commitment to God, was spilling out. This night's events would culminate his years of loving and contending ministry. Here, in the context of the ceremonial memorial meal, celebrating the ancient and continuing liberation of their gracious God, Jesus called his disciples to faithfulness within the new community of the Messiah.

Jesus in a new way brought together for them themes of the old covenant – committed community, pure life-sacrifice, and celebratory memorial meal. In naming and passing the cup of the new covenant, Jesus reminded his disciples then and reminds us today that we participate in his new community, in new shared life, and in a joyful feast of liberation.

The writers of the Gospels showed Jesus as the Fulfiller of the old covenant and the One who inaugurated the new. The accounts in the Gospels of Jesus' last few days leading up to his crucifixion reverberate with allusions of covenant language and ritual.

The Lord's Supper itself was the Passover (covenant) feast. It highlighted liberation and deliverance by the sacrificial death of Jesus, the Lamb of God. Through their shared meal, Christians established their covenantal relationship with their Lord. The moment of Jesus' death coincided with the ripping of the temple veil; its purpose had been to conceal the ark of the old covenant. Jesus fulfilled the messianic prophecies. Through his death and vindication, he established the new age of the new covenant.

The eucharistic community which joyfully celebrates its identity and its liberation through the lifeblood of Christ poured out will grow in deep inner commitment to each other and to Christ. This depth is the maturity which holds the community from wavering or collapsing when under pressure, a fruit quite different from that of superficial or over-personalized understandings of eucharist.

Discipline at the Table

In chapter 14, "An Open Table?" we will consider questions of who is invited to the Lord's Supper. In contemporary discussion, concerns arise for the loving inclusion at the Lord's table of seekers, strangers, small children – any who would like to come. The key idea is inclusion, equated here with the warmth, love, and hospitality which were hallmarks of Jesus' own character. Jesus welcomed children, sinners, foreigners, as well as religious folk – everyone has access to God's mercy and love. The implication some draw is that the church should welcome all to take part in the Sunday communion.

Boundaries worked out in the liturgy
Such questions as these were never thought of in the early Christian communities. Only the baptized took part in the eucharist. Christian worship was not a public event, so the question of pagans taking part never arose. However, their assemblies did include people ineligible for the eucharist. Christians worked out this problem within the framework of their liturgy, the form of which was shaped by the Greco-Roman banquet.

Boundaries were clear – candidates for baptism should attend the first part of the worship along with the "faithful" (the baptized), listening to the Scripture readings and sermon. They could take part in some of the prayers of the church but not all. They were dismissed while only the baptized members continued with further prayers and the service of eucharist. Those who had fallen into sin could be excluded from the table until proper restoration and reconciliation.

After infant baptism became the norm, the link between baptism and eucharist remained strong. And when baptistic reformers insisted on believers baptism, they also insisted on the continuing integrity between baptism (their understanding of it) and the Lord's table. Orthodox, Catholics, Lutherans, and Anglicans continue to link baptism and eucharist. Only some inheritors of the Protestant Reformation now seem willing to lay aside theological, historical, and practical connections between the two.

The church's Supper is just that – a form of worship inaugurated by the Lord Jesus but shaped by the early Christian communities in light of their experiences of fellowship within, of the presence of Christ in their communion, and of pressure from without. It was not primarily shaped by Jesus' story of the master sending servants out to bring everyone from highways and hedges to the banquet.

Jesus' vision of the grand inclusive table of the kingdom need not be taken as instruction to take away all boundaries from Christian communities. Jesus made a great point of the inclusive invitation to all, but he also insisted that choices be made. It was not a light thing to acknowledge the kingdom and to enter into its costs and joys.

There is good reason to have community boundaries. They help to shape identity and a sense of belonging. Traditionally, the church has bounded the Lord's table with baptism, and to break apart this connection could be disastrous. Baptismal initiation would make no sense if entry to the church's deepest communion could be gained by any other door of choice.

Baptism has in long Christian tradition been the recognized gate to the eucharist. Excommunication was the opposite. It meant literally to be put out of communion with the community, a severe penalty imposed for grave sins – murder, adultery, or apostasy. This practice the Christians inherited from Judaism, both in transgressing the law and in the removal of the transgressor from fellowship. In Christian communities the purpose of excommunication was to restore the offending person. This is the deeper meaning in Matthew 18:17: "Let such a one be to you as a Gentile." Penitence was the path to restoration, even if often public and humiliating. Peace was the goal and reward of restoration to fellowship.

Many churches have laid aside this penitential and disciplinary aspect to their communion table. In some places the discipline and removal from active fellowship calls for absenting oneself from the church's business meeting rather than from the Lord's Supper.

Christ's Offering and Ours

"Now the ushers will take up the offering." Could there be any words in a worship service more limp than these? The sorry fact is that for many this sentence expresses exactly what the offering is about. Seated quietly and accompanied by soothing music (the offertory), we solemnly place our little envelopes or cash on wide platters passed along the pews. Then as the minister holds the stack of offering plates, we stand and the minister leads in a short prayer. Later the treasurer counts the money. Eventually, in the annual accounts, we find out how much we gave and to what purpose.

For Christians throughout the centuries, offering has meant much more than this. Certainly gathering up money in a worship service is a derivative meaning for offering. Primarily, offering has referred to Christ's own giving of himself. From that meaning has come the memory-keeping of that gift in the eucharist. The eucharist has been called the "Oblation," which is simply the Latin word for offering. The bread and wine of the eucharist are called "offering," and the word also refers to the act of worshipers in the eucharist.

Within these four points of meaning have raged divisive arguments. "What the church does in eucharist is to identify with Christ's self-oblation." "No. Christ's offering was unique, and we cannot call the bread and wine of the table *offering*." In recent years a mellowing of attitudes has allowed Christians of various traditions to agree to emphasize the bread and wine as fruits of the earth but fashioned by human labor. As the bread and wine are prepared for use in the eucharist, God's gifts of provision for our sustenance and the gifts of our own work come together.

Some feel that this bypasses the question of earlier debates: what does

116

this have to do with Christ's offering which we celebrate in the eucharist? The challenge is to bring together the dual themes of Christ's loving gift and our grateful response in giving all that we have and are to God.

Offertory is an ancient term which refers to the presentation and preparation of the bread and wine within the eucharist. I think of a side table in a Greek Orthodox church, heaped with material goods and offering plates of money. I didn't ask about it the morning I attended the liturgy, but I have a good idea it was for distribution to the poor. That is what happened in early Christian communities. Justin Martyr describes what they did in the Roman Christian communities at the mid-second century.

> All gather together for a communal celebration ... Those who prosper, and who so wish, contribute, each one as much as he chooses to. What is collected is deposited with the one presiding, and he takes care of the orphans and widows, and those who are in want on account of sickness or any other cause, and those who are in bonds and the strangers who are sojourners among us. He, in short, is the protector of all those in need.   (Justin, *Apology* 1.67)

People brought gifts to the worship meetings. They put them all on the deacon's table near the door. It is striking that from that one table of offerings made by the whole congregation came the bread, wine, and water for the eucharistic service, and also the food distributed after the service to the needy within the community.

Another mechanism in the early Christian communities, one with the same root history as Justin's Sunday eucharist, was the agape meal. This was a continuation of the early fellowship meal which we saw in 1 Corinthians 11. It served a number of functions – for socializing, teaching, freer prayers and thanksgivings, and also for economic care of the poor.

> Our feast shows its motive by its name. It is called by the Greek word for love. Whatever is reckoned the cost, money spent in the name of piety is gain, since with that refreshment we benefit the needy ... As is so with God, there is a greater consideration for the lowly; since the agape is a religious duty, it permits nothing vile, nothing immodest. We do not recline at the table before prayer to God is first tasted. We eat the amount that satisfies the hungry; we drink as much as is beneficial to the modest.
>
> (Tertullian, *Apology* 39)

When you are all assembled to eat together, eat sufficiently, but so that there may remain something left over. Your host may send it to whomsoever he wills as the "abundance of the saints."

(Apostolic Tradition)

The early Christian communities didn't sharply divide spiritual from material activities and benefits. "If you have what is eternal in common, how much should you have what is transient?"[7] Their religion was earthy – with tangible expressions of what they believed. In their rituals at the table, and in the distribution of bread and wine, clothing and food, they worked out what it meant to "*do*" the memory of Jesus at table.

As we saw in Justin's mid-second century description of eucharist, bread and wine and water are brought to the one presiding. They were brought from the offerings-in-kind which the people deposited with the deacons as they came to worship. In the baptismal eucharist of the third-century *Apostolic Tradition*, honey and milk are brought forward as well as the bread and wine.

In the fourth and fifth centuries, in spite of the increasing complexity and control of the liturgy by the clergy, the laity had their part in bringing gifts to worship and presenting them for use in the eucharist. In the large church buildings, worshipers developed elaborate processions for taking the elements forward to the presiding clergy. In later times the clergy came out among the people and gathered up the gifts, both those used in the service and those for distribution to the poor.[8]

It isn't surprising that the offertory should have become a theological flashpoint. It is, after all, the coming together of representations and declarations about the created order and the order of redemption. Ordinary bread and wine, through our memory, our words, and our actions, meet the unique sacrifice of Christ on the cross. What indeed does happen at such a moment? And how can we talk about it? Offertory prayers and hymn texts perhaps best express the mystery and power of this conjunction. But as we shall see in chapter 18, "Offering Ourselves and Our Gifts," there are also things we can do to express in a richer way how these two offerings – Christ's and ours – come together.

11

Communion Themes
for Mission

Christ the Conqueror

CHRISTUS VICTOR, the Latin title for "Christ the Conqueror," is one of the oldest Christian themes and builds on and expresses a buoyant confidence in Christ. A eucharist centering around this theme will be joyful, bringing together the cross and the resurrection in one powerful celebration. The world around us agonizes over the manifest power of evil. Why must the innocent suffer? Christian communities which celebrate Christus Victor focus on one of the world's most urgent questions. When we celebrate and honor Christ, the One who conquers evil on a cosmic scale as well as in our lives, we become missionary people in the best sense of the word. We articulate the good news that God's reign of justice has begun. This name for Christ – Christus Victor – spells out our confident Christian hope.

In the eucharist we remember and celebrate the whole work of Christ in our human redemption. In Western tradition, the focus of Christians within the eucharist has been on the cross of Christ. The bread has signified Christ's broken body, the wine his life poured out.

Hence, the questions are posed: What really happened on the cross? Why was Jesus' death necessary? One of the oldest lines of explanation is this "dramatic" or Christus Victor view. This is a theme of conflict and struggle between God and his enemies, worked out at the crucifixion. At the cross of Jesus Christ, much more was happening than appeared. Spiritual powers stood behind the Roman and Jewish ruling establishments, the groups which condemned and crucified Christ. We read about these enemy powers in Colossians 2:

> God made you alive together with him, when he forgave us all our trespasses, erasing the record that stood against us with its legal demands. He set this aside, nailing it to the cross. He disarmed the rulers and authorities and made a public example of them, triumphing over them in it (Col. 2:13b-15).

Christ overcame the powers at the cross. The Christus Victor explanation requires the resurrection to complete the understanding of Christ's triumph over the rebellious powers of evil.[1]

Following Jesus

The most vivid visual image for most people of Jesus with his disciples is a depiction of the Last Supper. Artists in every time and place have imagined the scene. As we look at the pictures, we too are at that table. We take our places among the original twelve. We are disciples. Jesus offers us the bread and the cup. Jesus invites us to walk in his way. The communion table is the table of discipleship for all who would follow in Jesus' steps. Jesus gives us a solemn and sobering invitation: the call to follow him in life and in death.

The theme of discipleship appears most clearly in passages which concern the suffering or cross of a Christian, especially in relation to the suffering and cross of Christ himself.[2] Why does the Christian suffer? Surely not to pay off an offended God. To this question sixteenth-century Anabaptists made a distinctive insight. They insisted that "the *benefit* of the death of Christ applies only to the person whose acceptance of it includes discipleship. That is, the inward appropriation of the broken will and the outward following in the steps of Jesus."[3]

In Appendix B is an example of how one Anabaptist, Balthasar Hubmaier, developed this theme in the communion service. The Pledge of Love is a corporate promise made by the whole congregation just before they take the bread and the cup.

The theme of discipleship is strongly developed throughout the Gospel of Mark. It colors the way in which the Last Supper is recounted in chapter 14. In this version of the events, Jesus gives no explicit command that the meal should be practiced after his death. The story of the Last Supper is woven into the narrative as part of an overall Gospel theme of discipleship. In chapter 8 Jesus calls the disciples to take up the cross; in chapter 10 Jesus uses for discipleship the symbol of the cup. "The cup that I drink you will drink" (Mark 10:39). In Gethsemane, referring to his impending death, Jesus prays, "Remove this cup from me." Both cross and cup refer to Jesus' martyr death and the disciples' call to follow him.

This context of disciples pledged to their rabbi makes all the more tragic the betrayal by Judas. To dissent with one's rabbi or to leave the rabbi was bad enough, but for Judas to deliver up his Master was scandalous. Doing so, Judas rescinded his covenant of discipleship. To make it immeasurably worse, he arranged the handover during a hallowed mealtime. No wonder Christians have perpetually remembered that dark evening as "the night he was delivered up." Judas broke two covenants at once: the bond between host and guest and the bond between rabbi and disciple. Is it any wonder that Jesus chose that very evening to speak of covenant, a new bond of commitment between the Master and his disciples?

120

In Mark's version of the Last Supper, Jesus takes and gives thanks for the cup. When he gives it to them, they all drink from it. Jesus' cup words are "This is my blood of the covenant, which is poured out for many" (Mark 14:24). Through this account the Markan community is called to the path and the pledge of discipleship.

In John 15:20 Jesus warns his followers that they will receive persecution even as he himself did. If they pattern their life on his teachings, the consequences are predictable. "Servants are not greater than their master." But this warning is in the same chapter as that most beloved of communion texts – Jesus the true vine (John 15:1-17). There is much to recommend using the entire chapter 15 in communion readings and meditations.

John 6:53-54, with its metaphor of Jesus' self as bread eaten, stands in another favorite communion chapter. Here Jesus, bread from heaven, calls people to respond in faith. His followers are to eat their Master, literally to chew him up. This means to take into our lives by faith all of his teachings. We eat and drink Jesus, and we thoroughly assimilate him into the fiber of our lives. This metaphor is not strange in English usage. People often say of someone who has a compelling hobby, "He eats and drinks" it. Such a person both consumes and is consumed by his passionate interest.

And so, week after week, as we take part in the Lord's Supper, we renew our commitment to our baptismal pledges. We are nourished at the table. We "feed on him with faith" and go out together into a life which bears witness to Jesus' life-giving way. Not isolated individuals, we are Jesus' own disciple band. People will see us and be either repelled by the cost or attracted to join Jesus' way.

Serving One Another and the World

With the theme of service, we come to a play on words. The meeting around the Lord's table is itself called a service. And one of the truest outcomes of communion is a community which pointedly fulfills its calling to serve one another and the world in the Spirit of Jesus.

In the expression *communion service*, we have a beautiful combination of several aspects of the Lord's Supper. Communion, as we have seen, points toward the intimate and interdependent friendship Christians have together, and also to the mystic and sweet relationship with Christ that each Christian enjoys within the company of the larger body of the church. Communion has to do with secure and energizing relationships both with God and with other disciples of Jesus.

The service part of the expression reminds us of the active, outgoing expression of those relationships within the church, and beyond. Our word comes originally from the Latin word *servus*, which means slave. It has formed a great array of applications, none of which actually relate to slavery but usually refer to the performing of work which meets a general or specific need. The sense of performing something that needs to be done applies to service, whether in the context of a game of tennis, the running of trains, or providing food.

Jesus spoke of service in describing the mode of his own ministry. "I am among you as one who serves," he said (Luke 22:27), inviting his disciples to model the life of their community on his own example. Though he was the Rabbi, the Leader, and Teacher of his disciples, he didn't pull rank and expect them to do everything for him. His way was both to give and receive service. He listened and taught; he blessed and fed; he healed and encouraged. But we also know that he was comforted and cared for by others. Among Jesus' disciples, loving mutual service was to be the hallmark.

To explore this mark of humble service within the worship of an early Christian community, we will look closely at John 13. In this Gospel, we find two traditions concerning the Last Supper: John 6, the bread-from-heaven passage; and John 13, with no mention of the bread-and-cup ceremony, but portraying Jesus' act of washing his disciples' feet. John 13 thereby emphasizes Jesus' command to his followers to imitate his act, serving one another in humility and love.

Jesus and his disciples were at a fellowship meal. Many assume this was the Lord's Last Supper in the upper room, the same meal "on the night he was betrayed" appearing in four other passages.[4] It was at the time of the great Passover festival. John's account of this meal is in the context of Jesus' "farewells" in chapters 13 to 17.

Jesus scandalized his disciples at the table by interrupting the meal to act out a parable, taking up basin and towel, kneeling down, and washing their feet. Then he sat again and explained what he meant by doing that service. So often Jesus had baffled his disciples. But this time Jesus made it completely clear. In washing their feet, the action of a minor servant, he had set them an example. They were now to do the same to each other. Jesus said it not once, but three times: "You ought to [do this]" (John 13:14), "You also should do [this]" (13:15), and "You are blessed if you do [this]" (13:17).

The Gospel of John contains no specific words of institution ("Take, eat. This is my body ...") in a Last Supper scene as recorded in the other Gospels. But it is fascinating that John includes this detailed account of a Passover meal with Jesus' acted parable of foot washing as the centerpiece. Did his disciples understand Jesus? Did they obey him in this?

John 13:4-17

Recent work on this text throws new emphasis on certain neglected aspects of Jesus' teaching and dramatic action in John 13. In the first place, the disciples would have been thoroughly familiar with the ritual. A number of meanings were attached to foot washing. It was an everyday courtesy of a host to his guests. Before coming to the dinner, they would have bathed, but on arrival their feet would need cleaning and refreshing. This form of hospitality could join hygiene with comfort and aesthetics in the anointing of the feet with aromatic oils. Certainly, the one performing the washing and anointing was a person in a position of humble service to the guests. Besides these meanings, foot washing also referred to a strand of religious or cultic cleansing which was widely known at that time.

In all of these instances, foot washing served as a preparatory action. An idiom to describe a person who rushed into something without properly getting ready was that they acted "with unwashed feet."

There can be little doubt that the community of John's Gospel could quite easily obey and practice foot washing in a literal way, particularly since the text records Jesus' repeated commands to do so. The first time (John 13:14) Jesus underlines the act itself. What Jesus did for them wasn't just an illustration of a desirable type of action. They were to do this particular act. The disciples would not have seen it as a general illustration of an act of humble service. The second injunction (13:15) emphasizes the authority of Jesus as their Master. They should do it because Jesus told them to. The third command (13:17) is in the form of a blessing. In doing this act, they will receive blessing. That blessing is the continued fellowship with Jesus alluded to in verse 8, where Jesus promises to Peter a "share" with him. In the image of John 15, to be blessed is to "abide" in close communion with Christ.

When compared to the words of institution for baptism and for the Lord's Supper, these words of Jesus seem the strongest. How could his command have been mistaken for anything but the establishing of a rite of religious significance?

What was foot washing really about, in Jesus' intention and in how the first disciples understood it? It is important to remember that this account is within Jesus' "farewells," that it follows after the story of Mary's anointing which Jesus related to "the day of my burial" (John 12:7), and is followed by the departure of Judas the betrayer from the common table.

All of this connects with a number of allusions to Jesus' impending death. He is preparing his disciples, even though they will not fully understand it until later (13:7). When Peter protests Jesus' action with basin and towel, Jesus tells him, "Unless I wash you, you have no share with me" (13:8b). This word *meros*, "share," on one level referring to verse 3, means eternal life, the "all things" in Jesus' hands. But the word also indicates a person's destiny or identity. If the disciples were to share Jesus' destiny, that meant his death. Fellowship with Jesus meant to share his identity and his calling. Ultimately, it meant joining his mission and his martyrdom.

In John 13:10 we can distinguish between Jesus' words for bathing and washing. This relates to the custom of the time, in which a person bathed all over once a week, but washed only their legs and arms daily. Jesus alludes to this practice when he says, "One who has bathed does not need to wash, except for the feet" (13:10).

For the disciples there could have been only one allusion – to the bathing of baptism, which was done once, not to be repeated. This was the bath which had cleansed them. The reference is to the death of Jesus, which effected this cleansing forgiveness of sin. The "washing" then, according to a number of writers, could well refer to the cleansing needed for ongoing sin after baptism.

So Peter who had bathed (been cleansed from sin through his baptism) does not need to be rebaptized. When Jesus washes Peter's feet at the Last Supper, he points to cleansing from sin in his daily walk of life.

The meanings in Jesus' foot washing ritual center on the cleansing efficacy of his death. Forgiveness is available for all. The context is within the farewell materials. The potent terms *meros*, which means shared communion and destiny with Christ, and *makarios*, which refers to blessings of eternal life, are joined to an easily understood cultural act. A hospitable, hygienic, and aesthetic action became Jesus' parable for the disciples' participation in the benefits and blessings of his impending death. Foot washing was a cleansing, preparatory action which compelled them to their knees before each other, remembering the humiliation and sacrifice he was to offer on their behalf.[5]

Christian groups which have spelled out humility and mutual service as a central meaning have focused on Jesus' taking on the form and deeds of a servant and his injunction that they should do the same for each other. The theme of reconciliation and mutual love comes from the verses a bit later in the account – after Judas has gone out.

It seems essential to put the theme of cleansing from sin and the link to Jesus' death at the center of the rite. There can be little doubt that this community observed the rite of foot washing at their memorial meal, the meal at which they experienced communion with their Lord, and received cleansing forgiveness by his death for their daily walk of faith. The rite of foot washing brings rich meanings to the context of the Lord's Supper. We are indebted to the community of the Gospel of John who kept this tradition alive.

There is plenty of evidence that early Christian communities, across a wide geographical and contextual distribution, remembered Jesus' injunction and practiced the rite of foot washing. Although quite a few contemporary Christian groups observe the ritual of foot washing, to most Western Christians it is puzzling at best and downright embarrassing at worst. It is especially hard for those of us who live far away in time and space from Jesus' cultural and religious bombshell – this potent acted-out parable of a menial servant's task. In hot and dusty climates and in cultures closer in ethos to the Palestine of Jesus, the ritual of foot washing in connection with the Lord's Supper may be more easily grasped and appropriated to spiritual benefit.

In summary, the foot washing ritual inaugurated by Jesus has most often stimulated interpretations of a call to mutual service in a spirit of humility. But as we observed in John 13, several other themes run parallel to humble service. Allusions to Jesus' impending death fill the adjacent passages. Jesus calls his disciples to fellowship in his death and also to participate in the Father's gift of eternal life. There are intimations of baptism, cleansing, and forgiveness of sins. Christians going down before one another on their knees with the basin and towel will rise up as changed people. In obeying Jesus' command and invitation to "Do as I have done to you," we will take in his Spirit, and take on a true mark of his human life.

Making Justice

"The simple, central action of the eucharist is the sharing of food – not only eating but sharing. The simple, central human experience for understanding this action is hunger."[6] Monica Hellwig persuasively calls Christians to explore the meaning of eucharist through the reality of global human hunger, which largely results from violence, greed, and injustice. She puts hunger for food in a larger picture of spiritual hunger and depicts hunger as the "fundamental level of meaning that precedes all systematic theological explanations."[7]

In the theme of justice within eucharist, we conjoin concerns for physical and spiritual peace. Christians neglect this theme at their peril, and all too easily fall into self-absorbed complacency. If we explain to ourselves that everyday food nourishes our bodies but communion nourishes our spirits, we diminish and deprive the Lord's table of its deepest significance. By integrating justice concerns with the sharing at communion, we put God's people into the heart of the mission of God. We dare not separate ourselves from God's own passion for making things right.

Eucharist liturgy and justice – these two concepts are closely intertwined. For the many Christians who choose the name *liturgy* for the Sunday communion, the word refers to the actions of corporate worship. More than ceremonial, however, liturgy means the heart of the worship of which the ritual actions are outward signs. The rules and regulations, and the traditions and trappings can be drawn aside to reveal the heart of liturgy.

At that heart is a meeting between God and the people because all the actions of the liturgy form a kind of conversation, coming first from one side and then from the other. In this interaction the people hear God's heartbeat for love and for justice, for "creation healed." And in liturgy

God hears the people's cry, their yearnings for love and justice, their thanksgivings and their hope. *Litourgia*, a Greek word meaning public service, is the work both of God and of the people in the service of the public – the world God loves. That public service is God's justice – making things right again.

Co-workers with God – what a remarkable calling we have been given. We have caught a glimpse of God's vision for restored relationships, for creation healed. And now God calls us to take our part in the great task as that vision comes to fulfillment.

In the "working lunch" of the liturgy, we gather round Jesus' table and see the possibilities of an outworking of God's will, God's justice-making. God chose Jesus in order to show his hand – in which the high cards are for restored relationship with God, reconciliation with each other, and harmony among all created beings. Jesus tells us at the table what the costs of this vision will be. Can we share the cup of our Lord's destiny? Can we enter into his broken body? The upside-down wages for this kingdom work will be persecution, sufferings, a painful entering into the agony of the world and of all creation. The surprise in the wage packet is that with the pain will come "life to the full" (John 10:10) and joy unmeasurable.

A strong justice movement within the liturgy is one we have already glimpsed in the theme about God's desire and provision for reconciliation among ourselves. Jesus has gone ahead of us, acting out his teaching concerning peacemaking, truth-telling, and mercy-sharing. If this concern of Jesus doesn't have regular and effective expression in our corporate worship, there is something drastically amiss. When Paul found abuses of the Lord's table in the Corinthian church, he had sharp words and a remedy to offer.

Paul felt free to accept the tradition he had received (not the only Jesus tradition around) and to adapt it. In 1 Corinthians 11:17ff. he passionately calls the congregation to account because of abuses regarding the Lord's Supper. Paul's concerns are for order and for economic justice within the body. He calls the community to faithful witness and active remembering of the whole story of Jesus' redemptive acts. Paul puts together Jesus' self-giving love, Christians' willing identification with the cross, and a right observance of the Lord's Supper. This is what constitutes the true proclamation of the Lord's death, the proper meaning of God's salvation. (These ideas are developed above, with the theme about reconciling and making peace.)

A second justice movement in Christian liturgy is the concern for the healing of all of creation. In the Genesis 1 creation account, God gives to humankind the responsibility for careful stewardship of "every living thing that moves upon the earth." In this task we have failed more than we have succeeded. Surely the first thing we need to do is to repent of our disastrous misdeeds. All of creation belongs to its Maker; every living thing has its place in God's design. But we Humans have managed to distort, interfere with, and exploit virtually every aspect of God's good creation.

Our prayers at the communion tables can reveal our appreciation of the natural world and our recognition of responsibility for it. They can show our close observation, our delighted enjoyment, and our gratefulness to be part of God's creation.

The earliest prayers at the liturgy were Christian adaptations of Jewish blessings. In them we see a deep awareness of humans' place within natural creation.

> Be blessed, O Lord our God, King of the universe,
>   who feeds the whole world with his goodness, grace,
>   loving-kindness, and mercy;
> He gives food to all mankind,
>   for his kindness endures forever.
> Because of his great goodness, food has never failed us;
>   may it never fail us forever and ever,
>   in fulfillment of his great Name.
> He feeds and nourishes all, and does good to all,
>   and provides food for all the creatures he has created.
> Be blessed, O Lord, who feeds all.[8]

The tone of respect and honor for creation carried over into early Christian thanksgivings, along with the unfolding story of redemption. Prayers and blessings within the communion service can be vehicles for us to say we are sorry and to commit ourselves anew to our creation task – the responsible care of the natural world.

A third justice movement in Christian eucharistic liturgy is involvement with local, national, and global issues of suffering because of greed and exploitation. This concern can take practical forms of sharing as well as disciplined, passionate prayers within the service. The next part of this book includes suggestions on both levels of involvement – prayer and action.

Jesus calls his disciples to hunger and thirst for justice. We are truly living and will be "satisfied" when we enact that hunger and thirst in the communion liturgy. The world is watching us in this matter of justice. If we truly reflect God's passion for making things right with nature and within human societies, non-Christians who already have these deep concerns will be drawn into fellowship with Jesus' own justice-making community.

More Metaphors

There are many more word pictures and symbols in the Bible which can enrich our understanding, expression, and experience of Lord's Supper services. These may be related to themes already mentioned or may suggest new and fruitful links.

Geoffrey Wainwright[9] presents detailed and fascinating material on Old Testament background to the longed-for messianic banquet of the kingdom. Besides the themes of the Sinai covenant meal and other sacred meals, imagery of meals appears throughout a wide range of wisdom and prophetic texts.[10] In Wainwright's discussion of New Testament texts concerning the theme of feasting in the kingdom of God, the following important examples arise:[11]

The new manna from heaven

A crucial Hebrew memory was of God's miraculous provision of bread from heaven in the great Exodus story.[12] In the intertestamental period the Jews believed that when Messiah came, such a gift of manna would again descend from on high for them.[13] Several New Testament texts touch this expectation and its fulfillment: the miraculous feeding episodes in Jesus' ministry,[14] Jesus' discourse on the bread of life (John 6:25-58), and Paul's pointing to the bread of the eucharist (1 Cor. 10:3) as fulfillment of the meaning of the Exodus manna.

Inclusiveness

One of Jesus' pictures of future salvation was of the many who "will come from east and west and will eat with Abraham and Isaac and Jacob in the kingdom of God" (Matt. 8:11; Luke 13:29). Jesus refers here to the prophetic vision of the nations of the earth streaming to Zion, the holy mountain of God's dwelling, to receive life and salvation.[15]

Beatitudes

Jesus used the imagery of hunger and satisfaction in two of the Beatitudes:

> Blessed are you who are hungry now, for you will be filled.
>
> (Luke 6:21a)

> Blessed are those who hunger and thirst for righteousness, for they will be filled. (Matt. 5:6)

Luke's version seems to indicate Jesus' typical prediction that God's kingdom will bring surprises. The humble will be exalted (Luke 14:11). Only those who become like children will be great in the kingdom (Matt. 18:4). The first will be last and the last first (Matt. 19:30). Jesus' words here apply to those who are physically hungry.

But Matthew's version reminds us that there is longing both for food and also for God to establish his justice on earth. In the kingdom all human longings as strong as hunger and thirst will be satisfied.

Jesus at Table

Meals formed an important focus in Jesus' ministry, sometimes with his own disciples. Pleasant human fellowship has value, Jesus implied, in his well-known enjoyment of the table. But Jesus ate not only with his close friends and relatives. He also shared table with publicans and sinners.

Jesus invited sinners to eat with him (Matt. 9:13; Mark 2:17; Luke 5:32); and sinners invited Jesus (Matt. 9:10; Mark 2:15; Luke 5:29; 15:1-2).

In these meals Jesus dramatized God's offer of salvation (Mark 2:17). But just to eat and drink with Jesus did not guarantee salvation. At Levi's great banquet, Jesus declared, "I have come to call not the righteous but sinners to repentance."[16] God's kingdom isn't just a free lunch, Jesus reminds his hearers (Luke 5:32). Sinners are invited to the feast, but there are to be big changes ahead. Life can never be the same for those who have shared the Lord's table.

The Lord's Prayer

The petition "Give us today our daily bread" from the Lord's Prayer has given rise to many interpretations. It obviously touches many levels of association, from the ordinary bread of our human sustenance to the bread for the "great tomorrow" when God's kingdom comes in all its fullness. Wainwright lays out the range of meanings put forward by Christian teachers through the centuries.[17]

Joachim Jeremias discusses in detail[18] the Aramaic word which stands behind the English adjective "daily." He suggests that a good translation would imply not only the sustaining bread for today, or even for tomorrow, but the "heavenly manna" or the "bread of life," which is sustenance for the "great tomorrow." This is the bread of "the age of salvation." Jeremias emphasizes that this is not a "spiritualizing" meaning. "It does not sever everyday life and the kingdom of God from one another. It encompasses the totality of life." This expanded understanding points to a daily bread which embraces all of our needs and sustains our total well-being.

Mystery

The Eastern Orthodox development of mystery is different from the idea that lies behind *mysterion* as used, for example, in Ephesians 1:8-10: "With all wisdom and insight [God] ... has made known to us the mystery of his will ... set forth in Christ, as a plan for the fullness of time, to gather up all things in him." This mystery is a revelation, an opening up of God's intention for the redeeming of all things.

One of the oldest Christian confessions is found in 1 Timothy 3:16, introduced by the phrase "great is the mystery of our faith."

129

> He was revealed in the flesh,
> vindicated by the Spirit,
> seen by angels,
> proclaimed among Gentiles,
> believed in throughout the world,
> taken up in glory.

(NRSV, note)

Atonement

The New Testament includes a range of ways of understanding the work of Christ. No one way can contain all the truth, so we need to say it in many ways, and somehow hold them together. When we talk about the atonement, we are trying to explain Christ's death. Why was it necessary? In communion services we can evoke these different images and combine them with moving ritual and symbols.

The root of the word *atonement* is visible in the word itself: at-one-ment. That is what it meant – reconciliation, reunion, or bringing back into unity. The word came to include a whole range of meanings about the saving work of Christ, such as propitiation, satisfaction, vindication. Atonement had become a general label for a whole area of discussion, rather than one way of answering the question of sin. A further shift in meaning has attached a particular and narrower meaning to atonement – making things right, reparation, or satisfaction.[19]

Here is a list of atonement themes in the New Testament:

Christ's victory over the powers of evil
Christ's (and our) victory over death – the resurrection
Human guilt and suffering
Reconciliation with God
Revelation of God's love (John 3:16; 1 John 3:16)
Righteousness of God – God makes things right again
Jesus' death as sacrifice
Adoption into family of God
Redemption
Christ the pioneer
Christ the new Adam[20]

Proclaim the Lord's Death

Proclaiming the death of Christ in the context of a communion service has often been explained as equivalent to the obligatory sermon preached before the ceremony of bread and wine. In most churches it would seem improper to have the service of the table without the preached Word. And how strange it would be even to consider

130

reversing the order, to focus first on the table and then turn to the pulpit.

As we saw in the historic and classic shape of Christian worship, both Word and table are equally important and both were always present. Over the course of Christian history, the expectation and practice of preaching changed a great deal. At first it was probably a simple reciting and application of gospel to life situations, in the form of a conversation or dialogue. When church buildings and congregations grew large, the sermon became a rhetorical event. Later the table overshadowed the pulpit, and eventually the reverse held true in the Reformed traditions. Today congregations need continually to hold together the two parts of eucharistic worship, both table and pulpit. This needs to be done creatively, sensitively, and with great care.

However, to equate modern preaching with Paul's word *proclaim* doesn't do it proper justice. Paul in 1 Corinthians 11:26 is summing up his entire argument in the preceding passage. This includes his rebuke to the Corinthian church for their abuses of the fellowship meal and his appeal to the true tradition of the Lord Jesus at table. He follows directly with a summons to repentance and restoration of their worship.

Communion Themes

When the church worships in a worthy manner, it does proclaim the Lord's death. That is, the meaning of the cross can clearly be seen. Christ's own humble self-giving is mirrored in the relationships within the church. In this service the church identifies with Christ's cross. They die with him. They align themselves with the ideals for the Christian church as the body of Christ. Paul corrects the community and builds it up through reminding them of the true eucharistic tradition. They must hold fast to it not only in ritual manners but in their ethical behavior. In all of this, they truly show forth the significance and the value of the Lord's death, the meaning of the cross.

We proclaim the Lord's death through the entire action of the communion service. We do it by the liturgical actions of blessing and breaking bread in his name and memory. We proclaim the Lord's death by the story we tell to accompany the actions. We proclaim the Lord's death with the words of our sermons before the table. We proclaim the Lord's death by giving ourselves up in loving service to others. And we do it all in sure expectation of his coming again.[21]

This theme was Paul's summary idea, preserved in the "interpretative words" tradition of 1 Corinthians 11:23-26. But it must be held together with the other strand of New Testament supper tradition – that of the worship meal as a joyous foretaste of the eschatological messianic banquet.[22]

The moods of these two strands seem contradictory. They are difficult to hold together. How can we celebrate and sing happy songs when we are

131

trying to honor Jesus' death on the cross? That seems a dilemma to people who are searching for one right way to order a communion service. In fact, there isn't just one way. We need many ways in our search to explore and express such a wide range of appropriate biblical themes. (We will explore this further in the rest of this book.)

Each of the many themes we have looked at contributes to a whole. Though distinctive, the themes are interrelated. Our challenge is to weave them together in our communion understandings and observance, into a luminous tapestry of eucharist and honor to Christ.

Churches that explore and express these communion themes with greater freedom and vigor will change and mature. They will no longer remain stuck in one mode or attitude. Deeper reverence will combine with active reconciling. More serious commitment to each other will overflow into innovative justice-making service. Innovative symbol and language will inspire greater joy and freedom in praise. How we "do communion" shapes our character!

COMMUNION SHAPES
CHARACTER

Introduction: Communion That Nurtures

HOW WE celebrate communion makes a difference. It's not just that it matters. It actually makes a difference! For example, do we sit in hushed rows waiting to be served tiny pieces of precut bread? Do we move from our seats and stand closely around the table, sending the loaf and cup from hand to hand? How we do it shapes our understanding of the church, its ministers, and the nature of Christ's presence in the communion service. We act out our communion theology.

This section of the book deals with many practical matters having to do with the syntax of worship language – the lighting of the room, the time of day, how the invitation is given, our manners and habits. Many of these things have to do with the traditions of our churches, with patterns which persist across generations within a denomination. But other practices may be more transient, influenced by style or local culture. Everything about the way we celebrate communion may be laid open to scrutiny. What is strong will be stronger for being examined. What is less important may be altered to create better coherence or communication.

The purpose of all this is to nurture the church community to become a people of truly Christlike character. In Philippians 2:1-10 Paul calls the church to have the same mind as the mind of Christ, to imitate Christ's humility in their life together. This means encouraging one another, consoling one another in love, sharing in the Spirit, and showing compassion and sympathy. All these qualities are fostered within a church gathered regularly and often at the Lord's table.

Communion is not the only aspect of a congregation's life where this happens. Many other settings of prayer, study, common work, and fellowship nurture the common life. But the witness of the churches over the centuries is that the Lord's table provides a special focus. At the table the people acknowledge the Lord's presence. He offers them the bread of life and the cup of joy. In receiving these gifts, they are shaped by the Spirit into a compassionate community of love.

12

The Language of Ritual

Protestant Ritual, Empty or Full?

PROTESTANTS, ever since the sixteenth century, have condemned "empty ritual." Parroted words and repeated religious ceremonial, the Reformers insisted – all are devoid of spiritual integrity. What counted more for Protestants in matters of faith were an experience of God's gracious love, proper perceptions about it, and well-stated beliefs. Repeated ceremonies were unnecessary and showy. Set prayers were "meaningless repetitions." After all, Jesus himself had cautioned his disciples: "Use not vain repetitions, as the heathen do; for they think that they shall be heard for their much speaking" (Matt. 6:7, KJV).[1] Empty ritual was anathema. It was dangerous, probably even pagan.

Dead ritual is easy to spot. A moribund rite becomes a substitute for reality. This is clear, for example, in a ceremonial breaking of eucharistic bread and pouring out of wine in a congregation of people whose lives are in no way broken for the world or poured out in love for their neighbors. The ritual may be corrupted by an underlying consumerist attitude. People may have come to *get* something (religious feeling or forgiveness), but at no personal cost.

Perversely, Protestant reforming rigor did not connect Jesus' warning against vain repetitions with the "much speaking" of super-wordy worship and lengthy, often cliché-ridden prayers. Through the centuries these wordy patterns became strongly ritualized actions that gripped much Protestant worship. Our religious forebears wished to reform worship solely on biblical grounds. But in pursuing those reforms, they too often adopted unrecognized and unhelpful rituals.

This powerful anti-ritual legacy, born out of reaction, has produced some apparently unchallengeable practices, many of which are themselves highly ritualized. Some people call them sacred cows. Some of these may not be properly termed rituals, but they are habits characterized by verbal cliché or routinized physical actions in worship. These practices do not provide a theological underpinning of worship and have often formed a straitjacket of worship patterns for Protestant groups.

Through the Protestant ages, troublesome questions keep surfacing, ones which refer to religious ritual habits that are apparently without deep significance. Must we always stand up for the prayer at the offering? Why do we always sit down to pray? Why are Protestant prayers so full of clichés? Why do the women sit on one side and men on the other? Who thought up this way of serving communion?

Ritual Reformed by Protestants

Is every part of our worship really based, as the Reformers intended, on scriptural precedent? Of course not. Initially, a powerful factor was simply to avoid whatever the Catholic Church did. This negative principle ruled out such activities as processions, clerical ablutions, lighting candles, ringing bells, or elevating the host. It also cut off many Protestants from using biblical canticles, hymns, and ancient prayers.

The most clearly articulated positive principle was that everything in reformed worship should be done "decently and in order" (1 Cor. 14:40). Thus simple gestures and austere manners became typical of Protestant worship. Orderliness and simplicity were not the only concerns. Somber dignity and solemnity have always been important to Protestants, particularly because of the persisting focus in communion services on the suffering and death of Christ.

Sometimes without fully realizing it, churches have acted out their theology in visual and dramatic ways. For example, when they insist that ministers wear special clothing, antique in design, somber or celebratory in color, that separates a community into distinct orders: the clergy and the laity. Whether we see eighteen elders solemnly seated behind the raised Presbyterian table or a full complement of vested clergy around an Orthodox altar, the visual message is similar. Rank and function separate people from their ministers, and the visual message is that the ministerial function involves privilege. If priests, deacons, and elders wore clothing conveying the status of servants, a different message might come across. We can vividly vest our theology.

In some denominations the senior deacon always prays at the communion table. In other denominations particular words at the table are reserved to specified persons. These are rituals of church tradition, established over many generations.

One Christian community sits in a circle around a real-meal communion table. They read the Gospels, they invite probing and open reflection, they pray together toward corporate, faithful action in following Jesus' cross-way. Breaking bread and drinking from the common cup, they renew their baptismal vows and seal their pledge of costly discipleship. This "anti-ritual" tradition also uses rituals. Its particularly dramatic manner reveals a distinct eucharistic theology.

Let us keep communion rituals open to reconsideration. Let us observe keenly what actually happens. We must choose our questions carefully.

There are biblical, theological, and pastoral questions. There are also questions of aesthetic values and of effective communication. We wonder about enculturation: is what we do comprehensible to neighbors and inquirers? How do we express solidarity with Christians across time and space? Are we willing to give significant effort to this process of observing and evaluating our church's eucharistic practices?

The Language of Ritual

Ritual is a kind of language. Ritual fuses words, symbolic actions, and some form of material into unique communication. Good rituals inspire the imagination and the will so that good action may follow. Individuals, families, and groups develop rituals and use them for many purposes which range from the therapeutic to the celebratory.

A sad but simple ritual was devised by a couple at the time of their final estrangement. Three days before the wife moved out of the home, they laid two big circles of string on the floor.

> We both stood in them and said: "I release you totally. I release you from the bonds that we agreed on. I release you from responsibility for me." We both cut the string, moved our circles away from each other, then picked up our circles. That was it. We took the string away. I burnt mine. I don't know what she did with hers.[2]

This homemade ritual was simple, yet included all the typical elements – words, actions, something material, and an inner intention. The separating couple felt that their ritual helped them cross a painful bridge.

Numerous rituals surround us in our secular communities. There are newly developed ones for grieving parents who have suffered miscarriage or for people bereaved through disasters, AIDS, or Alzheimer's disease. And there are the classic social rituals such as New Year's celebrations and Remembrance Day ceremonies.

The church has developed especially subtle and moving rituals to mark entry into the community, and to make pledges of faith and different commitments throughout our lives. The special language of ritual says more than simple words alone could do. The water of baptism may be ordinary water, but it gains a powerful voice when combined with its unique actions and formulas of renunciation, adherence, and covenant. The language of ritual is the complex language with which a church can address the big questions it faces.

Ritual Connects with Real-Life Situations

The language of ritual speaks most powerfully when it is deeply connected to the circumstances of the people. Two moving examples come from

Christians in places of extreme pressure. In both cases the ritual spoke its unique word of hope and strength for participants who were alert and expectant, needy for God's presence and intervention.

In August 1994 Father Meienberg had a dream calling him to visit the refugee sites in Kibumba, Zaire, just across the border from Rwanda. He said it was like Paul's vision calling him to Macedonia.

> While Claire Rutambuka, a refugee from Kigali, summoned people with a bullhorn from the back of a blue pickup truck, Father Meienberg unpacked his mass kit from a brown leather bag. He selected readings that signaled hope, including Ezekiel 37, in which the prophet walks through the valley of dried bones and God brings the bones back to life, signifying the renewal of the spirit "which is Jesus," according to Father Meienberg. The people were disheveled after spending weeks in squalor. They gathered under gray skies, with a chilling breeze whipping in from the south and smoke from thousands of wood fires choking the air like smog. "We have faith," said one man, "and here our faith is made stronger. We understand what it is like to be persecuted." The refugees formed a circle about ten deep around Father Meienberg. As he read Scriptures in Swahili, an assistant translated into Kinyarwanda, Rwanda's official language. During pauses, the refugees broke into soaring, joyous hymns. Their voices and rhythmic clapping filled up the afternoon, drifting over the horrific, smoky landscape like cleansing rain. Several refugees offered prayers. One woman, a baby strapped to her back, asked God "for a new heart to love those who have been hurting me." Another woman asked God for "guidance in this time of distress." And then they took communion.[3]

Baltimore City Jail was the site of an austere communion. The Catonville Nine were serving sentences because of their antiwar protest.

> For eight days we fasted and prayed and waited. On the final day we decided to break our fast with a eucharist. Someone brought us a loaf of freshly baked bread. We asked the warden if we might have a bottle of wine. He acceded on condition that he himself might be present. Whereupon, around that board table began one of the simplest and most moving of communal actions. "Do this in memory of me," which is to say, "In remembering me, re-member yourselves. Put your lives and your souls together again."[4]

Unfortunately, ritual may become repressive. This would be true in a community in which a priest might make the people dependent upon him because he alone has access to the means for forgiveness. "The ritual of the mass can then become a substitute for reality, the benefits of the mass a consumer object. The pouring out of Christ's life, signified in the chalice, should inspire and engage the poured-out life of the people." Only that would be "genuine evidence of a proper sacramental life of the church."

A number of churches have explored the positive and flexible openness of ritual, and have employed ritual to reflect on and work out meanings and ways through their difficulties. Sometimes this means developing new rituals. But even old ritual which seems dead or empty can be filled with new significance for the community. Old rituals can find fresh life. Communities of faith can develop new rituals and use traditional rituals in creative ways.

The Shape of Three Christian Rituals

Three rituals closely associated with early Christian churches' practice of Lord's Supper are the bread-and-cup ceremony, the foot-washing service, and the kiss of peace. What do these three have in common? In the first place, they all involve material in some way – people's bodies, water and towels, wine and bread. Second, each has particular words associated with it: "Take and eat." "If you know these things, blessed are you if you do them." "The peace of Christ be with you." Third, certain gestures accompany the words: breaking the bread and sharing the cup, kneeling in front of people to wash their feet, exchanging a solemn embrace.

Fourth, the material, the words, and the gestures are bound up with an inward will or disposition which can direct or change lives. This transformation operates in the realm of the imagination, the inner vision. As we take part in the bread-and-cup ritual, we experience and pledge ourselves to a closer following of Christ. When we kneel with a towel and a basin, we empty ourselves of pride and determine anew to walk the way of Christ's selfless service. When we take part in a general exchange of peace greetings, we grasp the potential beauty of a reconciled and reconciling community where the peace of Christ truly energizes and heals. We commit ourselves to this vision.

These rituals may be relatively empty for a community which performs them in a perfunctory way, perhaps through routine or a sense of duty. The overt patterns of using material, word, and gestures are the easiest things to perpetuate. It's that fourth one, the inward disposition, which is the key to filling up a dry ritual.

A South African friend described the electric moment of seeing a father and daughter, estranged for years, meeting and greeting at "the peace." Suddenly the perfunctory words and desultory gesture of an arid communion service revealed the Spirit's power to transform, to make a broken relationship whole again.

I have heard people scorn the service of foot washing as culturally repellent, irrelevant, disgusting, or meaningless. But when they actually got down on their knees before their brother or sister, and did so in the Spirit of Christ himself, it took on a wholly new cast.

A racially mixed church desired to hold a foot-washing service. But one African-American brother protested: "It is not possible for me, for cultural reasons, to do this. It is too difficult, because of the history of my people, to wash the feet of a white man. Please excuse me."

Another man, of European descent, nodded his head. He heard and accepted the pain. He said, "That's all right. But will you let me wash your feet anyway?"

Neither man was prepared for the powerful effect of this ritual, for the tears that flowed, or for their new inner grasp of the Christian vision of reconciliation across the barriers of human pain.

"The servant is not greater than the master. I have set you an example. You are blessed if you do this" (John 13:16-17). If we allow Jesus' words and example to set our inner will and imagination alight, a potentially disgusting and meaningless, apparently impossible ritual will fill up with truth and meaning, right to the brim. The ritual might draw out repentance and confession. It might call for new recognitions or reconciliation. It might show us a new step of the way of Jesus.

So it is with the bread-and-cup ceremony. We can get through it in a few minutes' time, with our minds a mile away. But the apostle Paul might say to us, "It is not really to eat the Lord's Supper that you come together" (1 Cor. 11:20). Sometimes we have not just an empty ritual but an abused ritual, one which demonstrates a contradictory significance. Careless of the inequities in the church, unmoved by a lack of love, inattentive to a fragmented congregational life, we can wring an empty ritual dry and thoroughly abuse the table our Lord has spread for us.

Four Steps in Filling Up an Empty Ritual

How do we fill up an empty ritual? We begin with a proper connection with the realities of our community's circumstances, its inner dynamics and outer setting. As we saw in the stories of eucharist in a prison and in a refugee camp, the respective settings made a great difference to the manner and content of the services.

Most of us are not in either of those situations. But we are always in some situation! Ours might be a small inner-city congregation, a retirement home, or perhaps a large and successful suburban church. Wherever we are, the ritual forms and words we use in communion services need to connect with the truth of our community's life. This may have to do with questions such as excessive mobility and turnover in membership, issues of racism, fear of local crime, bereavements, sensitivity to justice concerns, the pressures of parental responsibility, or incentives toward material prosperity.

One role of the leaders of a church is to perceive and name the primary arenas of faith struggle. Through this clear insight, the eucharistic ritual can be planned and led. It might become dangerously relevant. Communion services can become blindingly full of God's challenging life.

Second, we take up the tradition that is handed down to us. The Christian eucharist has a strong outline structure as well as flexibility to serve us in whatever situation we find ourselves. We can use Scripture, silence, song, ancient words, and improvised words. We can move around and use gestures that express what words cannot say. We can use the symbols of materiality: bread and wine, water, cross, offering plate. And we can go on to use other material symbols as well, to express our thanksgiving, puzzlement, or our anguish to God.

It is important to create open spaces within the ritual. Evidence from early Christian worship shows that a number of people took part in eucharistic prayers. There was room for the Spirit. There was an interplay of forms with flexibility and freedom. Many denominations have narrowed the great tradition, and in so doing have induced amnesia and have stifled spiritual imagination. The Christian eucharist tradition is rich and awaits our fuller and more creative appropriation.

A third step is to do what Father Meienberg did in choosing Ezekiel 37, the vision of dry bones brought to life, as one of his Scriptures that day in the refugee camp. We need to find the passages that genuinely speak to the circumstances of our life together. Many churches use lectionaries with suggested readings for each Sunday. These often are surprisingly apt, but there is no law against substituting or adding further Scripture readings. It takes time, thought, prayer, and imagination to work in a creative way within a tradition. But it is well worth spending time on the choice of Scriptures. In doing, this we feed our religious imagination through the rich biblical materials. Metaphors, visual symbols, parables, testimonies, and hymns – all will spring into place. The raw materials, words, and gestures of the biblical tradition are all available for us. But we need to keep feeding our communion rituals with the nourishment of the Bible.

Finally, we enrich and fill up the ritual by the fourth movement, getting in touch with the inner will and imagination. We engage our deepest intentions and promises when we allow the great story of God to grasp us in new ways. Preeminently at the communion table, we retell that story of God's creating and redeeming and liberating love. With joy we join the thanksgiving song and find our places within the people that Jesus calls to his table fellowship. This is the work of the Holy Spirit, the One who continuously encourages, enlivens, and unites us together.

A Model Proposed

Here is a model developed to illustrate ways of enriching a church's eucharist.

1. Connect with the realities within the church. Let us say that there seems to be excessive self-absorption, individualism, and lack of concern for others.

2. Work within the church's tradition. Retain the familiar order of elements (e.g., readings and sermon precede the communion, intercessions come afterward). But choose a new action which may help to address the pastoral concern. Do one thing differently which reclaims and dramatizes a traditional value of communion (the Lord invites people to come to the table).

So perhaps you might ask the people to come and stand around the table at the communion prayers. Stand physically closer to each other, receive the bread and cup from deacons who come to serve each person, and at the conclusion sing together a familiar song – such simple things enable people to be more aware of each other than is possible when they are sitting in their routine places and looking at the backs of other people's heads.

Introduce only one change at a time, and prepare carefully for it. Explain it well in advance, such as at a previous congregational meeting or in smaller groups of the church, so that people know what lies behind the idea. You can explain that it is a concern for making more personally warm connections with each other in the whole of life, and to dramatize this in the way we observe communion.

There may be other ways of addressing the concern within the communion pattern. Instead of moving people forward, you might choose to move the table (but keep everything else familiar!). Explain that because we experience the Lord's presence in our midst, it is appropriate to place the table symbolically in the middle of the people during the communion service. So we move the table to a central position to remind ourselves of this vital truth. As people turn to face the table, they are also turning to face each other in new ways.

Or you might use the traditional symbols of cross and cup in ways you have not done before, to underline Jesus' call to compassionate mutual care. Perhaps someone in the church is prepared to give a testimony of loving care from another church member. Such a testimony grounds the communion in the church's local life. These are a few simple ways which, introduced sensitively, might open out and fill up a familiar ritual. Make the changes gently and with good preparation, and always link them with gospel values which people honor.

3. Choose Scripture well. Link the sermon more closely with the service of the table. Virtually all gospel readings can link more directly than we imagine. The parable of the waiting father (the prodigal son) is a perfect

example, as are related parables of the lost coin and the lost sheep. Many stories of Jesus' ministry relate closely to the values of the eucharist. Passages from the Old Testament Prophets, Psalms, and Writings bring unexpected riches. The words of the service are vital. In general, use fewer words but choose them carefully.

4. Allow for development of the inward vision and commitment in response to the communion. At the close of communion, we always give thanks to God for feeding us. At the same time we acknowledge the renewed energy and hope for God's love to flow through our individual and corporate life. We should make opportunity for new pledges or commitment and perhaps provide simple ritual ways of signaling this. For example, a church might have memorized a particular biblical blessing (such as "the grace") or a benedictory song. Simply asking people to stand up together and sing or say together these words of love and pledge can be helpful. Joining hands, keeping silence, turning to face the doorway by which we move away from the Lord's table – these and any number of other simple actions can help to internalize the connections between what God has given to us in the breaking of bread and the everyday life that awaits us as we leave the table.

This is how ritual can be enlivened and filled up. Let us keep connected to real congregational life, build on the tradition, feed on the Scriptures, open up the ritual, and allow space for the Spirit to bring it all to life again.

13

Thanksgiving Sets the Tone

MY CHILDHOOD memories of free-church communion services evoke solemn men standing beside round chromium tray towers of tiny glasses. They drew aside white linen napkins from the plates of pre-cut white bread. In the hushed moments of preparation, everyone's eyes were lowered, every heart turned inward.

The atmosphere was similar to the eucharist I recently attended on St. Stephen's Day at an Anglican cathedral. This time there were no trays of tiny glasses, and the surroundings were awesomely grand. The officiants were again, however, solemn men standing a good distance away from us pew folk. They moved around, they gestured, they chanted. They invited participants forward to kneel at a low barrier and administered the sacraments of bread and wine, not ordinary food but "elements." Quiet flutey "communion music" covered shuffling shoe noises as the people returned to private meditation at their seats.

What would Priscilla and Aquila of Ephesus, or Lydia of Thyatira, make of such services? Wouldn't they comment on the contrast to the joyful, confident atmosphere of their own communal meals? Perhaps they would be puzzled by the introspective, even dour, atmosphere. Their own church fellowship meals were the social and worship center of their lives. Even in hard times, they found hopeful encouragement there.

The joyous tone of those meals, however, was not due to memories of that meal we call the Last Supper. Surely, that was the saddest of mealtimes Jesus ever had with his friends.

After the crucifixion, "at the table" is where Mark's Gospel places the disciples (Mark 16:14). John's community remembered the disciples, in the desperate hours of Friday evening and Saturday, huddled together in a house, the door bolted for fear for their lives (John 20:19). Their reflex was to meet each other where Jesus himself had so often met them, in a domestic place. Probably they shared food in those hours. The atmosphere of the disciples' first reunion meals must have been unbelievably sad. Everything was finished. Their hopes, their lives were crushed. Yet they drew together, and they needed to put bread and drink on the table. That heavy mood was reminiscent of the foreboding and dread of their

Last Supper with Jesus, that unhappy Passover meal in the upper room.

We cannot fully imagine the stunning effect of Jesus' resurrection appearances at his disciples' meal tables (Luke 24:41; John 20:20). Suddenly the mood was jubilant. Jesus' greeting of peace and his transforming presence charged the atmosphere with joy. If our communion services have any sense of heart-lifting celebration, it is surely because of these post-resurrection meals. The early church remembered gladness, not gloom. We remember Jesus not only at a Friday table in an upper room, but also at a comradely picnic on a beach. We remember exhilarating reunions of Jesus with his friends.

Not Always the Same Mood

These days, when people are asked to name an appropriate tone or a desired mood for a communion service, they often list serenity, peacefulness, or stillness. Some want a sense of commonness and unity. Others long for a joyful, celebrative occasion. All of these and more besides may be appropriate and possible. But perhaps not all may be emphasized at the same service. The season of the year, the life experiences of members of the church, and pastoral concerns – these all come to bear on the tone of the communion service. In a church which observes communion frequently, there will be variety in tone from one service to another. Fine. There is not just one right way to do it, though many churches strive to find such a way.

Here is a comment from a young man who is uneasy with the prevalent tone of his church's communion services.

In our church everything about the communion service is extremely solemn, and I can accept that. After all, it is about Christ's suffering and death. But I wish it wasn't all so stiff and we could at least have some brighter music sometimes.

This young person's experience is all too common. Some churches, out of a proper concern to honor the death of Christ, have nevertheless allowed communion services to resemble somber funerals. But simply to add brighter music would not help in the long run. They must see that in proclaiming Christ's death, they honor not only Christ's suffering and death but the effects of his death. They honor also his resurrection and ascension and the powerful presence of the Spirit among the worshiping people. While retaining the solemnity in communion services, they could also reclaim praise and thanksgiving for Christ's completed acts of redemption.

Thanksgiving Is the Keynote

The best antidote to a heavy communion piety is to broaden and

146

strengthen the quality of thanksgiving at the Lord's table. One important way to regain this spirit is to draw on the Jewish character of thanksgiving and benediction so characteristic of Jesus and of early Christian worship. We can allow the ethos and scope of the Jewish thanksgiving blessings (*berakoth*), Jesus' own prayers, and the early Christian eucharistic prayers to influence our communion prayers.

From the *berakoth* we can retain the simplicity of dependence upon God who provides everyday needs. With Jesus, we can yearn to know Abba (our heavenly Father, Daddy) and follow his self-giving way. With the early Christians, we can honor not only Christ's suffering and death, but also his resurrection and ascension, and the powerful presence of the Spirit among the worshiping people.

Several Jewish table traditions stand behind the Lord's Supper. One was the everyday family meal with its simple benediction. A second was the Friday evening Sabbath meal, celebrated more formally within the family with its special blessings and ceremonies. Most important was the annual Passover meal celebrated according to the ancient Seder (order of service).[1]

The Passover is the feast that commemorates liberation from Egypt and the covenant with God established at Sinai. In retelling the ancient Hebrew story, we Christians can join the Jews in valuing liberation on several levels. We can celebrate human freedom within situations of social repression and mark the possibility of inner dignity even within personal servitude. In the words of Gustavo Gutiérrez, we can also appropriate liberation from sin

> which attacks the deepest root of servitude; for sin is the breaking of friendship with God and with other human beings, and therefore cannot be eradicated except by the unmerited redemptive love of God, whom we receive by faith and in communion with one another.[2]

There is no better way to deepen and strengthen the profoundly thankful tone of eucharistic worship than to probe and pursue the liberation themes of the Passover background to the Lord's table. This is to do immeasurably more than to add a few brighter songs. It is to enter into the universal pain of peoples in bondage, into the compassion of God for those who suffer, and into the longing for a liberating Messiah. It is to recognize with ecstatic joy the fulfillment of these yearnings in the life and death of Jesus, and in the resurrection which vindicated him and conquered the forces of sin and separation. The Passover and (how much more!) the eucharist celebrate all these themes together in one feast.

Many churches celebrate an annual Seder during the week preceding Easter, acknowledging the Passover context of Jesus' Last Supper on the night of his arrest. Some Christianize the Seder by making it into a communion service, explaining all the symbolism and readings in light of Christian fulfillment. Another approach, which I prefer, is to celebrate the Seder in a way which maintains its distinctive Jewishness.

Appendix B gives further information about the Seder and ideas for celebrating the festival meal. Some Christian bookstores sell booklets giving the Haggadah, the ancient text which prescribes directions on how to host a Seder.[3]

Another way to strengthen thanksgiving, enriched from the Hebrew background, is to broaden the use of Scripture within the communion service. You could include (read or sing) hymnic materials embedded throughout the New Testament writings[4] Many other texts can also serve as bases for expanded extemporaneous prayers of thanksgiving. The major suitable themes are thanks for creation, thanks for redemption, and joyful, confident hope of the kingdom coming. There is great scope for elaboration of these themes of praise.

In nonliturgical churches, the thanksgiving prayer at the table can be shared by a number of people. First, several people can offer prayers, giving thanks for specific events in the life and compassionate ministry of Jesus, for his faithfulness to the Father as well as for his atoning death and God's vindication in the resurrection. Others can give thanks for the Spirit present and active, thanks for forgiveness, thanks for the particular work of God in the congregation's life, thanks for healing and preservation from evil. Prepared prayers and extemporaneous prayers can weave together, both musical and verbal. Spontaneous contributions, exclamations, free prayers, and responses – all can contribute to a great multi-voiced Thanksgiving Prayer.

In sum, then, it is vital to make sure that the prayers at the Lord's table are the collective prayers of the whole community at praise, filled with thanksgiving and joy. Expressing repentance and asking for forgiveness, healing, and restoration must always be components of worship. But they are not the first matter, the primary content of our prayers at the table of the Lord. We come because we accept the Lord's invitation, and we come with grateful hearts.

Thanksgiving, the predominant tone of eucharist, may be expressed in a variety of forms. Sometimes thanksgiving can ride on a serene line of music, or it can flower in a still and meditative ethos. The peaceful tone which many people desire can carry a profound inner concentration and focus upon the immeasurable grace and goodness of Christ's presence. Any congregation will have a variety of personalities, a variety of experience and preference in expression of prayer at the table. We who lead services do well to serve the wide range of people who make up our congregations.

A sensitive woman, a church member for fifty years, commented,

> I get sort of scared when communion comes around. I know I daren't take it unless everything is okay in my relationship with God and other people. But I never feel really worthy to take it, and wonder if I ever will.

This statement from a devout free-church person illustrates a deeply ingrained, graceless piety which induces fear of unworthy reception at the Lord's table. She was born in the 1930s, but a woman of ten centuries before her might have felt much the same way about communion.

In Western Christianity we carry this heavy legacy. It bears theological error and pastoral cruelty, and it cramps the church in its mission. Even though the scholars and historians of worship are advocating a eucharistic piety of thanksgiving and joy, it takes a long time pastorally to bear fruit in local churches. Those who lead communion services have both the responsibility and the opportunity to correct the balance between a proper, reverent sense of our unworthiness and an equally appropriate, joyful confidence in God's merciful acceptance.

Call It Eucharist

One way to establish genuine eucharist is to call the service by this name. The name of an activity helps to shape people's attitudes toward it. It makes a psychological difference, for example, if we are faced with a test, an evaluation, an indicator, a quiz, or a profile. The name matters.

If substituting *eucharist* for *Lord's Supper* or *breaking bread* seems strange and off-putting to some congregations, it would nevertheless be a useful discipline always to refer to the Lord's Supper as "a service of thanksgiving." To conclude a service, thanksgiving prayers following the bread and the cup are appropriate.

14

An Open Table?

Who Can Come to the Table?

WHO CAN COME to communion? One form of bidding, based on an understanding of Jesus' meal-sharing in his earthly ministry, insists on a fully inclusive "open invitation." In this mode, any person may come to the table, precisely because Jesus himself does the inviting. Jesus is the Host. It is not up to the church to sort out the suitability or the state of conscience for any person who wishes to take communion.

In contrast, some groups invite only baptized persons. Others practice a more severe "close communion." They may strictly fence the table. For them, communion fellowship is limited to the disciplined, face-to-face community of faith, in which unity in prayer, in spirit, in discipleship, and in lifestyle prescribe suitability for participation. In some traditions, a semiannual communion service is preceded by a special period of time and a preparatory service for self-examination and mutual confession, with reconciliation of differences within the congregation. In certain traditions which practice a weekly Sunday communion, only congregational members are included in the invitation. All of these practices grow out of particular interpretations of 1 Corinthians 11:23-32 and deeply held understandings of who actually constitutes the church.

Which Adults Do We Invite?

Close communion

Churches which practice close communion emphasize a period of preparation. In North American Mennonite churches of this type, for example, personal self-examination is encouraged, and a congregational meeting on the penultimate Sunday provides time for prayer, meditation, reading of Scripture, confession, and the declaration that all differences among participants have been reconciled. A service of foot washing is often part of the process. These actions are understood to be founded on the teachings of Christ and are never minimized. The purpose is that the fellowship of the church be preserved pure. Unworthy communion by any one person would bring reproach on the whole assembly.

A similar pattern of rigorous preparation was practiced in Puritan congregations. Participation was only for members of the covenant community, and taking part was a way of continuing to identify with the community. Self-examination, confession, and giving and receiving of forgiveness took place throughout the community during the week prior to the service of the Lord's Supper.

The open-but-bounded table

A so-called "open table" implies that Christians accept the validity of each others' baptisms and journeys of faith. It is, however, a table with boundaries. This is distinctively different from an open-to-all invitation which welcomes anyone to the Lord's table, regardless of whether or at what age they were baptized. Participation at the open-but-bounded table recognizes the baptism of other Christians. It affirms a common and ancient Christian heritage and allegiance to a common Lord. In that recognition Christians welcome one another to the Lord's table. Open fellowship at the open Lord's table is for all baptized (and confirmed) Christians. Some sample invitations follow.

1. The invitation to communion at one large free-church congregation of this type begins with an explanation that participation at this table is for those who have chosen to be disciples of Jesus and have received baptism. Then follows a beautiful invitation to anyone present to come to faith in Jesus and to receive the grace of baptism, too. The invitation isn't a put-off but a genuine invitation to Jesus, into baptism, into the community of faith, and so to the table. Those who do not take the bread and cup are nevertheless welcomed to be present, to witness, and to be drawn closer toward the community of faith, commitment, and love.

2. Another example is the following invitation, which usually serves as an introduction to a prayer of confession at the beginning of the eucharist. The emphasis in this early part of the service is on preparing participants rather than on the Host (Christ) who invites.

> You who truly and earnestly repent of your sins, you who are living in love and goodwill with others, you who lead a new life following the commandments of God, and walk in his holy ways, *you who desire a testimony of your unity with all other believers*, draw near with reverence, faith, and thanksgiving; take this holy sacrament *(the supper of the Lord)* to your comfort.[1]

3. This invitation might suit churches which have an open table. It could encourage fearful ones or Christians who feel weak in their faith. But it is ambiguous on the question of whether those invited to participate have made a public commitment to Christ. The idea of the table bounded by baptism or by a public declaration of faith is strengthened and made more clear by the addition of the verses from Hebrews.

Come to this sacred table, not because you must
   but because you may.
Come not to testify that you are righteous,
   but that you sincerely love our Lord Jesus Christ,
And desire to be his true disciples.

Come not because you are strong,
   but because you are weak.
Come not because you have any claim on heaven's rewards,
   but because in your frailty and sin,
You stand in constant need of heaven's mercy and help.[2]

(followed by)
Therefore, brothers and sisters, since we have confidence to enter
the Most Holy Place by the blood of Jesus, by a new and living way
opened for us through the curtain, that is, his body, and since we
have a great priest over the house of God, let us draw near to God
with a sincere heart in full assurance of faith.

(Heb. 10:19-22, NIV)

4. The following invitation is typical in many English Baptist churches
and gives the impression that all that is needed is to "love the Lord Jesus."
Baptism and church membership seem "quite irrelevant as far as the
Lord's Supper is concerned." In his critique of this "limp and
undemanding" invitation, Baptist theologian Paul Beasley-Murray asserts
that "the Lord's table is for the Lord's People, for those who are believers
and are in good standing in their local [Christian of whatever
denomination] congregations."[3] Some people expand the invitation
slightly, as in the second, amended formulation (indicated in italics) of
example 4b, below.

    4a. If you love the Lord Jesus, and desire to love him more, you
       are welcome to this table.
    4b. If you love the Lord Jesus, *have confessed your faith in him*, and
       desire to love him more, you are welcome to this table.

5. Here is a strong, modern hymn which could be memorized and sung
by the whole congregation as they come to stand together around the
communion table. They affirm their acceptance of Christ's invitation, and
they call each other to the joyful sharing.

      Jesus calls us to his table rooted firm in time and space,
      Where the church in earth and heaven
        finds a common meeting place.

Share the bread and wine, his body;
    share the love of which we sing;
Share the feast for saints and sinners
    hosted by our Lord and King.

(Iona Community[4])

6. The sixth invitation clearly marks out potential participants, and specifies three conditions for inclusion: baptism, right relationships, and accountability. Participation in communion is open to

all who have been baptized into the community of faith, are living at peace with God and with their brothers and sisters in the faith, and are willing to be accountable in their congregation.

7. The following invitation is clear but may sound complicated to visitors. It has been worked out as one church's solution to disagreements about the possible participation of young children and visitors. The large bowl of fresh grapes on the table, not yet pressed to make juice, symbolizes the maturity of commitment still ahead for the young and for those who are exploring faith in Christ. The invitation, given with generous warmth, is to a service which provides participation and blessing for everyone.

Everyone who is here is invited to come to the table. There is something here for you. All who have committed their lives to Jesus Christ and have been baptized are welcome to come forward to receive the bread and the cup. Also those who have made a commitment but have not yet made it public and those who anticipate making a commitment are welcome to come forward to receive a grape and a cracker as a symbol of their intention. All the children are welcome to come forward to take a grape and a cracker, as a symbol of belonging here in the church.

8. Here is a Spanish church's solution to the invitation dilemma. It is a hybrid, combining qualities both of the bounded table and the open-to-all invitation. Their concern was to be inclusive and welcoming to children and to visitors, yet to mark off the baptismal pledges of committed and mature Christians. This invitation is eminently unambiguous.

All are welcome to this table. We all share the bread because Jesus, the bread of life, laid down his life, and he offers his life to each of us. We all eat of the bread. Not all of us will drink of the cup. Those who do so, give witness to their baptism and to the promises they made. Jesus invites all of us to enter into the new covenant which he inaugurated.

The open invitation

Some people object to limiting participation in communion. Listen to a young woman, a new Christian:

> The most beautiful service I ever went to, they served the bread and cup to everybody who was there – visitors, children, and everybody. They didn't ask any questions about whether you were okay with God or whether you'd been baptized or even if you called yourself a Christian. It was so inclusive and welcoming. I think that's what Jesus was like – didn't he invite everyone?

And here is a puzzled challenge from a student at a large church in a university town.

> How can you justify excluding people from the Lord's table, maybe those who want to learn more about Jesus? A Muslim visitor at our church took the bread and drank from the cup. Was that wrong? I think Jesus would have welcomed her, so how can it be right to refuse people when Jesus ate with all kinds of people, even sinners?

These questions address the sensitive issue of who is welcomed to the communion table and who does the welcoming. The key idea in the controversy is "inclusive," equated here with warmth, love, and hospitality, hallmarks of Jesus' own character. Jesus welcomed children, sinners, women, and foreigners, as well as religious folk. Through Jesus everyone has access to God's mercy and love. Surely in communion services, Jesus continues to welcome all comers. The good news of Jesus seems clearly to embody an open invitation.

The implication is that the church too should welcome all to take part in the Sunday communion. To do otherwise would seem to contradict Jesus' own free invitation. It's important to be clear about the term "inclusion." In this discussion, inclusion in participation at the Lord's table must be more than an invitation to a free meal, such as a new pizza restaurant would advertise. Invitation and inclusion at the Lord's table must always involve body, mind, and soul. The invitation has to be clear and faithful to Jesus and communicate some sense of the meaning of crossing that frontier into the kingdom where the Lord's table stands, of crossing into protection and solidarity within God's loving community. Jesus' own invitations invariably implied challenge as well as generous welcome.

Although the meal of church tradition, the communion service, is not modeled on the feeding of the five thousand and similar Gospel events, the impulse and Spirit of Jesus' open hospitality are the ideals that mark the communion table of churches who practice the fully open invitation.

Here is an invitation to the open-to-all table. The ambiguous but poetic quality makes its appeal to those who prefer to blur the boundaries and to allow attenders the freedom to decide whether or not they wish to participate.

You Are Invited

This is the Welcome Table of our Redeemer,
   and you are invited.
Make no excuses, saying you cannot attend;
   simply come,
   for around this table you will find your family.
Come not because you have to,
   but because you need to;
Come not to prove you are saved,
   but to seek the courage to follow wherever Christ leads.
Come not to speak but to listen,
   not to hear what's expected,
   but to be open to the ways the Spirit moves among you.

So be joyful, not somber,
   for this is the feast of the reign of God,
   where the broken are molded into a Beloved Community,
   and where the celebration over evil's defeat
   has already begun.

                             (Hope Douglas J. Harle-Mould[5])

Two of the earlier examples of invitations are crossover types. Example 4a without the additional phrase in 4b is ambiguous. Number 8, the Spanish invitation, separates the bread from the cup and thus provides for both bounded and open communion. Quotations from Jesus may be used in both bounded and open types, as in the following two examples:

Jesus said to them, "I am the bread of life. Whoever comes to me will never be hungry, and whoever believes in me will never be thirsty. Anyone who comes to me I will never drive away."

                                       (John 6:35, 37)

Let us celebrate this joyful feast. People will come from east and west and north and south and sit at table in the kingdom of God.

                                        (cf. Luke 13:29)

A completely open invitation addresses an entire spectrum: self-confessed Christians in many "states of grace," children of Christian families, children with no Christian background, people of limited mental facility, infants in their parents' arms, unbelievers, doubters, people of other faiths, saints and criminals alike. The invitation goes out to all in the lanes and hedgerows: "Come! the banquet is prepared!" (cf. Luke 14:17, 32)

In churches which practice an open invitation, it is especially important to state it clearly. For example, if ministers in the church have taken charge of a funeral for a person with many non-Christian relatives, this could be the approach and the manner of addressing the invitation:

> In this time of communal pain and family grief, the action of communion expresses many mysterious things, among which is the openness of God to all people. As we share this meal, we symbolize our sharing in your pain and holding you in our hope. We stand with God in the pain of the world, that by God's solidarity and ours, hope may be kept alive. If you wish to join us in signifying that, please feel free to do so. We invite you to take the bread and the wine with us.[6]

Those who hold to a bounded Lord's table would not consider a communion service to be appropriate in the context of a funeral with a mixed assembly of people. But to those who hold an open-to-all understanding, the communion table can serve as a vestibule to faith. The table can be a sign of inclusion in God's love and thus can function as the invitation to the covenant of baptism.

Baptism, then, the sign of adherence to Jesus Christ and his way, follows participation at the table. It's not the other way around. The steps of the covenanted Christian way are not fully known at baptism, not fully grasped by the mind. Nor is the life cost to be fully weighed in advance. In baptism, people profess the desire to cling to Christ and to walk in his steps. They are never wise enough to take this step. But they know the need to be close to Christ and to his people. That closeness, that fellowship of communion anticipated at his table, draws seekers onward into the Christian way and into the covenant of baptism.

Those who advocate a fully open invitation, point to the new covenant Jesus inaugurated. Who is included? The new covenant, they say, is dramatically characterized by its openness – it is for many, for all. Some will object, "But if the table of the new covenant is for all, is there no distinction between church and world?"

The theology of the open invitation, as advocated by English Baptist pastor Michael Forster, declares that the cross, not the table, forms the demarcation between the church and the world. The church is called to be distinctive at this point – in its willingness to be different from the world by its radical inclusiveness. The cross of Jesus breaks down the walls of hostility. "The frontier between the church and the world is the scandal of the cross, and we deny that, if we protect our God or ourselves with barriers."[7] Radical inclusiveness, advocates of this approach argue, should be the hallmark of the Christian community. The church's table is the proper place to act out that inclusiveness.

This position calls for an abrupt break in church tradition. Forster believes that a positive function of tradition is to put the brakes on change until issues have been fully explored. But when church traditions counter the Spirit of Jesus and the gospel, then, Forster insists, they must no longer be allowed to be obstacles to change.

Considering the varied understandings of participation in eucharist, it is vital to be careful in preparing the words of invitation in the service. They set the tone and clarify the meaning of the actions. It is especially important for visitors to know precisely how they may or may not take part. A poorly phrased or altogether absent invitation can cause confusion, a sense of rejection, or embarrassment. A clear invitation puts at ease those who will simply stay quietly among the congregation as well as those who will participate. Has your church worked through the questions of adult participation in communion services?

Do We Invite Children?

In churches of several traditions, conflict and confusion centers around the exclusion of children from communion. Sometimes the question appears like this: "Should we include children in communion?" Some are offended by the implication that excluding the children could even be an option. Others are keen to hold back for young people the experience of communion until an age of maturity when it can be "properly meaningful." What is the shape of the inclusion debate, now narrowed down to a particular subgroup, children? The discussion is especially focused on children of the families within the church. Here are some of the questions.

Can We Settle It from the Bible?

Churches of the Reformation, those who claim to worship in forms based on Scripture alone, ask this kind of question: Wasn't communion commanded by Christ? Isn't the shape of the communion service determined in Scripture? Who are we to counter the biblical way? The Lord took his Last Supper with only the inner circle of disciples, those who knew the Lord Jesus and followed in his way. There were no children present at that table.

It must be clear to us that our churches' eucharistic practices are not based on direct patterns in the Bible, either Old or New Testament. They are based on traditions which involve interpretation of Scripture. Some

157

eucharistic traditions strongly reflect Pauline texts, others root more in Johannine or other gospel passages. Many churches build their rites on a collage of various biblical texts.[8]

The church's table is not an equivalent to the Last Supper table, as we saw in chapter 1, "Last Supper to Church Supper." There is no record of women at the Last Supper. One traitor attended. There were no Gentiles, only Jews. It is true that we have no record of children in that upper room. But the configuration of participants around the Lord's Passover table has never prescribed the church's tradition of participation. The exclusion of children from communion is derived from strands of church tradition, not directly from Scripture.

If biblical tradition centering on the Last Supper were to hold full sway in determining church practice on participation at communion, we would need to recall that the background to the Last Supper was the Passover Seder, a family meal which children not only attended, but in which they had distinctive parts to play. The action which Jesus referred to in the phrase "as often as you do this" was undoubtedly in the sense of "whenever you have your common meal." Those common church meals were family meals. It would be impossible to exclude children on the basis of biblical tradition.

Is Communion for the Whole Community?

In the past twenty-five years the Western churches which practice infant baptism have probed church tradition on the matter of infant and child communion. They have had to face the anomaly of baptizing children but not admitting them to the eucharist. It has come to seem indefensible to separate in time a person's baptism and the first reception of communion.

In fact, the Eastern churches have continued infant communion up to the present day. But in the Western churches, the practice was discontinued after the twelfth century. Erosion of infant communion in the West proceeded through four phases: in separation of baptism from eucharist, the refusal of the chalice (the wine) to the laity, the injunction against "reserving" both the bread and the wine, and the loss of any sense that actually taking communion was a normal part of the mass, whether for lay or religious folk.[9]

A first important move to restore communion to the whole Christian community, including children, was in the fifteenth century among the Hussites of Bohemia. The *regulae* of Matthias de Janov reveal the theological rationale for a radically reformed eucharistic practice. He insisted that eucharist was for the whole community, that the priest could not take communion on behalf of others, and that the eucharist should be celebrated frequently and by all – the poor and the weak as well as the powerful and religious.

John Holeton sums up his discussion,

Once the community accepts all in its corporate life despite age, or intelligence, or social status, the question of universal participation in the eucharist becomes a real one. Once all the community shares in the eucharist, the experience becomes a conversion.[10]

Among the Hussites communion practices shaped the community, and the experience of renewed community, in turn, shaped their communion theology.

In sixteenth-and-seventeenth-century England, church leaders, for and against infant baptism, volubly debated the question of children taking communion. This discussion has yet to be resolved, though the outposts of the debate are clear. The biological understanding of the sacraments (an assertion that baptism is for infants, confirmation is for adolescents, communion is for adults) has been undermined.

What determines suitability for individuals to take communion – rationality, faith, literacy, repentance? What is the relation of the eucharist to the faith community? All Christians, either within traditions which practice infant baptism or believers baptism, need to work through these questions.

Many churches have carefully worked-out reasons for distinctive communion practices in relation to the children of their families. These reasons are based on fundamental understandings of who constitutes the community of the church and on the relation between baptism and eucharist. The careful articulation of these understandings forms a primary statement of identity, and it will stand up to rigorous scrutiny. In the following section we will hear several voices in this discussion.

Can We Tamper with Church Traditions?

Many people are torn and confused by this question: Can we tamper with tradition? If our church has worked out a way to understand and celebrate communion, who are we to question it now? Isn't that audacious or even foolhardy? Lots of children have grown up perfectly whole within churches which asked them to watch adults communing and not take part in it until later, at the "right time." And yet ...

Christian tradition is the big story within which we live. It is a great relief not to have to make everything up as we go. We are linked through the generations of the church with the stories and the wisdom of Christians who have faced big questions before us. It would be foolhardy to pay no attention to Christian tradition, audacious to give only original and relevant answers to modern questions. But if we go any way toward accepting Michael Forster's view of tradition – that it puts useful brakes on change, but needs continuous and reverent reevaluation – we must be willing to look freshly at what we have received in the light of Scripture and Spirit.

Let us take one tradition originating in Reformation times as an example of the process of necessary scrutiny and reevaluation. Churches of the Anabaptist tradition have emphasized that communion is for the baptized, for a disciplined and reconciled community of believers. To be a believer implies personal trust in Christ and a commitment of loyalty to him. It also requires a measure of intellectual understanding. Communion is for grown-ups who can count the cost of discipleship commitment which is signed with the covenant seal of baptism.

Children are to be patient. Baptism and communion will come in due time. Following Jesus in community requires self-knowledge and mutual correction, which is beyond children's capacities. Communion celebrates a reconciled unity in spirit and in prayer. It is a declaration of things made right among a face-to-face community of Jesus' disciples. There is little sense that the making-right and the reconciling are to be born out of the communion itself. Things have to be put right first, then all are fit to take part. Preparation is as important as the communion itself.

This statement of an Anabaptist communion tradition does not reveal that present-day communion practice and values among some Mennonite descendants of Anabaptism have in some respects changed. The traditional counsel meeting and foot-washing services, held the week before communion, are still maintained in a minority of churches. Mennonite congregations are passionately concerned about communal questions these days – how to incorporate their own children into the faith community, how to draw others to faith in Jesus, how to deepen church fellowship, how to relate to the weak and needy members, how to serve the crying world. All of this care for each other has to be generated and nurtured out of less and less communal and worship time.

In struggling with the modern setting, Mennonites are reshaping their tradition. They need to reverently work at this revaluation of communion. It is important to honor the values of the past and not arbitrarily throw out "folkways" simply because we do not understand or enjoy them. But we should hold up the traditions for scrutiny, to be sure that they continue to express and build Christian community on gospel principles.

In the past, the deep sense among Mennonite children of belonging to the community has been forged in a variety of ways, but all those ways were distinct from taking the bread and cup. As long as Mennonite communal life built and conveyed to children a strong sense of belonging, the issue of children at communion did not arise. Now, however, Mennonite communal life, like that of most contemporary Christians in the West, is eroded by modern lifestyles. There are few hours for worshiping together and for sharing work and life. So more has to be asked of the truncated community life that remains. Mennonites, and, indeed, all Christians, want their tradition to live, and their children to embrace it. That means we must work with the tradition, and yes, be ready to make changes where necessary.

How Does the Presence of Children Affect Communion Piety?

If communion becomes an inclusive, cross-community event, what happens to the piety of introspective self-examination and of private devotion which has become so precious to many Christians? Is a healthy, multi-generational church community possible? Do communion services help or hinder in building it?

Highly individualized communion piety is widespread among all Christian traditions. It would be cruel to declare it inadequate or mistaken. Many Christian churches will continue to foster this piety, and people will continue to meet Christ through it. But what riches of resource we will find if we widen our understanding of eucharist, perhaps by establishing different types of communion services within a congregation, so that it truly shapes and nurtures a distinctively corporate Christian faith community.

These days people talk about "target" groups within a congregation, groups which long for different styles of worship. Agonized questions arise: Should we have 5:00 p.m. services specifically for elderly members, using their favorite music or older versions of the Bible? Should we have youth services full of videos, drama, and rock music? Should we have special invitation services for non-Christians, in which people are not asked to sing hymns or pray prayers? Should we have "missionary communions"? If we target special groups, how can we build a community in which the founding tradition is passed along? Don't the young need the old? Don't the new Christians need the music and words of ancient Christian tradition?

Whatever we do in meeting the heart-needs of various groupings, we must continuously build the multi-generational community. We have to find commonality across apparently irreconcilable parts. New Testament models of Christian community show a radical joining of disparate and even formerly hostile parties. The unity-making work of the Spirit sometimes seems mad, hopeless, and impossible. But if we give space to the Spirit on this matter, and if we become willing to try out some new ideas, miracles beyond our imaginings can happen.

Even if we have special-interest worship services for various groupings within a church, there can be eucharistic worship which crosses all the groupings. The very nature of eucharist as a meal and as a storytelling event in which Jesus is remembered makes it the most flexible and accessible form. The focus is on Jesus, his fascinating activities, his wonderful stories, his provocative teachings, his comforting and grace-filled presence. The ritual of bread and cup, especially in its proper context of a real meal, knows no generational boundaries for participation, access, and comprehension.

The unexpected and uncontrollable aspect of our eucharistic worship is that Christ meets us there. If we are open to the Spirit, our encounter with the God of Jesus changes and shapes us, personally and as a community. If we are willing prayerfully to risk evaluating and reshaping our eucharistic worship, we will find the Spirit in the middle of it, showing us the way.

Working Through the Questions: Five Approaches

1. Ritual

In a church I know well, there was a big discussion about how members might help themselves function as a genuine community. How could they share their lives, serve each other, draw new people in, learn together, work together? That discussion was the context in which the question of children and communion came up. They realized it was not just another question in the list. Here, in the way they "did" communion, was potentially an arena in which to work out the way forward on a number of other issues as well. This is exactly what a living ritual, communion, might be able to do. Chapter 12, "The Language of Ritual," provides more guidance on how this can work.

2. Disciplined discussion

Once I took part in a vigorous discussion on the question of children and communion. It was during a training conference on how to work toward agreement within a group which included wide variation in views.

This conference group, not a congregation, was a collection of Christians from a variety of backgrounds. Because they represented a range of communion practices, the question of children in communion was a good issue for practicing constructive conflict. The method we used of disciplined listening to each other's understandings could be useful in congregations dealing with this controversial question or others.

Here is how it worked. We each took a place in the room, standing along an imaginary line representing a spectrum of views. One side was for the position "Serve children at communion," and the opposite side of the room was for the position "Never serve children at communion." The ends were for people secure in their categorical positions. Between the two extremes would be people who had questions about it, leaving them unsure or unwilling to declare a prescriptive position.

Then along the line we grouped ourselves into three huddles representing the range. Those in each group cooperated to write out the rationale of its particular position – for children communing, against children communing, and the questions of the middle group.

Next we sat in a ring of chairs one person deep around the room. A representative from each of the three groups presented one or two points. There followed a well-disciplined group discussion, supervised by two "animators." Each person wishing to speak could do so without interruption. People could address questions directly to those of divergent views.

This method avoided the "hot speech" often characteristic of open discussions in church business meetings. A scribe wrote the points on an overhead transparency as we went along. Every person taking part said that they had learned a number of new angles on the question by going through this disciplined pattern of corporate thought.[11]

The following is an outline list produced in that discussion, to stimulate you in thinking through the issues. In another group, of course, other views would come out.

Serve Children
Dichotomy: open worship, closed communion
The covenant meal, children included
Ecumenical weakness in refusing the child: the outsider is
    unexamined, but child is refused
Christian distinctiveness on inclusion
Full gospel includes communion
To exclude reinforces wrong idea of "magic" event
Children respond best to symbol, visual, story
Passover precedent – children's central role
Jesus: "Let them come." "Become like children."
All come – not dependent on left brain abilities

Never Serve Children
Can't take it seriously; cheapens communion
Inappropriate for young children
Safeguard the integrity of baptism
Recognize stages of faith development
Make faith their own, not extension of parents' faith
NT model: disciple band shared Jesus' "cup"
Value in secrecy for religious integrity, bonding
Private events are good, valuable
Historic tradition in linking understanding to readiness for baptism
    and communion
Counter to the modern "now" impulse
Value in anticipation of future communion

Question Stance
Rationality: What is the difference between an adult with learning
    difficulty and a child?
Baptism as borderline between childhood and adulthood, not
    communion?
Communion is a benefit. How withhold it from anyone?

163

Who decides? Should each person, including a child, decide
whether or not to participate?

Some children don't want to take part, some do. How discern
God's calling to them?

Some adults resent children's participation. How to deal with this
pastorally?

3. Practices based on convictions

For twenty-five years Mennonite minister Donald Steelberg has shared
communion with the unbaptized children of church families. This practice
is based on convictions and not on parents' complaints or children's
wishes. Some of the assertions that lie behind it are:

1. Scripture does not exclude children. Church tradition has often done
so.

2. Taking communion enacts Christian discipleship. Children readily
understand enacted stories.

3. Accepting children at communion is in line with Jewish Passover
tradition.

4. "Breaking bread" in the New Testament refers to ordinary day-to-day
meals, the churches' "common meals," and refers to the entire
community's sharing of material substance. Jesus' command "Do this"
refers to the shared meals of the community.

5. Early Christians shaped their tradition. We can take similar
responsibility today.

6. The Lord's table can be a prelude to baptism, not always vice versa.[12]

4. Practices first, theology second

Stuart Murray, an English Anabaptist who teaches evangelism, reports the
practice in an inner-city free church made up primarily of people from
"unchurched" backgrounds. It was a new church and there were no
precedents. Over a period of twelve years, a pattern became apparent.
Children were taking part in communion according to the guidance of
their parents, though it was really left up to the children themselves. The
little ones were keen to take part, but as the children approached puberty,
they became more reticent. Though they attended the services, they might
not take communion for a number of years. Then when they took a faith
stand and were baptized, they again took part in communion.

In this church there was no big issue about whether or not people took
the bread and the wine. Communion was observed in small groups of the
larger congregation, usually in an informal and mealtime setting in homes.
They saw the home as a more conducive setting for breaking bread than
the larger congregational meetings of from 150 to 200 people.

When the church began to think this through, they developed three
ways to consider the children in relation to the church and communion:

1. Children are not included until baptized.
2. Children are not regarded as members, but as potential members.
3. Children are regarded as full members until they decide otherwise.

The third option is the one they came to accept. Children played a full part in church life, appropriate to their age. Children came to faith over a period of time, and baptism became appropriate when a child was ready to make an independent decision. They have baptized children as young as nine years old.

Three questions engaged this church:

1. How do we strike the right balance? It is important not to be too prescriptive with the children, not to coerce them to take part in particular ways. They should be allowed to choose not to take part. We want them to know they are accepted at every stage as members of the church community.

2. Including children in communion affects our style of services. It can be serious and dignified but not overly solemn and ponderous.

3. Church members wonder, "What next? Children praying, prophesying, teaching?"[13]

why not ?!

5. "A time of wondering" for the children

Marjorie Waybill, an experienced Mennonite educator, has persuasive advice for churches which hold strictly to the view that communion is only for baptized and covenanted church members. This view grows out of a concern that children need to observe the central faith rituals of the church, even if they will not actively participate until years later. Sometimes children have been left at home with babysitters or taken out of the room during communion. Perhaps they would make noise and disturb the solemn atmosphere. But these children had no idea what communion services were about. They never saw or heard what actually went on.

Children should be present to observe the ceremonies, to listen to the Bible readings, to sing the special hymns, and watch as participants solemnly take the bread and the cup. This is a "time of wondering" and a time to observe, even if they do not participate fully; a time to remember Jesus' life and to look forward to the day when they will join baptized believers to participate fully. "For now it is enough for the children to join their families in this sacred event, and to feel the pastor touch them and say, 'God bless you, child. Jesus loves you, and we love you, too.'"[14]

These are just five examples of ways in which Christians from nonliturgical traditions have worked with the question of children and communion.

Who Presides at Communion?

We should not consider the question of children's participation in communion apart from the roles of the adults in the congregation, especially of those who are in positions of leadership. One of the greatest impediments to Christians sharing at communion is posed by the question, Who presides at the Lord's table? Entire sections of Christianity refuse to recognize "validity" in the ministry of other groups. Catholics are forbidden to receive communion in Protestant churches.

Because of their theology of the priest representing Christ, some Anglicans and Orthodox refuse to acknowledge the possibility of a woman presiding. Complicated arrangements are necessary (involving "lay" administration) in French parishes for whom no priest can regularly preside at mass. Many churches pay no attention to these prohibitions and clashes. Instead, they ignore questions of exclusive Christian practices. They narrow their sights within their own biblical understandings and their own church culture. They just carry on as usual. Each Lord's table stands in its own windowless dining room.

In the free churches there is a range of theological positions on this question. For some, to preside at the table is a function accorded through the authority of the congregation, and not necessarily through an external rite of ordination. Any designated member, a person of recognized spiritual maturity, may be asked to serve the church in this role.

Other churches hold to what is sometimes called a "higher" view of the ministry. Certain people are called, set apart, theologically trained and ordained. Only they may preside at the table. In some churches it is appropriate for only the local minister to preside, not visiting ministers. Perhaps the deacons pray or serve in particular ways.

These are matters of church traditions and church culture. As with all traditions, these matters may be laid open to prayerful scrutiny and evaluation. If the practices are well founded, they will be strengthened by this process. But perhaps some changes will need to be made in light of fresh biblical insights, or because of local circumstances.

Following Jesus

My intention has not been to prescribe solutions but to consider creative and responsible ways in which we can vitally observe the breaking of bread together. This means that we will value baptism, welcome the children, and honor the roles of ministers, members, and friends. Jesus' words of challenge, inclusion, and servanthood are relevant to our practices in communion, and they address us all: "Follow me." "The greatest among you must become like the youngest and the leader like one who serves." "Allow the children to come to me."

15

A Community of
Many Tables

ONE GOOD REASON to learn Christian history is that we can develop fresh and practical ideas for church life from old events. Earlier in this book we read about the Greco-Roman banquet as a familiar cultural form for the early Christians. We saw how they adapted it to their common fellowship meals. This poses a question for us today. Is it possible that we might transform hospitality and meal traditions from our own culture into distinctive types of Christian fellowship and worship? How would such hospitality relate to traditional communion services?

If a church tries a variety of communal meal forms, and relates them to the meal traditions of Jesus and his community, people's understandings, expectations, and manners in communion will develop. The purpose in this section is not to advocate replacing Sunday communion patterns with modern formats. It is to suggest more frequent, intentional table fellowship of many types within a church. All of these forms and experiences of meal fellowship can be considered as significant parts of the overall eucharistic fellowship of the church.

Three Forms of Modern Table Hospitality

First we will look at three modern forms which are not very helpful in developing eucharistic fellowship. In one instance a church has tried adapting breaking of bread to a modern buffet table. The other two are even less suitable.

A church of several hundred people I visited was trying out new ideas. After a "normal" service of singing and preaching, the leader announced that we would continue singing praise songs. During the singing anyone who wished to could go over to the table in a side aisle to receive bread and wine. At the table stood two servers who were prepared to pray for people as they came or to offer them the bread and the cup, whichever they chose. The congregation stood for an extended period of singing while various people drifted over to the table. This church was experimenting with putting a traditional service of breaking bread into a culturally familiar form, the buffet table.

However, this seemed to contradict the biblical pattern of breaking bread as a corporate act. The focus was on the music group leading the songs from the front. Everything about breaking bread was privatized. People probably said inwardly, *Shall I go over to the table? Will someone pray with me? Should I do it all in silence? Maybe I'll wait to see if John goes first.* The take-it-or-leave-it buffet table is not a suitable form for the Lord's Supper.

What about the cocktail party, another familiar social form in our society? It is apparently useful to hosts who wish to discharge a large amount of social obligation all at once while assuming that guests may have little in common. The only common factor is the host's social obligation to the guests. Everyone circulates, encounters are superficial and fluid, people come and go. This form of social hospitality seems to offer little for Christian transformation.

Mercifully, no one has yet proposed a take-out communion, or TV-meal bread and wine for use in conjunction with religious television services.

Eight Forms of Eucharistic Fellowship in a Church

Churches can celebrate both generously open meals and bounded ceremonial meals. In each type they work out different aspects of their life together. The various forms express a unique commitment within the membership, yet strengthen the distinctive character of the church community as generous and hospitable folk. The whole range of shared meals may properly be called "eucharistic." The following types can be seen to supplement traditional ways of observing communion.

1. Sharing food with the hungry

Feeding stations for the homeless and indigent, unlike a "communion take-out," offer possibilities. Everything depends on the motivation and the manner in which people serve and are served. The mercilessly caricatured rescue mission format may be demeaning and alienating. Recipients of food have to endure an evangelistic message before receiving a meal.

A different vision comes from the Community of St. Egidio in Rome. In 1968 some high school students began meeting together once a week. They talked about their dream to create something different from the loneliness their parents' society offered – in their words, something *hot*.

In a simple way, they started reading the Gospels, virtually unknown to them. They decided to try out some things they found there. They noticed Jesus' challenge to radical hospitality. God used the willingness of that handful of young people to take the gospel seriously. From them has grown a Christian community committed to hospitality and care for the homeless of Rome. They offer friendship and food to all comers.

Jeanne Hinton describes her visit to St. Egidio's soup kitchen:

I had come to help. "Work her hard," Mario had said laughing, as he left me there. There was no problem about that. This was no self-service, cafeteria-type soup kitchen, but one where those who come are served. I had to serve two tables; all five courses are served separately: a pasta dish or soup, a main dish of meat and vegetables, cake, fruit, coffee. Bread rolls and fruit are piled up in wicker baskets, and served not with your hands but with tongs. Many asked for several rolls and pieces of fruit. That would be their breakfast tomorrow. While I served two tables, other community members were there to sit and talk with those who came, and came not only for the food, but for the conversation and friendship, too.[1]

The Community of St. Egidio is a eucharistic community, celebrating mass regularly in the church. The members go directly from mass to soup kitchen. The hospitality of their soup kitchen dramatizes and extends Jesus' invitation to his table and expresses the heart of Jesus' vision for the kingdom banquet among the marginalized of Rome.

2. Ordinary meals at home

Recently we had a meal for a few Christian guests in our home. At the end of the main course, we broke bread and shared the cup together. We offered prayer for each other and a period of quiet thanksgiving and recognition of Christ, present with his people in the simple meal routines of ordinary life. This was not exactly a communion service but was surely eucharistic in the broadest sense. At a domestic meal, we explicitly acknowledged the presence of Christ, gave thanks for the new life we have received in him, and prayed the Lord's kingdom prayer together. If members do this kind of fellowship in their homes, with their families, and with guests, it will make a positive difference in the expectation and quality of participation at the corporate Sunday communion.

3. Coffee mornings

Coffee mornings for shoppers or for the elderly and under-employed of the neighborhood have potential for becoming more than merely social events. They could become eucharistic in the sense of extending hospitality in the name of Jesus and offering the happiness and safety of his presence to those who take part. Banner prayers of thanksgiving could hang on the wall, or printed blessings could be given out to each person served. To speak words of blessing as well as to receive such blessing could open up a relationship of caring love. We become a blessing as we say a blessing!

4. Parents and children

"Moms and Tots" groups meet a great social need but can do more than that if there is a vision for transforming such meetings with religious significance. Young children are especially open to symbols and little rituals of love, hospitality, and sharing. This can always be done in the name of the Lord Jesus, who welcomed children and blessed them. The dominant tone can be that of saying thank you and of sharing God's love together. Such activity needs to be seen as a valid thing in itself, not just a hook to get people to do something else, such as coming to church on Sunday. This kind of event can be one of many eucharistic expressions of the church community. Here is one of the places where we can literally act out Jesus' vision of invitations to all who will come to God's banquet of love and mercy.

5. Picnics

Ordinary picnics offer a meal tradition of our culture that could become more overtly eucharistic. By definition picnics are outdoor events in natural surroundings and so can easily link with Christian commitment and concern for the natural world. A eucharistic picnic is like any other picnic, except that it includes an intentional element of acknowledging Jesus as Host and giving thanks for his spirit of generosity and hospitality. Jesus ate many meals on the road, so what would be more natural than to acknowledge his presence when we too eat a meal along a wayside?

I can hear an immediate objection: "But I would feel embarrassed by presenting 'religious intrusions' upon such informal hospitality. Picnics and coffee mornings are just ordinary human activities, so I can't imagine myself imposing prayers or holy talk upon them."

This objection generalizes timid Christians' religious embarrassment. But is it fair to pre-guess others' responses to a church fellowship or Christian family which overtly and happily acknowledges God's provision and Jesus' presence as foundations of their "ordinary" life? And since when do other people's responses guide what Christians do as a community?

6. Combining Bible study with an agape meal

Here is something unusual, not just a bring-and-share "faith lunch." It is a study of the book of Romans done through role play and simulation. Various members of the group choose to role-play specific characters who might have been in the five house churches (cells) that made up the Christian church in Rome.

Each person finds out as much as possible about who they are – a free-born man, a slave girl, a Jewish conservative, a shopkeeper. As the group studies the text of Romans, members stay in their chosen roles and imagine how it would affect them, what their questions and responses might be. After nine Bible study simulations, the group prepares and celebrates an agape meal together as the tenth session.

This meal might demonstrate "continuing rivalry and tension between those who have dietary scruples and those who do not, between those who observe holy days and those who do not."[2] Or depending on the simulation, it could be a time for reconciliation and healing worship. In this shared meal, Bible study meets real-life emotions in surprising ways!

7. Saturday breakfast

Once I attended a delightful Saturday church breakfast. The hall was bright and attractive; the tables were set with colorful cloths and great baskets of rolls and breads. Flasks and pots of coffee and tea, and generous bowls of jams and marmalades hardly left room for plates and mugs. Music boomed from a cassette player on the windowsill. The atmosphere exuded a wonderful sense of generosity and joy.

This was a monthly event for all members and any friends they might invite. It was both social and religious, everything woven together with prayers and friendship. Each month there was a different theme, talk, Bible study, discussion, or just plain socializing. This church found that the church breakfasts helped to build up the character and personality of their community – they could become more hospitable, more generous, more able to receive and give prayers, as well as share food within and outside the church family. They enjoyed working together to plan and organize the details of the breakfasts. They could have had as their motto Jesus' own words, "Come and have breakfast!" (John 21:12).

8. A dramatic meal

"Picnic 5000" was what one church called an annual summer event at a regional forest preserve with lakeside picnic tables. This was part of a long-running project of acting out various Bible stories in the open air, involving everyone in the church. Picnic 5000 wasn't as complicated as crossing the Red Sea, but everyone considered it a high point of the summer program.

As recounted in all four Gospels, the story of Jesus feeding the multitude beside the Sea of Galilee was obviously central in the early church. We had to work out how to act the story, how to say the words, how to mime and gesture so those at a distance could see and understand – all of this preparation required that the participants be dynamic theologians. "And then what do we do with the twelve baskets of leftovers?" Good question – one that the Gospels do not answer for us. Because this story is traditionally interpreted eucharistically, Picnic 5000 is a powerful way to enter into the rich and evocative symbols involved.

I hear an objection. "Our church has lots of elderly members, and I simply can't imagine them going in for dramatic and innovative communion services. They would enjoy the social events, but you wouldn't get far trying to describe as 'communion' anything but the traditional, quarterly Sunday morning event."

171

How Changes Can Happen in Communion Observances

Perhaps Edward de Bono's advice would be useful here. In proposing changes he suggests retaining traditional patterns but introducing parallel events or patterns which experiment with alternative ideas. It would be wrong to jettison the established forms in favor of untried ones. So much is invested in the old ways, much that is valuable and precious. But those older forms might be renewed.

I think of a small inner-city congregation meeting in a large building almost a century old. With many ethnic groceries, foreign-language book shops, small abandoned factories, the neighborhood has changed dramatically from its proud heydays. The elderly members of the church observe the Lord's table once a quarter as they always have, using the same hymns, words, little pieces of cut bread, little cups of grape juice. For these folks, bewildered by frightening changes in the church's neighborhood, there is reassurance and safety in the repetition of the familiar words and rituals.

It would be cruel to impose drastic changes in this situation. And yet, as de Bono reminds us, good ideas can move by osmosis from an experimental site into familiar territory. For example, if some younger members in this church have developed table hospitality with eucharistic overtones, they might sing different songs or use loaves of bread instead of tiny fragments. Perhaps elderly members have been invited to these eucharistic meals in homes and have begun to feel at ease with a broader range of language, manners, and music. Eventually the quarterly communion services can include some of these elements, which have come to belong to all the members of the congregation.

We can continue the familiar services and at the same time enrich our entire life of hospitality and table fellowship, letting everything be inspired by Jesus' unique manners. My suggestions here are simply for ways to expand our desire for becoming eucharistic communities and to enrich our practices together. Our churches can truly become communities of many tables.

16

Words and Stories
at the Table

THE EUCHARIST places its principal focus on Jesus' words at the Last Supper included in the so-called narrative of institution. There are Jesus' words of ordinance or command in which he established the Lord's Supper for the church. Accounts of the supper appear in four places, and each is a bit different.

A useful exercise is to parallel the accounts of the Last Supper in the three Synoptic Gospels and in 1 Corinthians 11:23-25. Besides obvious overlapping, these accounts vary in key details. Church traditions have selected and fused various phrases into an authoritative patchwork for the words of institution used at the heart of the service of eucharist. One sentence is usually left out, however. The liturgical words of institution are found in Matthew 26:29 and in its parallels in Mark 14:25 and Luke 22:15-16. This is Jesus' reference to not drinking the fruit of the vine until he drinks it anew in the kingdom of God.

Parallels in Words of Institution

Who in the same night that he was betrayed (1 Cor.)
took bread and gave [you] thanks. He broke it (Matt. Mark, Luke, 1 Cor.)
and gave it to his disciples (Mark) saying,

"Take (Matt., Mark), eat (Mark); this is my body (Matt., Mark, Luke, 1 Cor.)
which is given (Luke) for you (1 Cor.).
Do this in remembrance of me" (Luke, 1 Cor.).

Then in the same way after supper (Luke, 1 Cor.)
he took the cup (Matt., Mark, Luke, 1 Cor.) and gave [you] thanks (Matt., Mark);
he gave it to them saying (Matt., Mark),

"Drink this, all of you (Matt.),

this is my blood of the [new (Luke, 1 Cor.)] covenant (Matt., Mark,
    Luke, 1 Cor.)
which is shed for you (Luke) and for many (Matt., Mark)
for the forgiveness of sins (Matt.).
Do this, as often as you drink it,
in remembrance of me" (1 Cor.).

Among all the accounts, the words in common are few:

Took bread, gave thanks, broke it.
"This is my body." Took the cup.
"This is my blood of the covenant."

Through scholarly comparison of the original texts and a thorough
knowledge of the Aramaic language, Joachim Jeremias has proposed this
as the core of the oldest form of the words:

Take. This my body / my flesh.
This my blood of the covenant (or: the covenant in my blood)
Which ... for many.[1]

Often in liturgical use the words of several of the biblical accounts are
melded together, smoothed out, and given a parallel structure. Here is one
form used by the Church of England.

... who in the same night that he was betrayed
took bread and gave you thanks;
he broke it and gave it to his disciples saying,

"Take, eat; this is my body which is given for you;
do this in remembrance of me."

In the same way after supper
he took the cup and gave you thanks;
he gave it to them saying,
"Drink this, all of you,
this is my blood of the new covenant,
which is shed for you and for many for the forgiveness of sins.
Do this, as often as you drink it,
in remembrance of me."[2]

Jesus' Last Parable

How do we understand these words? Liturgically, they serve as
legitimation of the eucharistic rite. They are the command of the Lord

Jesus and so are considered binding on the church. They are sacred words; we treat them with the same immense regard we pay to the Lord's Prayer.

Perhaps there is yet another level on which to consider these words. Jesus so often taught in parables, and it is possible that these words constitute Jesus' last parable. On that fearful night in the upper room, he might well have been thinking and talking in his typically parabolic way.

In John's Gospel we read a whole series of "I am" teachings: "I am the door. I am the good shepherd. I am the resurrection. I am the light. I am the bread." Jesus' Last Supper words, "This is my body" or "I am the living bread," might be considered in a similar way. Jesus was not speaking as a rationalist but was using language to convey something deeper than a blunt "this equals that." With his parabolic picture, Jesus tells us vastly more than the words simply say.

Markus Barth explores this mode of speech and points out the difference in John's Gospel between "dark speech" (parabolic, figurative, or symbolic) and "plain talk." To perceive what Jesus meant, we can go to Old Testament use of key terms such as *shepherd, vine,* or *light.* These are poetic metaphors. Jesus reveals himself as "the eternal archetype, now descended from heaven."[3] His images always include the implied attitudes and responses of his disciples or others to himself.

If Jesus is the Shepherd, who are his sheep? If Jesus is the door, who enters through it? A literal interpretation of these images would be absurd. If we are Jesus' sheep, we are not impelled to bleat in unison. Sometimes traces of "plain talk" are present in the "dark speech" of Jesus' parables. For example, the Good Shepherd actually does die, not literally torn apart by a wolf but on the cross of humiliation.

Barth reminds us that if we take in a literal sense Jesus' parabolic words of John 6: "I am the living bread" (6:51a) or "Those who eat my flesh and drink my blood have eternal life" (6:54), we can only be scandalized and perplexed.

> The Bible student who is so blind, dumb, insensitive, and hard-hearted as to sense nothing behind the bare words ... would indeed understand nothing. What good could come of chewing up a person or a god, and drinking the blood – together with, or instead of, plain bread and wine?[4]

Barth concludes that the whole of John 6 deals not just with the eucharist but with the whole meaning of the incarnation and of Christ's sacrifice. These verses are entirely appropriate to use in the eucharistic service, the meal at which Christ's life and sacrificial death are "remembered, proclaimed, and praised."

Jesus' words about the broken bread and the covenant cup were terse and undoubtedly puzzling to his disciples who first heard them. But upon those sparse phrases have grown complex theologies and convoluted practices. All too often Christians have read the accounts of early Christian practice through the prisms of doctrine and conflict belonging to later ages. The temptation has been to read in a backward direction, from the churches' developed practice into early experience.

Although it is important to take into account Christian experience through intervening centuries, it is essential to try to uncover the meanings held by the earliest Christian communities. The eucharistic words of Jesus are a vital link. But we must do more than venerate them, more than endlessly repeat them. We need to probe the words, meditate on them, and appropriate their allusive power.

We Retell the Old Story

In every Christian eucharist, we "pass on the tradition." We repeat the narrative of Jesus' inauguration of the rite. We retell the old story. This is a crucial point. Eucharist is rooted in history, in the painful memory of events "on the night when he was betrayed." Eucharist is not just a beautiful ceremony which gives us good feelings. It connects us with history's most remarkable conjunction of the human and the divine, the story of Jesus of Nazareth. It is essential that every eucharist retain the connection through conveying once again the story of a particular meal which has put its stamp on all other meals of the church, right through the ages.

Liturgical churches regulate the way this story is told. There are many variants among parts of an Anglican eucharist, a Catholic mass, or the divine liturgy of the Orthodox. Yet the precise form of cup-and-bread words must remain constant. One strength of this is that the story is always told. Most Christian denominations specify the use of a biblical form for the words of institution. But unfortunately, some become careless on this point. Informal churches especially need to pay special attention to keep the communion service strongly anchored to its historical origins in Jesus' life story.

Informally Telling the Story

Paying attention to history may be done in an informal way. I once attended a moving service of breaking bread in which the people were seated around a meal table. At the beginning of the meal, the leader reminded us that we were gathered in the name, in the power, and in the true presence of the Lord Jesus. We were there to remember him, to give thanks, and to realign our lives to Jesus' way of discipleship.

The leader then led us in telling the story among ourselves. She asked us simple questions. We answered them informally in a dialogue. We retold the story as though each of us ourselves had been in that upper room. Her questions went something like this:

Seated here around this table, we remember Jesus at a table with his friends, all those many years ago. Who was there that night? Was that meal in any sense a special event? On that night was there one person who was especially disturbed? How did Jesus treat him? What did the other disciples say? Then what happened? What were the ordinary things about that meal? Did anything particularly surprising happen? Did everyone understand it? What exactly was said? What exactly was done? How did the mealtime come to an end? Do we know what happened after that meal?" And so we told the story to each other, and felt our presence to Jesus, and his presence to us.

Another informal way to tell the story is to draw on the tradition of questions asked at the Passover meal. In the Seder a young child asks, "Why is this night different from all other nights?" Then each of the symbolic foods and gestures comes under scrutiny. Why unleavened bread? Why bitter herbs? Why on this night do we recline at the table? As these simple questions are addressed, the story of the exodus from Egypt and the Passover festival unfolds.

Beginning with the same question, "Why is this night different from all other nights?" Christians breaking bread at the Lord's table could ask and respond to many aspects of the Last Supper tradition. In the way these questions develop, in the way the story is told, a simple but rich theological understanding could be evoked.

The Story Tradition That Measures Our Stories

In his letter to the Corinthians, the apostle Paul told the story and employed it as an antidote to what had been reported to him about the church's communal meals. After hearing the truly dreadful story about what was going on there – the richer members despised and humiliated the poor within the church – Paul addressed the problem by telling the story which is the measure of all communions. "I received from the Lord what I also handed on to you, that the Lord Jesus on the night he was betrayed took a loaf of bread ..." (1 Cor. 11:23).

Paul challenged them. He pleaded with them to realign their congregation story with the story of Jesus. He described events in that Last Supper, and he told them that they should clean up their corporate life in light of it. They should reshape their own story so they would truly "proclaim the Lord's death" through their life and worship. The story of Jesus' cross should somehow become a template for their corporate life. If this happened, their story would illuminate the meaning of Jesus' cross. Their story would explore ways of learning to lay down their lives for each other. Others could "read their story" (observe their corporate life) and begin to comprehend "the Lord's death until he comes." The abuses in worship at Corinth were directly related to their failure to remember and reenact Jesus' story in the right way.

This is what Paul meant by "unworthily partaking" of the bread and the cup. It wasn't that the people were individually unworthy, but rather that the manner in which they worshiped together was unworthy. The offense of economic injustice within the church was the problem. The word "unworthily" described the action. Paul retold Jesus' story and urged them to move ahead and once again live and worship in the light of Jesus' teaching and actions.

The Corinthian agape-eucharist fellowship meal was much closer than we are to the customs of the festive banquet of Roman times. It would have seemed natural after supper (during the symposium) to do a variety of things – read a letter to the church, report on a visit to a prison, introduce traveling friends, listen to a poem, song, or psalm from a child, sing, pray, argue, and converse. All or any of those things would have been entirely appropriate to the occasion.

Corinthian Christian worship could include both reasonably formal events along with informal contributions. Without their making a point of it, their everyday concerns could be woven into the web of theology and ceremony. Their individual stories and their congregation's story could run in parallel.

Telling Our Stories at the Table

The church family that tells and retells its story can become a strong community. Founding visions, minor foibles, disasters, hilarities, sorrows, and celebrations are all interwoven to form the strong historical canvas upon which they cross-stitch details of today's story. It is a human story, full of surprise and event, humdrum and puzzlement, dreams and commitments. Imagine that multifaceted tale spun out at the Lord's table. People are struggling to make peace with their neighbors. God has restored a broken friendship. Someone has lost essential property through a burglary, and friends have given emergency help.

As we tell our own local stories, we can also retell hero and martyr stories from Christian history, both global and local. In Central America, where people have lost their lives because of their faith, names of the martyrs are read out as a roll call before the bread and wine are shared. As each name is spoken, the congregation responds in unison, "*Presente!*" Each person, with a unique story of suffering and faithfulness, is specifically remembered. Through their stories the martyrs are alive to the church. They are present as "a cloud of witnesses" (Heb. 12:1). Such a ritual gives depth to the expression "the communion of saints."

One of the ancient prefaces of the eucharistic prayer goes like this:

Therefore with angels and archangels,
and with all the company of heaven,
we proclaim your great and glorious name,
evermore praising you and saying ...

What a beautiful way always to put our worship into the context of heavenly worship, with the witness and the stories of countless Christians who have gone before us. We all join together with the angels in praising and thanking God.

Imagine the institution narrative not intoned simply as the warrant for a ritual action but told as the story it is. This is the big story which enfolds our local stories. It has the power to transform our stories, to make ours new. The story of Jesus at table with his friends, on a night so dark, reverberates down the generations. Jesus loved his friends. He ate with them, he warned them, he recognized their disappointments and lack of understanding, he prayed with them, he struggled in the face of his dangerous vocation. In the middle of it all, one of his own disciples left the table to go out and arrange to hand Jesus over to his enemies. Yet he loved his disciples and told them to love one another in the same way. And Jesus invited them, as he does us, to follow him. What a story!

Communion Without Words

Have you ever taken part in a communion without spoken words? Perhaps you have members who are unable to hear. Would they be willing to lead a communion service? What kind of inner listening and sensitive communication would become necessary for the church to participate?

Churches of every tradition have an overall simple structure for their services. Such a silent observance would clearly reveal what that pattern is. Gestures, symbols, and movement would become especially significant. Those from a liturgical background have deeply internalized the sentences used in the communion service. Since they know the words of the service by heart, they can more easily reach for another language to express the content and feeling of the eucharist. Chapter 17, "Singing Our Communion Theology," provides more help in fleshing out this idea.

Bible Words During the Distribution

Older people in a Mennonite tradition often mention a practice now rarely heard in communion services. They remember the ministers repeating passages of Scripture during the distribution. As the ministers moved among the people, serving the bread and the cup, their voices intoned, "There is therefore now no condemnation to them which are in Christ Jesus, who walk not after the flesh, but after the Spirit ..." "I am the bread of life. He that cometh to me shall never hunger, and he that believeth in me shall never thirst ..." "The leper said, 'Lord, if thou wilt,

179

thou canst make me clean.' And Jesus put forth his hand, and touched him, saying, 'I will; be thou clean!'" "Truly our fellowship is with the Father, and with his Son Jesus Christ. This then is the message which we have heard of him, and declare unto you, that God is light, and in him is no darkness at all."[5]

The comforting words of Scripture, the promises of God, the mystery and hope of their faith – these were in this way inextricably wedded with the people's reception and sharing in communion. Some churches in the Reformed traditions have a similar practice.

Just as music is the interplay between sounds and silences, so the most effective use of words involves silences, the refraining from words. However inspired or comforting they may be, a continuous wash of words is counterproductive. Choose words carefully. Make space for silence.

17

Singing Our Communion Theology

IN A RECENT congregational discussion, "When I Survey the Wondrous Cross" was a hymn mentioned by a number of people as indispensable for a communion service. Its themes are rich: contrasting Christ's supreme gift of himself with our "richest gain" and pride; meditating on the costly love of Christ, flowing out in sorrow and pain; the only response to "love, so amazing, so divine" can be to give "my soul, my life, my all."

This hymn is a perfect example of the synergy of words and music. The total impact of words plus music is greater than the apparent sum of the two. Something extra happens in that last verse as the tune reaches up on the words, "Love so amazing, so divine." We do more than think about Jesus' love. We give up all that we have and are to our Lord, uniting ourselves with him and his destiny. The hymn mysteriously operates in that place of inner integration, the place called by the psalmists "the heart." Our thoughts, our emotions, our wills engage together in an expression of lyrical faith.

We sing our theology. What do we believe? We believe what we sing. John and Charles Wesley understood this well and with great care produced hymns which were at the same time didactic and inspiring. The texts overflowed with scriptural allusions which filled out the doctrinal themes. Then the words were bonded with music which captivated the voice and set the spirit soaring.

Here are a few illustrative lines from several Wesley hymns. As we sing them together, we receive and express a fuller meaning.

> Who thy mysterious supper share,
> Here at thy table fed,
> Many, and yet but one we are,
> One undivided bread.
>
> His presence makes the feast;
> And now our spirits feel
> The glory not to be expressed,
> The joy unspeakable.

Every congregation has its own "short list" of sung theology. Among this music of the heart are the communion hymns and songs. Perhaps lines embedded in our hearts include ones like these: "Let us break bread together," or "Hallelujah, our Father, for giving us your Son!" or "Opening our hearts to him, Jesus is our King!" All of this sung theology is deeply anchored in the core of communal life, along with the Lord's Prayer, certain psalms and benedictions, familiar manners and rituals, our memories and stories. These are indispensably central to our worship.

A useful effort is to determine which hymns and songs are on the congregation's short list for eucharistic worship. Informal conversations with members as well as a hunting trip through the printed songbooks might uncover some surprises. You may find some valuable but neglected pieces to restore. There may be new songs to put on your short list.

Look carefully at the texts. Notice the themes. Are they primarily about Jesus' death and sacrifice? Are there texts from different centuries of Christian history? Are they mainly from one denomination or stream of piety? Here is a list of communion themes from the Lord's Supper section of a recent denominational hymnal. A typical congregation would probably have precious hymns and songs which are not in the current hymnal, so an actual living list of themes might be longer. How does your list compare with this one?

Themes from the Lord's Supper Section of a Hymnal

Eating and drinking with Christ
Table fellowship in the church
Betrayer at Lord's table, we are not worthy, either
The cross of Christ, Christ's suffering and death
Our sins forgiven
Christ the light
Union with Christ – personal
Union with Christ – the church
Joyful feast, banquet
Victory of Christ over powers of evil
Healing
Liberation, freedom
Resurrection
Holy Spirit presence – effects
Eternal life
Offering our gifts to God at the table
Discipleship
Suffering with Christ

I have kept a more detailed listing of hymns and songs in current use by the congregation. Under each title I have quoted particularly distinctive lines, drawing from the entire text. My tendency had always been to remember the first line or stanza or maybe a salient line from a subsequent stanza well, but to be vague about the rest of the text. This list, a summary of key points, assists in selection of hymns and songs for the service.

We considered over twenty theological themes in the second part of this book. You could check your list of themes in relation to those themes. Perhaps there are gaps in your sung theology. If so, you might need to go out and find songs and hymn to enrich the scope of your congregation's communion music.

Find Your Poets

Musicians are usually more visible in a church than poets. Musical efforts are vastly more often called upon, to greater or lesser benefit. Why not search out your hidden poets and ask them to consider writing texts for the congregation? These poems might simply be read, or might be set for singing. They may not enter that essential core of the congregation's worship materials, but they serve a good purpose, drawing on the experience and expression of the members, and developing congregational prayer upon it. Compositions for one-time use, whether musical or poetical, are as important in their own ways as the pieces we use year in and year out.

Speaking and Singing

Earliest Christians used both Scripture texts and their own poems in their eucharistic worship. But in those days they did not distinguish as we do between sung and spoken words. In fact, the Hebrew and Greek languages have no separate word for music. In ordinary conversation people used the rhythm and intonation suitable for ordinary thoughts. But in a ceremonial situation, or when the expression became poetic or religious, words were delivered in a different way. This may not have been what we would recognize as singing, but it was distinct from the everyday speech of commerce or conversation.

The word for this kind of religious or poetic speech is "cantillation." The falling-third interval singsong of children making fun of each other on the playground gives an idea of what this might have been like, as does a caricatured recitation of nursery rhymes with an exaggerated pattern of rising and falling intonation. The call to prayer from a Muslim mosque is another recognizable mode of sung speech.

Sung speech can be expressive and extends the time through which a text is heard. Both of these qualities set apart and enhance the meaning of religious texts. Jewish and early Christian psalm singing was of this type, a cantor alternating verses or phrases with congregational responses.

There is plenty of early evidence of such song, either of psalms or of original texts. Tertullian tells us, "The Scriptures are read and the psalms are sung." He adds, "After the ritual handwashing and the lights, each one is invited to stand and sing to God as he is able: either something from the holy Scriptures or of his own making."[1]

We would do well to emulate both their singing of Scripture and also of producing their own texts. I have heard psalms sung solo in free churches, offered as a form of charismatic prayer. The music is an improvised and expressive form of cantillation.

Three Eucharistic Hymns from the Ancient Church

"Gloria in excelsis" is one of the earliest hymn texts associated with the eucharist. It was based first of all on the song of the angels: "Glory to God in the highest, and on earth peace, good will toward [people]" (Luke 2:14, KJV). It gradually expanded with a stanza addressed to God, followed by two stanzas addressed to Jesus Christ. All the classic liturgies include this song in the early part of the service:

> Glory to God in the highest,
> and peace to his people on earth.
>
> Lord God, heavenly King,
> almighty God and Father,
> we worship you, we give you thanks,
> we praise you for your glory.
>
> Lord Jesus Christ, only Son of the Father,
> Lord God, Lamb of God,
> you take away the sin of the world:
> have mercy on us;
> you are seated at the right hand of the Father:
> receive our prayer.
>
> For you alone are the Holy One,
> you alone are the Lord,
> you alone are the Most High,
> Jesus Christ,
> with the Holy Spirit,
> in the glory of God the Father. Amen.

The importance of this hymn can be gauged by its inclusion with the Psalms and Canticles at the conclusion of the fifth-century biblical *Codex Alexandrinus*, now in the British Museum. This hymn, translated into German as *Allein Gott in der Hoh sei Ehr*, entered English through Catherine Winkworth's rendition, "All Glory Be to God on High."

Though twice removed from its fifth-century form as found in the *Codex Alexandrinus*, it would contribute to nonliturgical communion services, bringing both historical and theological continuity with early Christianity.

Another ancient hymn, one which has its regular position within the eucharistic prayer, is the "Sanctus." Used first in the Eastern church, it entered the Western churches in the early fifth century. The text is partly derived from Isaiah 6:3.

> Holy, holy, holy Lord,
> God of power and might,
> heaven and earth are full of your glory.
> Hosanna in the highest.

A third eucharistic hymn text from the ancient church is the "Agnus Dei," a modified part of the "Gloria," and based on John the Baptist's words, "Here is the Lamb of God who takes away the sin of the world!" (John 1:29b). First referred to at the end of the seventh century, over time the "Agnus Dei" evolved to include its two additional phrases of prayerful petition.

> Lamb of God, you take away the sins of the world:
>   have mercy on us.
> Lamb of God, you take away the sins of the world:
>   have mercy on us.
> Lamb of God, you take away the sins of the world:
>   grant us peace.

This hymn has come into English through German versions. Nikolaus Decius' sixteenth-century German hymn was translated in the mid-nineteenth century by A. T. Russell. It follows the ancient three-part form. The three stanzas are identical except for the final phrase. The first two stanzas conclude "Have mercy on us, Jesu!" But the third stanza has "Grant us thy peace, Jesus!"

> O Lamb of God, all-holy,
> Who on the cross didst suffer,
> And, patient still and lowly,
> Thyself to scorn didst offer:
> Through thee our sins are healed,
> And God's great love revealed.
> Have mercy on us, Jesu!

Traditionally, this hymn comes near the close of the eucharist, before or as the people are taking the bread and wine. The text is appropriate for nonliturgical churches to use at that point, with its words of forgiveness, healing, and peace.

Psalms in the Eucharist

O taste and see that the Lord is good;
Happy are those who take refuge in him. (Ps. 34:8)

From earliest times Christians have chanted Psalm 34 in the communion service. It is as appropriate today as ever and remains a favorite choice, especially in proximity to taking the bread and wine. The whole, of the psalm sums up the hopeful dependence of the believer upon God, Redeemer and source of all goodness.

The Hallel Psalms 113-118 are associated with the Passover feast. These undoubtedly comprised the "hymn" that Jesus and his friends sang just before going out to the Garden of Gethsemane. For this reason, then, these psalms are closely associated with eucharist.

The penitential Psalm 51, "Have mercy on me, O God, according to your steadfast love," is often used as a prayer of confession at communion. It provides a place for inward contemplation for individuals in the service as a whole, which is primarily a corporate expression.

The much-loved Psalm 103 has traditionally been used to conclude a communion service: "Bless the Lord, O my soul, and all that is within me, bless his holy name." This is exactly where the Genevan *Service Book* of 1556 places it.

Equally appropriate are these verses from Psalm 145:

> The eyes of all look to you,
>   and you give them their food in due season.
> You open your hand,
>   satisfying the desire of every living thing ...
> My mouth will speak the praise of the Lord,
>   and all flesh will bless
>   his holy name forever and ever.

These can be used either in an introductory part of the communion service, or in a concluding prayer of praise and thanks.

Words with Music

Just as the Hebrews, Greeks, and Romans used their cantillations, we, too, provide musical lines for our special texts. It makes a great difference whether a poem is simply read, sung to an ill-fitting tune, or sung well or poorly yet with an appropriate tune. Nothing irritates the spirit so much as hearing a favorite hymn or song mutilated.

Why do we care so much? Professional musicians and liturgists ponder this question. They try to analyze why and how eucharistic music works, how it generates meaning. But we don't have to understand the psychological and spiritual mechanisms to know that these songs and hymns do enable an expression of meaning deeper than the words can do alone.

Singing together at the eucharist profoundly expresses its communal dimension. The ones presiding at the Lord's table serve the congregation, but it is the entire people who celebrate the eucharist and best give their thanks and praise to God through singing together. Many voices blend and join to make one voice – the voice of the entire group. To sing together like this expresses koinonia, the intimate sharing and unity of the body of Christ. There is no better way to express our unity in our diversity than to sing with our one congregational voice.[2]

Singing the psalms, canticles, hymns, and songs of the church through the ages enables us to express our part in global and even cosmic anticipation of the great banquet of the kingdom. We join the "festal gathering" and sing the "new song of the Lamb." We sing the "sacrifice of praise" with the tunes of our hearts' music.[3] Celebration calls for singing.

As Protestants, we have our job cut out to counteract the wordy, didactic tendencies of our traditions. Wordy, didactic hymns are some of our favorites, and we naturally reach for the ones we know best. This is fine, but we must provide a wider range of musical styles, ones that will support a broader scope of prayer for our people.

Many churches are using the simple music of the Taizé community to provide the time and space for a more contemplative expression within communion services. People respond warmly to this, if well led and supported, because the tunes are easy to learn, the bass lines are interesting, and people can breathe easily as they sing. The frequent repetition of the songs enables them to sing, to hum, to listen, and to pray through the song with a sense of ease and expansiveness. This contemplative quality is often missing in other parts of the service.

The "Agnus Dei" mentioned above is a fine example of a simple and repetitive text, based in Scripture, which can assist people in meditative prayer at a crucial point in the eucharist service. It may give time to reflect on the matchless gift of forgiveness and healing and to place ourselves within the wholeness of God's shalom. But we would not conclude the service with this music. We need another kind of song to close the eucharist, something that sends us out into faithfully and joyfully joining in God's own mission of love to the world.

Music Without Words

There are many right ways of using music without words. What we think is right is usually what we are used to. So for some, this means quiet, worshipful instrumental music during the distribution of bread and wine.

But others are incensed at the intrusion of music at communion. For them, it's a time for silence!

Instrumental music can convey a range of messages. Pre-service music might tell us the musicians aren't ready yet; they are practicing and tuning up. That's a definite message, but is it one we want to communicate? Maybe so. Or maybe the music before a service is very soft, perhaps a prelude by Chopin or a piece by Grieg played at half volume, which makes every other pianist present wonder, *What in the world is this piece of music doing at church?* We are used to associating them with piano recitals or practice sessions at home.

Sometimes musicians play mood music which establishes a soporific or funereal atmosphere. In some churches people sing "gathering songs" during the fifteen minutes before the service hour begins. In other churches priority is given to children and young people learning to play instruments, to make their musical offering. Why do we have music and a particular style of music as we gather? Does it contribute to the particular themes of eucharist we are developing on that day? Some days the mood might be upbeat and at other times more somber. But we must give it some thought and choose the musical form that serves best.

During the offering is another point at which instrumental music may be heard. But there is a sense in which the offering is the proper time for congregational singing, a communal expression to go with the gathering together of our material gifts, both of money and of the work of our hands represented by the bread and the wine. It is no substitute, theologically, to play innocuous organ music or listen to a young child play a Bach invention! Here is a challenge to each church. How do we make our decisions about music for communion?

Churches which use instrumental music during communion might do so for a number of reasons. To cover shuffling noises as people walk forward? To provide an atmosphere for private devotion and prayer? To justify the expense of the organ? Perhaps to provide a quiet musical basis for congregational song in a contemplative mode? Or to allow time for special intercessions following the communion? These reasons raise practical and theological questions the congregation must address. Music is too potent to be left to tradition or unconsidered habits.

Singing a Whole Service

Have you ever been in a communion service which is entirely sung? A "sung eucharist" is such a service, although there are always some spoken parts – the reading of Scripture, the sermon, and some of the prayers. People in a liturgical tradition learn the music of their services by heart. It is literally in their hearts, and so they can easily take an active part in their eucharist. This might seem complicated to those from other Christian traditions.

Eucharist in Music and Mime

This might be something to work out at a retreat weekend, or in a workshop exploring how to express ourselves with gesture. Perhaps small groups could each work out one segment of the service, then it could all go together with music to accompany. Perhaps you could retain some spoken parts among those that are sung and gestured. If you have people in the congregation who know sign language, they could contribute to the process. It is remarkable to experience the difference between simply saying or singing the words, and pairing words and gestures. A next step, removing the words, and using only music with gesture, would introduce you into the exciting realm of liturgical dance.

Either independently or joined with words and movement, music is a rich resource for the corporate praise which is our eucharist. Let us use it wisely, not allowing it to dominate or distort but to serve.

189

18

Offering Ourselves
and Our Gifts

EARLIER WE traced something of the history and meaning of eucharist and offering. It has, first of all, to do with Christ's offering of himself on the cross, the supreme gift. But it also has to do with offering ourselves and the fruit of our work in shaping God's gifts of sustenance through creation. The offering brings together the themes of creation and redemption. How these themes work out in the eucharist has historically been the source of acrimonious debate. I suggest that arguing about it isn't as useful as simply doing the offering more seriously, more creatively, and more joyfully.

We will consider this from several angles – presenting the bread and wine at the Lord's table, collecting money gifts, and offering ourselves in response to Christ's own offering of himself to us on the cross, and at the table. How we do these actions reflects our understandings of them, but also has the potential for shaping us, our living and loving response to God's gracious gifts of forgiveness and mercy.

Four Stories: Presenting the Bread and Cup

1. I once attended a conservative Bible chapel, a congregation which had as its visual focus a shining drum kit in a central position on the elevated front platform. The drum kit stood just under a large wooden cross. On the left, akimbo, stood the communion table and opposite to it, on the right side, also placed at an angle, stood the pulpit. The morning service began. After fifty minutes of singing and testimonies, someone entered the platform through a side curtain and placed the bread and wine on the table. I was concentrating on singing, and so I almost missed this action altogether. Into my mind flashed the thought, *Oops, they forgot to put the things on the table. They'd better get it done before we're finished singing this song.*

2. Another memory picture is of an Anglican service in which a family of parents and several children, accompanied by a joyful song, walked forward, the length of the center aisle, carrying bread and wine to the communion table. No one in the congregation missed seeing them, even though we were all vigorously singing. The children's faces, excited and happy, brought smiles from members of the congregation. Carrying the

bread and wine forward, the family led the congregation into the next movement of the worship.

3. Robert Webber records his own childhood memory of communion Sunday. "I would walk into the church on the first Sunday of every month, see the table covered by a white cloth, and say to myself, 'Oh, oh, another downer Sunday.'"[1] People put on somber faces. The hymns were slow and heavy. A child immediately picks up the non-verbal signals.

However, there is another side to that tradition. One church I know well has dedicated members who lovingly and carefully prepare the linens and the little cups and the bread for communion Sunday. Looking at the snowy cloths and shining vessels, I am always moved by the labor of people behind the scenes, giving hours of their time both before and after the service. They truly offer themselves and their work to serve all the others.

Without the offertory procession of the liturgical churches, however, the free churches have to consider what is communicated by the way bread and wine are physically and visually presented. Gently lifting the white cloth away, uncovering the bread and cup, can give an impression of great respect for what is revealed, perhaps of mystery, or of fragility of the elements. On the other hand, careless or unaesthetic handling detracts and demeans the action. In a culture where women prepare and serve the food in the home, seeing only male ministers handling bread and wine at a communion table removes that "meal" even further from connections with real meals or with Jesus at a meal table with his friends. Of course, in some instances that may be exactly the intention.

4. One Harvest Sunday I took part in a memorable communion service. As we entered the room, the empty table stood in the center with chairs ranged around it in a wide arc. During the vigorous singing of the first hymn, a motley procession of members, tall and short, old and young, came in from both sides. They carried armfuls of wheat stalks, baskets of fruit and vegetables, a brilliant tablecloth, flowers, loaves, plates, jugs, and cups for the wine. There in front of the congregation, and as we sang, they literally laid the table for the meal. Then, standing in an arc behind the table, they joined with us, the singing congregation, in completing the circle. Together we responded to the invitation to the table of the Lord.

I had never seen such a festive and joyful setting. An important part of the effect was simply that lots of people had taken part. They brought the fruit of their own labors. They actually set up a table that was recognizably a meal table. And it was all done right there in front of our eyes as we provided the joyful music in praise of the Host who had invited us there.

In these four examples, we notice a number of effects derived from the manner of presenting bread and wine at the table. The harvest communion and the family carrying bread and wine up the aisle focus for the whole congregation the joy and participation of all members in the action. The table prepared beforehand, however lovingly this is done, may set off special people who do special things with special cups and special bread.

This approach can stimulate a sense of false mystery and communicate "Don't touch!" which is akin to the very thing it most intends to counteract: that eucharistic bread and wine are extraordinary elements, distinctly different from the food of our tables, and only certain people can handle them. The table surreptitiously prepared while everyone was thinking of something entirely different – well, such an approach hardly bears comment.

The Offering of Money

As we learned earlier, money offerings replaced offerings-in-kind when the church set up institutions for the care of the needy. When we take up offerings, sometimes even special "alms for the poor" at communion services, we are remembering an ancient meaning of communion: sharing with the needy and thus doing redistributive justice. So it is right that our money offerings are placed on the communion table. Perhaps we could make more of this than we do.

The money offering serves as an important expression of thankful response to God. God has given so much for us. This is our opportunity to share generously of what he has given. Sometimes the offering becomes a perfunctory routine; at other times it is the most somber action of worship, as though parting with our money is a painful ordeal. Ideally, the offering is an act of joyful response.

We Westerners can learn from our African brothers and sisters, who make much of offerings. Multiple offerings take up a fair amount of time in the services. Often the offering is personal, accompanied by a testimony of God's protection and provision. Specific thank offerings, special project offerings, offerings from youth, children, or service groups – offerings are danced and sung to the Lord. It all seems to be fun, too!

An English church which has African members has learned to celebrate their offerings. This is a high point of the worship for everyone. They bring out several large baskets and place them across the front. Then as the band plays (anyone can join in playing at this point), they launch into their happiest songs. Singing, the people stream forward to throw their offerings into the baskets. It isn't at all orderly. It is noisy and chaotic. But they say that no one forgets to bring their offerings!

What if you had to stay at your seat when everyone else was having such a good time? They told us that in Africa deacons give out coins to the poor children so that everyone can join in the offering. So they watch and give each other money to throw in, and sometimes people return to the baskets again and again.

Usually more sedately, we Westerners bring the offerings to the communion table. There they take an important place, both materially and symbolically, expressing our response to God's gracious generosity in creation and redemption. The money offering, which represents the fruit of our work, will always be an integral part of the eucharist.

Some churches suggest that other kinds of offering can be placed in the offering baskets – pledges of services such as outdoor work, care of children, financial consultation, music lessons, pastoral visiting, planting a garden to share produce with others. Such suggestions remind us that all of our life can be brought to the Lord's table in response to God's gracious giving to us. At the table we remember God's greatest gift of all, Jesus our Savior. Often a theme for Christmas-time, we can develop this one all around the year.

One of the important outcomes of eucharistic worship is exactly this – that we offer ourselves to each other and to the world because of the love of God. Giving and offering ourselves do not come naturally. We have to practice. And the place to practice, in both senses of the word, is in the eucharist. We bring all that we have, in response to the Lord's invitation. We celebrate Christ's great self-giving in God's plan of forgiving mercy. In response we dedicate ourselves anew to life in the power of God's Spirit, life in which we pour our lives out for each other and the world.

A congregation that frequently practices eucharist like that will become distinctive and noticeable. Participants will be "changed from glory into glory." They will overflow with thanksgivings, and God will be glorified.

19

An Environment for Thanksgiving

The Environment Speaks

ISN'T IT amazing how completely different two eucharists can be! How is it possible, when they both seek to show and proclaim the same truth, and to perform the central Christian act of thanksgiving for God's work of redemption in Jesus? Differences in theology, language, or degrees of formality are factors that come quickly to mind.

Here we will consider some other aspects of the service. These have to do with the whole environment of the service. They include everything from pleasant lighting and fresh air through placement of furniture, flowers, and visual focus. They have to do with how people sit or stand in relation to each other and with the posture and manners of those who lead the service. Conducive visual and physical factors contribute greatly to the overall tone of the service. We honor guests in our own homes when we obviously and thoughtfully prepare the meal and the rooms for their arrival. Similarly, we honor the church as well as Christ among us when we make the effort to prepare a suitable environment for the deeply felt and joyful assembly.

Buildings

First we will consider the building, the room in which the congregation gathers to celebrate communion. The room itself has a lot to say. J. G. Davies[1] shows that worship buildings are either like paths or like places. The first type, the path, suggests movement and direction, perhaps a journey within the building. The second type, the place, revolves itself into a center, a place of rest.

Gothic cathedrals are *path* buildings in which everything is drawn in one direction, to one point. The arcades of columns, the side aisles, the floor design, and the ceiling patterns all work together, causing the eye to move to the focus of the entire building – the high altar. The altar is central in every sense. It is essential for the celebration of the eucharist. The altar dominates the visual field. The whole congregation stands facing the altar. When they do move, they move toward the altar. The cathedral's design profoundly expresses the meaning of the Anglican eucharist or the Roman mass: the sacrament is the central focus.

Baptists, too, can articulate a rationale for a *path* building. What they need, says John Newport, is an expression of "the biblical emphasis on journey, after the redemptive pattern of the Prodigal Son."[2] So a Baptist building might allow space and movement for response to an evangelistic appeal made from the pulpit.

The table usually stands below the pulpit, on a platform which covers the baptistery. This building design speaks volumes about the theological understanding of the relation of congregation, preacher, penitent, pulpit, baptistery, and table. Do Baptists primarily need to use the sawdust trail for their architectural motif? They need to ask whether their foundational emphasis on the congregation is expressed or contradicted by the design of their buildings. When the design and the theology cohere, it all goes better – preaching, baptizing, communion.

The communion service in a *place* building is no less influenced by its space than the mass in its cathedral. The congregation is not on a journey to the front. They are clustered, gathered together. In such a room, the table may be in the middle, completely surrounded by the people. Or it may be placed on a central axis, with the congregation in an arc. The feeling is nondirectional. The sense is that "we are here together in this place."

Unfortunately, some congregations hold a *place-space* theology for the congregation gathered around the table but own buildings designed on the *path* motif. All bodies face forward, all eyes are led to the central focus, a raised pulpit. A long central aisle with fixed pews rivets the people in their places. But the congregation cannot express a *place-space* communion.

I visited a church recently which holds strong principles of the gathered congregation, biblical simplicity in worship, and the centrality of breaking bread. I was surprised at the visual contradictions. Fixed theater seats ranged along a central aisle. The wall behind the central platform featured a large wooden cross. At the foot of this cross stood a shining drum kit, illuminated by spotlights in the ceiling. Beside the drums was a full complement of microphones, back-speakers, music stands, and further electronic instruments.

All of that took up the right-hand half of the platform. On the lefthand side was a pulpit with a microphone and a dark velvet curtain hanging behind it. I knew that this church observed communion every week. I kept thinking, *Where is the communion table?* I never saw it. After 40 minutes of singing and a further 35 minutes of sermon, someone pulled the red velvet curtain aside and from behind the pulpit produced the communion plate with bread and the communion cup. It was my first (and I hope last) experience of a hidden communion table.

Our buildings speak. We express our communion theology through them, and they in turn shape our communion theology. Here is an instance in which the very character of a congregation's togetherness was altered by changing the architectural message of the room they worship in.

This church, when it had grown in numbers, added an extension at the back. Now they could seat 200 instead of 135 people. The pulpit stood on a high front platform with the communion table on the floor below. The room was long and narrow, with fixed pews along a central aisle. Families with children sat in the back. Elderly folks sat in the front. Being shortsighted, the preacher could hardly see the farthest 75 people.

Then some new folks wanted to attend church. These were people in wheelchairs. There was no way to get them inside. So the church decided to build an additional room alongside with an elevator and an entrance at the front of the church for the wheelchairs. But the wheelchair people did not particularly like the idea of coming and going at the front of the entire congregation. What to do?

The church did something radical. They unbolted some of the pews and changed the orientation of the worship. They left the back third of the church as it was. In the front third of the church, they turned the pews around to face "backward." The middle third now has its (fewer) pews facing sideways toward a low platform along the wall, in front of two windows covered to prevent glare. The leftover pews from the middle third were installed on the platform at the end of the room.

Now the communion table and the pulpit are together in the middle of the congregation. The elderly still sit in the front, but the front is the middle. The families sit in the back, but now the back is near the middle, too. And the wheelchair people have space to come and go with ease. The communion service in this church is entirely different from in the old days. Their theology of the gathered congregation fits with the place-space of their building.

The Lord's table, set in the middle of the congregation, is a potent symbol of Christ's presence in the midst of his people. The very act of gathering around the table symbolizes and helps to make true the communion and unity the people experience.

Churches in the liturgical tradition are carefully designed to present the three foci which serve their understanding of their sacramental worship: pulpit, font, and table. These three must be in proper architectural relationship, to communicate their theological, sacramental, and practical relationships. Even Christians who do not live in one of the classic liturgical traditions do well to consider the prominence given to pulpit, baptistery, and table. How do the three central actions – preaching, baptism, and communion – interact? A good way to start looking at this is to observe our buildings and listen to what they are saying, what they reveal to us about how these important actions function.

The Table Itself

What kind and shape of table is best? It needs to be in proportion to its surroundings, neither spindly nor grandiose. It should be in a reasonable relation to the pulpit in size. It shouldn't be railed off, isolated into the proximity of just a few privileged people.

Some churches place enormous, ornate chairs behind the communion table, honored places for deacons or elders. What is the message of these elevated seats, looming over banks of rigid pews? Surely their occupants, the deacons and the elders, are in the same spiritual position as the congregational members in their serried ranks of pews, all equally receiving life and bread and wine from the hand of Christ. All too often, inappropriate furniture, expensive memorial gifts of previous generations, have outlived their contribution but are still so "good" and substantial that they cannot be moved out. Such furnishings can tie the hands of a church which needs to make changes to implement a theology which corresponds to the church's life.

One congregation I visited had a high central pulpit with elaborate oak panels below it running across the entire front of the church. The communion table with its ornate chairs stood on a small platform below the pulpit. The heavy pews sat much too close to the communion table. There was no room to move around the front of the church at weddings or funerals. In ordinary services, no one sat in those front pews. After long discussions, the church decided to abandon using the high pulpit. They took up the front pews, sawed them up, and used the wood to construct a spacious platform which held both a movable communion table and a movable lectern. Parts of the panels from the big chairs reappeared in the sides of the table and in the lectern. They threw nothing away but rather transformed the materials into forms and objects which serve the church in the present time.

Only the necessary and significant things find their proper place on the table, not extraneous decorative or practical items. When I took a group of students on a "church crawl" around the town, we tried to read the buildings. What did they say to us, even when no one was present? In one church we saw a huge silver ewer (a pitcher of antique design) on the central communion table. I cautiously asked the minister whether this ewer played an important role in their communion services.

"No," he said. "We always put it away in the kitchen on communion Sundays."

However, the devout person who had given it as a memorial to his wife wished that it would always stand on the communion table. Living relatives would be offended if the ewer were removed to another place. So it formed a permanent and central visual focus for the church's worship.

Father George, an Orthodox priest, was puzzled to see a bouquet of flowers on the Baptist communion table. "What is the meaning?" he asked. A good question! What is the interplay between aesthetics and significant religious symbolism?

Bread and Wine

We must not neglect the important part played by the physical substance of the bread and wine. The forms of bread and wine and the actual doing of the distribution – all are vital in our communication and perception of communion meanings.

The free-church habits of using tiny cubes of bread and trays of tiny glasses for grape juice seem peculiar to those from other traditions. People say the move away from common cups was for hygienic reasons, but in fact it was "due more to advertisers than to doctors."[3] Hygienic scruples reputedly account for the precut servings of bread.

Catholics use what they call "wafers" – tiny discs of pale material unlike anything we would call bread in everyday life. These wafers have a history of their own, and a staying power which some Catholic reformers are trying to counteract.

Why not use real bread, real loaves of a kind of bread that connects with normal life? Some communities use pita bread or *chapatis* (unleavened and non-crumbly). Others buy the biggest, freshest loaves possible, so the breaking and sharing of bread carries a message of generosity and delicious nutrition.

Feelings run high on the matter of how the cup is served. To satisfy apparently irreconcilable opinions, some churches serve the congregation in two forms – the people can go forward to one side and receive from a common cup, and to another side to receive individual cups.

In Nepal, Europeans introduced the use of tiny cups into Christian communion services. Nepalese Christians, because of cultural taboos, could not use a common cup, but the tiny cups were utterly strange to them. So instead they now use a pot with a long spout which makes it possible to have a common cup, yet the vessel does not touch the mouths of the participants. Culturally, this is a familiar mode, and so it communicates positively in contrast to the tiny cups which were so clearly a foreign import.

In churches where servers go out among the congregation, sometimes the bread is eaten as it is received (signifying individuals coming to Christ's table). The individual cups are held until all have been served, then taken at once (signifying the church's unity in Christ).

Some churches which have traditionally served people where they sit are moving toward inviting people to come forward or to a choice of positions to receive the bread and cup from pairs of servers. People unused to doing this have found it a remarkably profound act, moving out of their seats along with others, lifting their hands to receive from the brothers and sisters who serve them, hearing and responding to words of blessing spoken individually to them.

A smooth method of serving, in which people remain seated to serve each other, requires a simple instruction, easily learned. "Please serve the person on your left, say a word of blessing, and then pass the bread to the person on your right. That person will then serve you." The stewards serve each row from the left side, passing the bread to the second person in from the aisle. At the right end of the aisle, the steward serves the final person in the row. The same procedure works for serving the cup (with napkin to wipe the lip of the cup each time) or for passing the tray of individual cups along the row.

Recently I watched a free-church minister conducting a communion service. When he broke the small loaf into two pieces, he silently held them out and down in front of himself, at the level of the tabletop. How different from another minister who had an enormous loaf and a number of large goblets on the table before him. He broke the loaf and held the pieces aloft, high over his head, as he almost shouted the words, "Look! The body of Christ, broken for the world! Bread of heaven! Bread for the world!" Then we listened as he poured the cups full, the aroma of the grapes filling the room.

Moving Ourselves Around

How we move ourselves around in the service makes a great difference in the perception of communion. In a recent service in a traditional Anglican church, full of heavy furniture, choir stalls, platform risers, steps to a lectern, and steps to the pulpit, the celebrant did a surprising thing. He invited the whole congregation to come forward and gather around the table for the Thanksgiving Prayer and the distribution.

It was crowded, with little children peeping over the table at chin level, some people standing close to the priest, others on different levels of steps as they clustered as close as they could to the table. Singing the congregational parts of the service was wonderfully immediate: "Lift up your hearts"; "Holy, holy, holy"; "Blessed is he who comes in the name of the Lord"; and "Behold the Lamb of God."

The acclamations were led by the priest, and the little child standing beside him mimicked his actions. "Christ has died. Christ is risen. Christ will come again!" The distribution was not as orderly as it would be if people had come up, as they usually did, in single file to the altar rail. But they managed it with ease. Then it was time for the final blessing and joyful song. What a memorable service!

We tried this same idea at a seminary chapel not long ago. There were fixed seats in the room, which doubled as a lecture hall. A high stage had a heavy pulpit and table, which they wheeled in for religious services. On this occasion the long communion table stood at center stage, pulpit looming nearby.

After the readings, songs, and sermon, we invited the students to come up and gather around the table. It wasn't easy because not everyone could get on the stage. Some leaned on the pulpit, some balanced on the edge of the stage, others stood on the steps. But we did it. Five people led the informal prayers of thanksgiving, read the Gospel narrative, broke and distributed the bread, and shared the cup. Singing broke out during the distribution, bringing a beautiful sense of joyful peace. This could not have happened if they had all sat in their fixed seats and we had stood behind the table up on the stage!

Visuals

These days, preachers use visual aids in creative preaching. Slide projectors and overhead projectors make this easy to do. Color transparencies from photographs or from book illustrations can enhance any part of a worship service – prayers, praise, notices, sermon, and even communion. Recently we preached on the parable of the waiting father, a theme Rembrandt worked on many times. We showed a particularly moving version in which the son, his back to us, buries his face in the father's knees. The father bends forward toward the son (and us) as he places his hands on the son's back.

It is easy to imagine oneself in the place of the son, and almost able to feel the father's hands on one's own shoulders. Because the theme of the sermon could integrate with the theme for the communion service, the overhead slide remained illuminated. It was like a special banner for that service, communicating a sense of forgiveness and grace which could never have been done with words alone.

20

Praying at the Table

PRAYERS HAVE always been closely associated with the Lord's Supper. In fact, the whole service is an act of prayer. In Acts 2:42 prayers are in the short list of activities of the Christian community – teaching, fellowship, breaking of bread, and prayers. There were sure to be different types of prayer, including the Lord's Prayer. Without doubt, intercessions were important. The writings of Paul, Peter, and James testify to this.

Intercessions at the Eucharist

Why are intercessory prayers particularly associated with the communion table? We remember that Jesus' High Priestly Prayer in John 17 models fervent, loving intercession and is within the same farewell section as John 13, the foot-washing chapter. Praying for each other is one obvious way for us to obey Jesus' new commandment, "Love one another as I have loved you."

As we saw in the ancient two-part pattern of eucharist – Service of the Word and Service of the Sacrament – the intercessory prayers conclude the first part. This is precisely where intercessions are prayed in Lutheran, Anglican, and Catholic services. The form of these intercessions is often a bidding (e.g., Let us pray for those in need), a short prayer which might end with the leader's petition, "Lord, hear us," followed by the congregation's response, "Lord, graciously hear us." Then would come the next bidding, prayer, and response.

The scope of these prayers is wide. Concerns range over many areas: the global church, the government, those in special need, peace, the local church, and special local involvements. Many churches in the liturgical traditions model the active participation of the congregation in the prayers. They are truly, according to the ancient naming, the "prayers of the people" and not a "pastoral prayer" by one person, in one voice alone. This is not to eliminate the minister's moving intercession for the people but is simply to say that the pastoral prayer does not displace the prayers of the people.

Further prayers of intercession may come at the heart of the service, immediately after the Great Thanksgiving with the words of institution. In the Catholic and Orthodox services before the breaking and sharing of bread and wine, prayers are made for those who have died (the church triumphant) and for the living (the church militant).

I have observed churches in nonliturgical traditions that have placed intercessions in a similar sequence. After they give thanks for God's great acts of creation and redemption and retell the story of Jesus at the Last Supper, they pause before actually breaking and sharing bread and cup.

This is to draw close to the Lord's table all those who long for God, those who suffer, those with whom the church has strong solidarity. Thus believers can dramatize that the Lord's table is for many, for the forgiveness of the sins of the world. This makes a loving space beside themselves for the world, whom Jesus has also invited to his Lord's table.

Including generous intercessory prayers at this point in the communion is one way to counteract a tendency toward congregational self-absorption or individualistic piety. Some congregations include prayers of thanksgiving for the faithfulness, testimony, and memory of members who have died.

The Lord's Prayer and Intercessions

The prayer Jesus taught his disciples, the Lord's Prayer, is the hallmark of Christian worship, the prayer of God's kingdom coming. In it we express longings for God's will and name to be honored and lived, now on this earth. Tertullian described a practical way in which this prayer was used in North Africa, phrase by phrase, as a framework for intercessions.[1]

From earliest times this prayer was closely associated with the eucharist. Its placement within the service varied, probably regulated by the importance of certain phrases of the prayer. The petition for bread drew the recitation of the prayer to be near the actual reception of the bread. In other regions, because of the importance of forgiveness in the Lord's Prayer, it came next to the kiss of peace. We can accurately picture those early Christians at prayer, standing with uplifted arms, the people mirroring the posture and gesture of the one presiding at the Lord's table.

Third-century Christians, after a service, took some of the blessed bread home with them so they could partake of it on every day of the week. The Lord's Prayer probably accompanied this daily "home communion."[2] Christians took seriously, as a command, Jesus' injunction to "pray like this" (Matt. 6:9a). The Lord's Prayer was at the heart of their piety and their corporate worship.

At the Reformation, in spite of leaders drastically "housecleaning" the Roman liturgy, the Lord's Prayer survived in the communion services of Reformed, Lutheran, and Anabaptist traditions alike. Using this prayer in the service of the Lord's table may well be as ancient a tradition as the very words of institution. Its use unites Christian communities across time, culture, and geography.

Early Christian Intercessions

There is strong historical evidence that Christians from earliest times prayed in the eucharist service for each other and for the world. Though not a prayer within an actual service, the reported prayer of the aged Bishop Polycarp upon his arrest must give evidence of the impulse and shape of intercession among the Christians of the mid second century.

When the police burst into his home, Polycarp calmly came downstairs to meet them, offered them food and drink, and asked permission to pray before they bound and took him away. The old man stood for two hours and prayed fervently "for all who had met with him at any time, both small and great, with or without renown; and for the whole universal Church throughout the world."[3]

A beautiful prayer for the whole church appears in the table prayers of the *Didache*. God is petitioned to "bring the church together from the ends of the earth into your kingdom."[4] There was clearly a sense of global solidarity among the various Christian communities.

Christians in mid-second-century Rome prayed for themselves, those just baptized, and Christians everywhere. These prayers were integrated into their eucharistic worship. Similarly, fourth-century Syrian Christians prayed lengthy intercessions after the Great Thanksgiving (which included the words of institution) and just before the communion. These early Christians always included prayers for their rulers. Their prayers were addressed to God through the Lord Jesus Christ, their Intercessor and High Priest. Christ was himself at the heart of all Christian praying.

Prayers in the assembly were done corporately, not simply spoken by one leader. Egeria, a fourth-century Spanish religious tourist to Jerusalem, described how one of the deacons would read a list of petitions. As he called each one out, the crowd would answer, "Kyrie eleison" (Lord, have mercy). From Syria in the same period, we have the actual words of the petitions and the directive, "At each petition which the deacon pronounces, the people shall say, 'Kyrie eleison,' especially the children." These petitions were for the well-being of the whole church, for the leaders of the church, for all people and the emperor, for the sick, for those traveling, for the poor, for benefactors of the church, and for peace.

This kind of prayer, with its individual petitions and congregational responses, was called a litany. When introduced into the Latin-speaking West, the Greek response Kyrie eleison sometimes remained unchanged, although in some places it was expanded and translated into Latin. In the Orthodox liturgy of the Eastern churches, this precise form of intercessions with responses has continued unaltered to the present day.

The ancient litany with Kyries survived in a Western form called *Deprecatio Gelasii*, an extended text of fifteen petitions with congregational responses.[5] The petitions are on behalf of a holy and universal church, that it should have peace, protection from dangers, that it should bring forth fruits, that it be a leaven for divine power in the world, that it should know unity and love, and that the Holy Spirit should lead and govern its life.

This so-called General Prayer of the Church was dropped in the fifth century when intercessions and mementos for the living and the dead were inserted into the heart of the eucharistic prayer. Later, specific petitions in time of great need were inserted next to the Lord's Prayer. Unlike the Eastern churches, the Western Latin churches did not allow for prayers and petitions in the language of the local people.

Intercessions as Response to God's Goodness and Mercy

Whenever Christians remember the gracious gifts of redemption, healing, and forgiveness, it is utterly natural that we should turn in loving remembrance to those in need of God's shalom. We are selfish if we enjoy and celebrate God's kindness to us and simply neglect to pass on our experience of love and grace. Praying for others is one of the best ways to "love your neighbor." At the communion table, we focus on God's love for the world and Jesus' matchless gift of sacrifice for us. That love and that gift are for the whole of God's creation, and we have our part to play in channeling them onward.

Healing Prayers in the Communion Service

These days many churches include a ministry of personal prayers within the eucharist. In larger congregations, those who wish for special prayer may ask for it just before receiving the bread and wine. Or there may be an adjacent area set aside. Attention is not focused on this ministry, because others are continuing to come forward to receive the bread and wine. There may be soft singing or instrumental music accompanying the movement of the congregation as they go forward to receive. The person requesting prayer briefly states a need to the one offering prayer. The person who ministers then offers a brief prayer, petitioning a blessing for God's wholesome peace in every area of life – forgiveness of sins and healing and restoring of the spirit and body. It is appropriate to use a simple form of prayer and blessing, perhaps the same words for each person.

Sometimes there is anointing with oil. This is never a counseling session nor an exorcism. A person might request prayer for someone else, or prayer for safety, healing, clarity. Anyone can go for these brief prayers – visitors, members, and particularly the elders and ministers of the church themselves. It is moving to see gifted pray-ers, members of the church, praying for those who are called as ministers and pastors to the church.

A Sample Prayer in Healing Service

May God grant you the powerful presence of the Holy Spirit,

forgiving your sin, releasing you from suffering, and restoring you to health. May God deliver you from all evil, preserve you in all goodness, and bring you to everlasting life, through Jesus Christ our Savior.[6]

I once saw a whole family of parents and children go forward for prayer for their elderly relative who was ill. I shall never forget the sight of the little children kneeling there, intent and serious in their intercession of love. Meanwhile, the congregation moved past them to receive the bread and wine, and then to return to their seats, singing, Jesus, Lamb of God, have mercy upon us. Grant us your peace."

However, this happens not only in the liturgical churches. Free churches too are learning ways to extend forgiveness, healing prayers, and compassionate silence to those in need, all in the context of the communion service.

We confess our sins and receive God's forgiveness when we come to the Lord's table. Now we need to learn better ways to become people of forgiveness and healing. One way to do this is to make space and time within our communion services for God's healing love to flow through us. We may always include a "Shalom Prayer" in the intercessions. This could be an informal prayer, but it would include the same concerns as the one above: affirming that it is God's Spirit who brings forgiveness, release from suffering, deliverance from the power of evil, and restoration of the whole person to wholesome goodness.

When the congregation prays the Lord's Prayer, "Forgive us our sins as we pass on that forgiveness to others," the whole people will become a channel of healing. As God heals their infirmities, they pass on prayers for healing for those who suffer around them in the world. This is what it means to become a people of shalom.

Thanksgiving Prayers at the Table

We have considered prayers of intercession and of healing at the eucharist. All our prayers are clothed with thanksgiving. That is the essence of Christian prayer in response to the mercy and faithfulness of God. And so we come to the heart of the eucharist service – the Great Prayer of Thanksgiving. It would be inappropriate for free-church congregations simply to use eucharistic prayers from the service books of the liturgical churches. But it can be helpful to look closely at those prayers, and to appropriate key phrases and the general scope of the prayer. Here are some specific ideas for enriching the thanksgiving prayers at free-church communion tables.

1. We do well to emulate the thanksgiving prayers of early Christian communities. From earliest times these prayers had certain characteristics. Typical of such communion prayers are the following:

a. Thanks for God's goodness in all of creation
b. Thanks for the faithfulness of God's witness through holy people and prophets throughout the ages
c. Thanks for God's acts of redemption in Jesus' life, ministry, and death
d. Thanks for Jesus' faithfulness to God's will
e. Thanks for God's vindication of Jesus in the resurrection
f. Thanks for the confirming and empowering presence of the Holy Spirit in the church

2. These same qualities will typify our prayers at the Lord's table. Whether we use set services or pray extemporaneously, the whole point of the communion prayers is "to give thanks and praise" to God. Here is the beginning of a New Zealand Anglican thanksgiving prayer which breathes a spirit of simple thanks, which delights in creation, and marvels at the mystery of redemption:

> It is the joy of our salvation, God of the universe,
> to give you thanks through Jesus Christ.
> You said, "Let there be light"; and there was light.
> Your light shines on in our darkness.
> For you the earth has brought forth life in all its forms.

3. Another example of a spirited thanksgiving prayer comes from the French Reformed Church. It begins like this:

> Yes, it is our joy,
> O God of love and holiness, our Creator and our Father,
> to give you thanks always and everywhere.
> In your image you made us all,
> your universe you put in our care;
> your creation you entrusted to our hands,
> with all its wonders and its travail.[7]

4. Baptists often begin their extemporaneous prayers of thanksgiving at the Lord's table with Scripture. They choose texts about God's redeeming love and care. A joyful response of thanksgiving springs naturally from the following verses:

> What shall I render unto the Lord for all his benefits toward me? I will take up the cup of salvation and call upon the name of the Lord. I will pay my vows to the Lord in the presence of all his people.   (Ps. 116:12-14, KJV)

Christ died for us while we were yet sinners, and this is God's own proof of his love towards us.   (Rom. 5:8, NEB)

God so loved the world that he gave his ... only Son, that whoever believes in him shall not perish but have eternal life.
(John 3:16, NIV)

For you did not receive a spirit that makes you a slave again to fear, but you received the Spirit of sonship. And by him we cry, "Abba, Father." The Spirit himself testifies with our spirit that we are God's children.   (Rom. 8:15-16, NIV)

5. A thanksgiving prayer at the communion table which ensures breadth includes these elements:

Introduction – "Eternal, living God ..."
Adoration – Thanks for God's gifts
 in creation
 in providence and in society
 in the church fellowship
 in Jesus Christ
Memorial – of the incarnation, ministry, death, resurrection,
 ascension of Christ
Something appropriate to the day – season, events, texts
Invocation of the Holy Spirit
Offering of ourselves

6. The earliest prayers at the liturgy were often Christian adaptations of Jewish blessings similar to this:

Blessed are you, Lord our God, King of the universe, for you
 nourish us and the whole world with goodness, grace, kindness,
 and mercy.
Blessed are you, Lord, for you nourish the universe.

The tone of respect and honor for creation carried over into early Christian thanksgivings, along with the unfolding story of redemption. Prayers and blessings within the communion service help us to commit ourselves anew to our creation task – the responsible care of the natural world.

Prayers and Thanksgivings for the Holy Spirit's Action

We now come to a sensitive area. It has to do with the theology of what happens to the bread and wine at the time of the Prayer of Consecration. This is sometimes made quite clear, as in the Catholic mass; sometimes it is less clear, as in Anglican services. Compare these phrases from Catholic and Anglican sources:

> May the Holy Spirit sanctify these offerings. Let them become the body and blood of Jesus Christ our Lord ... Father, we bring you these gifts. We ask you to make them holy by the power of your Spirit, that they may become the body and blood of your Son, our Lord Jesus Christ ... (Catholic mass[8])

> Grant that by the power of your Holy Spirit, these gifts of bread and wine may be to us his body and blood. (Rite A, 1; Rite B, 2)

> Grant that by the power of your Holy Spirit we who receive these gifts of your creation, this bread and this wine ... may be partakers of his most blessed body and blood.
> (Rite A, 4; Rite B, 1;Church of England[9])

One point of conflict among Christian traditions has been over whose gifts are the bread and wine. Does the emphasis fall on our gifts, or on God's gift? The words *offering* and *gifts* touch sensitive nerve ends. The words *make them holy* and the name *Prayer of Consecration* focus another debate – that of what it means to make the bread and wine holy.

Notice that in one of the Anglican phrases, the power of the Holy Spirit is to make a change in the partakers, in the people, rather than in the bread and wine. The other Anglican expression, "may be to us," is vague enough to satisfy people of varying theology.

Protestants reject the idea of praying for the Holy Spirit to enter objects, not persons. The New Testament records the coming of the Spirit upon individuals and groups of people. It is appropriate to shape communion prayer in a Trinitarian balance. The following are suitable prayers and expressions which ensure reference to the work of the Spirit.

1. We are your new creation in Christ;
   Fill us with your Spirit,
   to bring good news to the poor,
   to heal the brokenhearted,
   to announce release to captives
   and freedom to prisoners.
   As we eat this bread and drink this wine,

   (*response of the people*)
   Come, Holy Spirit, flow through us
   fill our sacrifice of praise and thanksgiving
   with your power and love.[10]

2. By your Holy Spirit sanctify us
   and these your gifts of bread and wine,
that the bread which we break
   may be the communion of the body of Christ,
and the cup which we bless
   may be the communion of the blood of Christ.
Give us grace to share his sufferings
   and to know the power of his resurrection,
that we may be made one and evermore abide in him,
   to your praise and glory.[11]

3. We beseech you, send over us your Holy Spirit,
   and give a new face to this earth which is dear to us.

   May there be peace wherever people live,
   the peace which we cannot make ourselves,
   and that is more powerful than all violence,
   your peace like a bond,
   a new covenant binding all people together
      in the love of Jesus Christ, here among us.[12]

WHAT COMES FROM COMMUNION?

21

Character

Communion Builds Community

COMMUNION BUILDS character. Throughout this book we have considered various facets both of communion and of character. We have thought about how the two are related. It isn't just simple cause and effect. We don't assume that the quick way to a good result – Christian virtues – is to schedule more communion services.

It might be more like a flowering plant. The blooms are Christlike evidences of the vigorous life of the plant. The roots reach down and draw up God's grace and love. Perhaps a healthy eucharistic life is represented by the green stems and leaves. As in Jesus' own parable of vine and branches, all is connected together. The life sap of God's love flows unimpeded throughout every fiber and cell of the vine. A healthy Christian community blooms and gives fruit true to its God-given character.

Continuing the image of the plant, we see that the structure and strength of the green stems matter. They must be strong and resilient. So it is with the forms of our eucharistic worship. We need traditions and patterns; we need familiar forms and disciplined freedoms. Through these strong stems, then, God's love sap can reach to all the cells, enabling them to flourish and become fully what God desires for them.

We Become Who We Are

Is there one facet or quality of character which is more important than all the others, one fundamental, distinctive mark of Christian character? I think so. I think it is the impulse toward commonality, an impulse which is so beautifully expressed and fulfilled in eucharistic worship.

Simply assembling together, the first act of Christian worship, is one of the most significant things we do. Why on a Sunday morning don't we just stay at home or drive around in our cars, listening to religious music? As we are drawn to common worship, we contradict the primary impulse of Western individualism. No longer just Miguel and Sarah and John, we gather ourselves in the name of Christ. We take on a corporate name – church. We become a coherent body, drawn to each other because of our shared commitment to our Lord and to his kingdom coming.

213

We come together not for separate praying but to assemble as the church. When we go to church, we go into that assembly to "constitute the church." We go to exercise what we became on the day of our baptism – "members, in the fullest, absolute meaning of the term, of the body of Christ."[1]

We come together not just to gain personal comfort, friendship, and strength. God draws us together to fulfill our calling to be the church: "a holy nation, a royal priesthood, a chosen people." We, together, manifest and confess the presence of Christ and his kingdom in the world (1 Pet. 2:9, NIV). How do we show and confess the mystery and power of Christ and his kingdom? No better symbol, no better drama, could we imagine, than the one we have been given – the table of the Lord. It is Christ's table around which we gather, the table at which we receive bread and wine, his gifts made holy. It is at his table where we offer prayers and thankful praise. It is in this table gathering that we become who we are – the true body of Christ in and for our world.

A Storied People

However, it is not enough just to confirm that we come together. What is it that calls us back again and again? What is the strongest characteristic of our gathering? It is our storytelling. There is enormous power in bringing individuals into "the orbit of God's love manifested in a story told, a rite repeated and a community committed to that way of looking at the world which reflects that story and shares the same experience."[2]

It works like the song of an old nursery rhyme. We tell and retell the story demonstrating God's love. We repeat the rite which retells the story demonstrating God's love. We constitute the community which repeats the rite and thus retells the story demonstrating God's love. The community, the rite, the story – all these mediums interplay to shape the character of our loving involvement in the world. Through retelling and reenacting the great story, we are enabled to incarnate in our everyday life the life of God, a truly sacramental and holy-making process.

The Holy Story Shapes a Holy People

Eating and drinking at the Lord's table is holy action for a holy people. Our holiness is of "a people who have learned not to fear one another, a people capable of love." We live freely, in truthfulness, with one another, without envy or greed. We receive and pass on forgiveness, using the symbol of shared food, made a holy sacrament in Christ's presence. We learn that "forgiveness of the enemy, even when the enemy is ourselves, is the way God would have his kingdom accomplished."[3]

In his exploration of enculturation of the gospel among Masai people, Vincent Donovan describes a ritual gesture, employed during a communal disagreement, of passing a handful of grass to indicate that no offense is intended, no violence will ensue. Preparation for mass involves praying for the sick, dancing, discussions, passing of the grass – every activity of the village. Yet it is not obvious that eucharist will emerge from all of it. The leaders of the village must decide when the time is right.

> If there had been selfishness and forgetfulness and hatefulness and lack of forgiveness, ... let them not make a sacrilege out of it by calling it the body of Christ. If the grass had stopped, or if someone had refused to accept the grass as the sign of the peace of Christ, there could be no eucharist at this time.[4]

Forgiveness and truthful transparency are two virtues that mark a graced community. Spinning out for the eucharistic community the implications of the "big three" – faith, hope, and love – a creative way, full of surprises, opens up. Living "out of control," the holy people seek not powerful effectiveness, but faithfulness. They live in expectant patience, yearning for God's justice. They are prepared for miracles. Expanding a well-known definition, Stanley Hauerwas observes that the church is truly known "where the sacraments are celebrated, the word is preached, and upright lives are encouraged and lived."[5] It all fits together. Word. Sacrament. Character.

22

Unity

One in Christ, One at the Table
"I ASK, ... [FATHER], ... on behalf of those who will believe in me, ... that they may all be one. As you, Father, are in me and I am in you, may they also be [one] in us, so that the world may believe that you have sent me" (John 17:20-21). We hear Jesus praying that believers should know unity through the Spirit and within the Father's will. He invites his friends and disciples to express and delight in this unity at his table.

Is there greater joy than in receiving this gift of sharing bread and wine at Lord's table with newfound brothers and sisters? Although I would not consider trying to take communion by false pretenses in a church which I know refuses such inter-communion, I have taken part in communions in the context of conferences or retreats with Christians of various backgrounds. As we worked through issues of common faith, biblically and practically, we truly became one in seeking fruitful discipleship to the same Lord. To share communion seemed not only natural but necessary. We received it together with joy, a gift from Christ himself.

However, such events are scarce. More common is the story told by a friend of mine, a young married woman. She had recently moved into a new neighborhood. She took her fourteen-year-old brother, who was visiting for the weekend, along to a small church on the next road. They hadn't noticed this church before, but they responded to a friendly invitational flyer in the mailbox and decided to visit one Sunday morning.

The brother was dubious, but the sister thought they should go. Their parents had raised them to regular participation in a church back home, and they hadn't found a local church home in this town.

The greeter at the door shook their hands and said, "You're new here, aren't you? You're welcome to attend the service, but of course you can't take communion with us. It's only for members."

The sister protested a bit, stating that they were both baptized Christians. But it wasn't good enough. If they had brought a letter from their church at home, maybe they could be eligible. Surprisingly, the visitors stayed on to sing hymns and listen to the sermon, but only to watch the communion service!

What word can describe the scene on that church porch? Insensitive? Principled? Rude? Inhospitable? Muddle-headed? What would Paul say of such communion? Would he be as severe as he was with the church at Corinth? "The supper you celebrate is not the Lord's supper!" Do we regard it demeaning when we ask people of faith to pass by the bread and cup just because they come from the "wrong communion"? What is more shocking than that Christians, indifferent to the scandal of "separation," refuse to eat and drink together at the Lord's table!

In their early days, the Taizé community dreamed of having one eucharistic table for Christians of all traditions. But they soon recognized that they had to face the reality of divided Christianity. On one side of the large central table, they had a table for distribution to Catholics, and on the other side they had one for Protestants.

For centuries, among major liturgical traditions, there has been the sense that the separated churches can share communion only after they have united in all matters of faith and life. Many have been unable to imagine eucharist as a means toward unity. For them, it must serve as a climax and proof of unity.

Radicals at the other end of the spectrum refuse even to use the term "inter-communion" because it falsely implies that there could be more than one communion. Has not the Lord invited all believers to join him at his table? Surely there is only one communion, one koinonia, one Lord with whom Christians unite at the Lord's table!

Most of the discussion ranges, however, around a middle ground. When is there sufficient common ground of unity so that Christians can share the eucharist? Is it possible both to express that sufficient unity and also to foster further fellowship? How do we resolve the dilemmas posed by different views of ministry and presidency at the table? Can we recognize the validity of varying practices of baptism and understandings of its relation to participation at the table?

Though the problems are daunting, there are reasons to be hopeful that some liturgical Christians are moving in the direction of table fellowship. Where their leaders and scholars have together studied the history and prayers of the early Christians, many Western denominations are adopting compatible eucharistic structures, formulations, and texts. There is a wide and growing consensus on many aspects of eucharistic practice.

For example, there is general agreement on a sequence of events within eucharistic services: In the service of the Word – Old Testament readings, New Testament readings, sermon, prayers of intercession; and in the service of the sacrament – taking up, giving thanks for, breaking, and sharing the bread and wine. Common lectionaries are increasingly used among varied denominations.

All churches accept the Scriptures as God's Word, authoritative for their faith and life. Surely this is a strong basis for unity.

The Apostles' Creed also is accepted by Eastern Orthodox, Western Catholic, and Protestant communions alike. It "gives verbal expression to the whole Christian mystery. On that basis, Christians of all these churches are one community of professed belief. They are not justified in keeping separate tables."[1]

There are three further areas of drawing together. Today the widely used expression "doing the memory of Christ" reveals a dynamic understanding of eucharistic remembrance. Remembrance is not static, nor is it just a verbal or mental process. There is also more emphasis on the eucharist as the eschatological banquet of the kingdom of God. In sharing the cup, we "share a destiny, and participation in the eucharist gives rendezvous with Christ in the final kingdom."[2]

Furthermore, the current Roman Catholic tendency to use language of "transsignification" rather than of "transubstantiation" moves away from concepts of change in the elements toward the importance of what the Lord makes of the elements in the gathering of his people around the table. The bread and the wine become vehicles of his presence.

In spite of hopeful movements toward shared communion, severe obstacles continue to block the path. They include unwillingness to recognize another tradition's forms of ministry, contrasting views on the relation between eucharistic participation and baptism, and church discipline.

If drawing together to a common table happens only slowly among the larger and liturgical Christian traditions, it seems among other Christian groups to have little hope of happening at all. The contradictory welcome to the young woman and her brother on the church porch illustrates it well. It is fine for a church to have private meetings for members only, whether for decision-making, prayers, or shared meals, including communion meals. But the shock comes in ineptly trying to combine mission invitations with close communion. That church did not have a theology clear enough to underpin the challenges they faced.

Such closed groups often delight in their own local unity in the Spirit. They give thanks for good times, for times of reconciliation, for foundational times of vision and empowering of the Spirit within their own circle. At their communion services, they celebrate their peace and unity, necessary in preparing for the table. But it is a unity they foster in other settings of the congregation's life. The table does not serve as a focus for effecting peace, nor as a locus for receiving peace as gracious gift. Anticipation of a mystical presence of Christ reveals an almost pre-Pentecost spirituality. Sharing communion with other Christians certainly is not on the agenda.

On the other hand, churches of Restoration movements make an open invitation for people to participate at the Lord's table according to the call of their own consciences. The Lord's Supper restores, expresses, and effects New Testament unity. Following Christ's institution, these churches consider the weekly Sunday Lord's Supper central to their own congregational worship life. Inviting others to participate, they perceive their emphasis on "taking openly" in line with an apostolic and Restorationist plea for unity among Christians "in essential matters."[3]

All traditions are ultimately accountable to Christ himself. Does our approach to accepting other Christians at our table fulfill Jesus' high-priestly prayer? Does our way of doing things "smell" like the gospel? Can any other criteria be more important?

23

Mission

JESUS HAS MARKED us with his unmistakable character. He calls us into communion both with himself and with one another, into a unity which is a miracle of the Spirit's love. At his table, Jesus also calls us to join his mission, drawing people into the freedom of forgiven life.

Pervading his teachings and life were Jesus' commitments to reveal the Father's character of loving mercy, and to invite people into fellowship with the Father. His favorite mediums of communication were story and acted story, shot through with the imagery of the kingdom and of the heavenly banquet.

In celebrating the Supper, we do it too. We retell and reenact the story of Jesus. The stories of the kingdom and of the heavenly banquet operate on several planes at once. They bring together in the present moment the past (memory of the liberating life, teachings, and suffering of Christ), with the future (prefiguring of the fullness of Christ's completed work of redemption, and the new creation). In the kingdom meal, these three planes come together – past, present, and future. The church, in three-part perspective, can truly understand the times in which we live and grasp the tasks to which we are called. In the Lord's Supper we explore the perspectives and express the practicalities of kingdom life.

The Lord's Supper, with its multiple levels of meaning, is a sign of the kingdom. It is a sign of Christ. It is a sign of hope. The Lord's meal is an open meal, shared at a big table. It is a meal of joyful fellowship in which the church declares and demonstrates "the peace and righteousness of God [for] the world."[1]

In this final chapter on "Mission," we consider a question which points to the future: How faithfully is the church declaring and demonstrating God's reconciling invitation to the "many"? We will look at church obstacles to Christ's vision. And we will look at Alpha, a form of mission. This may suggest steps toward a renewed quality of eucharistic worship flowing with Christ's vision for his table to be a delicious appetizer course of the heavenly banquet.

The Lord's Table Drawing People to the Lord

First, let us recount a story which reminds us that God works with people at surprising times and in spite of our unpromising ways. Here a woman's understanding that communion is only for proper Christians blinded her to the missionary moment. But she made a quick recovery. Christ slipped past her ineptness to receive a person whom he called to his table.

She was a Christian who was sitting with her unbelieving husband at a simple communion service. The plate of bread came along their row. She took. He reached.

She warned, "You can't. You're not a Christian."

"But I want to be one."

"Well, you'd better be quick."

Another story of the Lord's table as a place for conversion comes from a friend who was in charge of a young people's weekend retreat. One young man, not a believer, nevertheless during the course of the weekend, through earnest involvement in study and discussion, was drawn to faith in Christ. My friend led the closing service, communion, and invited "all those who are Christians to take part."

At that moment his eyes turned toward the young man. So he impulsively expanded the invitation. "If you would like to declare your faith in Christ by coming to the table, please freely respond to the invitation of the Lord. This is the Lord's table. You are welcome to meet him here."

The young man came to the table.

John Wesley would have smiled. He was so confident of Christ's presence in the communion that he spoke of the "converting power of the eucharist." Any who seek will find God at the table, where forgiveness and grace are poured out, where Christ's life in his people is broken open, poured out, and generously shared. Christ continuously refreshes and renews all who will come to his table. He gives an open invitation – one facet of his gracious mission.

The Shape of Jesus' Mission

The new covenant – God, church, "the many"

The missionary wife had unwittingly stumbled across one arm of the three-way covenant which God inaugurated first with Abraham, then anew in the work of Jesus. Jesus didn't just invent a new covenant and make up a new rite to ratify it. Jesus fulfilled the old covenant. He made it new in his death and showed the way the vision of the old flowed on through the new.

God gave Abraham more than a personal promise. God gave him a vocation which grew out of the fruit of the promise. With a new identity as God's set-apart people, Abraham's descendants would become vehicles for God's blessing. All nations, all peoples of the earth, were to be eligible for divine salvation. The three-point triangle of the old covenant put God, God's people, and the nations into relationship. Each of the three touched the other two.[2]

It is the same with the new covenant, brought into effect through Jesus' self-giving sacrifice. Jesus instituted the new covenant in its three dimensions in the cup of blessing at the Last Supper. The points of the new triangle again read: "God," "People of God," and "The Nations." The new covenant in Jesus' blood is simply God's new order of salvation. It is salvation not just for a righteous few who fit the right preconditions, but for "the many" (everyone). The new covenant is to be one of blessing and service (not domination), and it is for the benefit of "all nations."[3]

Churchy "drags" – theological, moral, hierarchical

If we call our communion service the Lord's Supper, then we must recognize that it is the Lord himself who issues the invitations, both to the feast which celebrates the new covenant, and to the vision it embraces. It is the Lord's invitation, not the church's invitation, which establishes fellowship at the table. If we limit the invitation, setting up our own conditions, don't we almost forfeit the right to call our communion Lord's Supper?

The Lord's table is where we celebrate God's liberating forgiveness. It is not the place to exercise "discipline" according to human worthiness in the eyes of oneself or in a church's evaluation. No one is worthy, except Christ alone. The Lord's Supper is not meant to be a meal of repentance. Precisely because of the church's undue emphasis on confession, absolution, and unworthiness, many sensitive and needy people excommunicate themselves from the table. The Lord's table is spread for a feast of joy, not of worrisome lament.

"Everyone whom [Christ] calls and who follows his call, has authority to break the bread and disperse the wine. The administration of the Supper is the 'ministry' of the whole congregation and every person who is called."[4] Is this true? Doesn't it contradict restrictions, elaborate or blunt, through churches' (hierarchical) ordination patterns?

Christ himself not only invites us; he is the one who serves (ministers) at the table. He invites the church, the whole body, to enter into his self-giving ministry at the table, too. No biblical texts specify "ordained" intermediaries. There is a sense in which the church's historic ministry structures, separating the people from the ministry of the Lord's table, have masked not only the nature of Christ's invitation to his table but also to the vision and to the task which the table represents.

The shape of Jesus' vision can inspire the shape of worship at the Lord's table. But it may mean pruning away what impedes – our need to control access to the forgiveness and joy of the Lord's fellowship, our traditions of control over who, when, and how the benefits of the table are dispensed. The Lord's own table is an open table, served by an open ministry, and leading to an open mission. How do the tables of our churches compare?

Open Friendship and an Open Table

Many churches are learning new ways to provide access to the converting power of the Lord's table. New forms of mission hold together a generous invitation to the table with a realistic reckoning of the personal cost of following Jesus on his way.

Alpha,[5] an approach to mission now gaining widespread application in a wide range of Christian denominations, unites Jesus' own favorite methods – friendship and table fellowship. It was devised in the mid-1980s as a ten-week practical introduction to Christianity for both nonchurchgoers and new Christians. One person described it as "cringe-free evangelism." Friendship is at the heart of Alpha. So is the shared meal. There are many permutations and local adaptations, so the following description of one Alpha course is not a universal model.

Norman comes to the table

Six members of a congregation each invited one guest to an early evening dinner in the church fellowship rooms. Two additional members of the church were present, preparing the meal, serving it, and joining at the table. Each guest was in some sense on the fringe of the church. Before the course began, the various pairs of host and guest had lots of conversation about church or about struggles for values and directions for life.

The intention of the first evening's after-meal discussion was clear. It was a time to air questions and discuss the attitudes that people had of Christianity. Is Christianity boring? Is it irrelevant? Untrue? It was to be a session for listening and finding out if Alpha would be a safe setting in which to explore participants' inner questions of faith.

This Alpha course had fifteen sessions, always with the same small group, always gathered around a meal table, ranging over question topics from "Who is Jesus?" and "Why should I pray?" to "What about the church?" and "How can I make the most of the rest of my life?" The meal servers were also teachers, prepared with prayer and Bible knowledge as well as with skills to listen closely to the guests for underlying questions.

One of the participants was Norman, a man in his sixties who never attended church. But he always drove his wife there, sat in the car, and read the Sunday paper until she came out. Church? They had stopped discussing it twenty years ago. They had just settled into a habitual pattern. He sat in the car. She went to church. Surprising the wife, another church member invited Norman to Alpha. Surprising himself, Norman agreed to go. So began his serious yet enjoyable journey to faith.

During the final session, the group decided to spend a half day together at a country retreat house where they could hold their common meal together after spending some time enjoying the grounds and the surrounding countryside. Their final dinner would be a eucharistic meal. In it they would specifically remember the Last Supper, give thanks with bread and wine, and receive through prayers whatever God wanted to give to any participants. The teacher suggested that during the afternoon they each walk separately. As they walked, they might initiate a conversation with God.

At the table that evening, the teacher asked, without using coercion, if anybody wanted to tell about their conversations with God. Norman, holding the cup of wine in his hands, told with tears how God had invited him "to come home." That was just what he wanted to do. He declared his intentions, prayed a simple prayer of faith, and drank from the cup, breathing out a great sigh of quiet relief.

Alpha allows the Lord's table to become a focus for mission, for the nurture of tender faith. Alpha courses are sometimes large events, using small groups within the larger for safe discussion and friendship. They are held in restaurants, in homes, even outdoors in warmer climates.

Covenant, friendship, and the shared meal – the shape of Jesus' mission
The new-covenant link to God's heart is friendship, desiring that all people be drawn to love, forgiveness, and freedom. This is well expressed in the shared meal. Such natural approaches marked Jesus' ministry. How can we do without them? Some, commending an approach such as Alpha, say that it is a mission strategy based on friendship and conducted with hospitality. It could help to "get them in." But, they would say, it has nothing to do with Sunday worship.

They assume that this mission method would be good for sinners but is not necessary for us who are already "in." I wonder. Isn't it possible that a way to renewal of Sunday eucharistic worship could be through reclaiming Jesus' own approaches of love for outsiders, his radical invitations, and his generous table hospitality?

The Great Song of the Supper

Why does Alpha ring bells for us? It resonates in the major key of the great song of the Lord's Supper. Among the many theological and practical themes that Christian communities have interwoven at the table, two principal tunes stick out:

1. Jesus willingly ate with sinners.
2. Jesus shared his table with his own disciples.

For much of Christian history, these two tunes have seemed dissonant. It seemed impossible at the same time to be both open and closed. Yes, the church should approve the openness of Christ's meals during his ministry, his imagery of the banquet of the kingdom, his association with sinners as well as with the righteous.

But how can that be done within the confines of a rite which memorialized the Last Supper? Shouldn't the Lord's Supper be for an inner circle of disciples, an occasion to reflect soberly on the sacrificial death of Christ? How can these two themes of Christian tradition be sung together? Is there any way to make them harmonize?

The meanings of Christ's open table with sinners and the disciples' meal share a profound theological foundation. They are both meals of the kingdom of God. They are both signs of the Christian hope of the kingdom, present and coming anew.

Jesus, eating with sinners and tax collectors, enacted a powerful and controversial sign of the gospel of the kingdom. Unique in those meals was Jesus' anticipation of the "feast of the righteous" with the unrighteous, who are made righteous through his presence. Jesus dramatically accepted the sinners, boldly shared God's forgiveness, all to the horror of the religious establishment.

However, what if Jesus had only said words of acceptance and forgiveness? What if he had never acted out what acceptance and forgiveness would look like in human society? As always, Jesus' actions and words reinforced each other. Jesus' provocative meal fellowship with sinners blazed a messianic sign, bringing to light what God's radical invitation to reconciliation and freedom could mean.

Meals with tax collectors and sinners were not Jesus' only ones. In the days of his earthly ministry, Jesus regularly ate and drank with his disciples too, and in doing so they anticipated eating and drinking together in the kingdom of God. Clearly Jesus understood it in this way. At the Last Supper he declared that he would "never again drink of the fruit of the vine until that day when I drink it new in the kingdom of God" (Mark 14:25). Jesus, in their shared meals, offered his disciples a foretaste of the kingdom banquet.

Through this enacted and dramatic image of the Great Banquet, Jesus drew his disciples into his own messianic ministry. The Last Supper was one in a sequence of such enacted signs of the kingdom – shared meals. In that upper room the disciples held fellowship with Jesus, and through the common bread and shared cup, Jesus called them into his own mission. That meal was not a prototype for exclusive meals enjoyed by a righteous few. It was "the meal of Jesus' friends, who participate in his mission 'to seek that which was lost.'"[6]

The church's memory of the Last Supper is overlaid with memories of post-resurrection meals, in which Jesus again ate with the disciples, and commissioned them through the Spirit into the mission that lay ahead for them. He sent them out to continue his own gospel vocation.

Thus the meaning of the upper room meal is not primarily in its remembrance of the historical Last Supper. Its full meaning can be received only in the living presence of the risen Christ. We grasp the Lord's Supper not only in the memory of Christ's suffering sacrifice but also in the light of Easter and in confident hope of the kingdom coming.

Both types of meals – the sinners' meals and the disciples' meals – were messianic feasts. Both types contribute to a unified understanding of the Lord's Supper. Through the sinners' meals, Jesus enacted the vision of the Great Banquet to which "people will come from east and west, from north and south, and will eat in the kingdom of God" (Luke 13:29). Through the disciples' meals, Jesus invited his friends into his messianic vocation. Open and outward – these are the impulses of both Jesus' vision and his vocation.

The Long View

In the last section of this book, we have stepped back to take in the bigger view. Recalling Jesus' vocation and looking with his perspective, we see that to the farthest horizon and beyond, all is marked out with the love of God. With his love God claims all of creation, and he longs to bring it all to fulfillment. In this loving mission, God has a surprisingly unique place for the church. God will reveal the richness of his wisdom through the church (Eph. 3:10).

The New Testament tells us that God's wisdom is Jesus-shaped. The world will especially learn to know God's love through the self-giving sacrifice of Christ and the corresponding self-giving service of his church. Our calling is to be directly involved in God's work of reconciling the world through Christ. We, as co-workers with Christ, are to enter into the divine ministry of peacemaking.

With such a job description, the church needs great vision and limitless resources. Fortunately, through the Holy Spirit, we are given what we need. One of the richest resources of all is the gift of eucharist.

The Table of the Kingdom of God

Let us picture a Sunday assembly of Christians gathered around the central table of the kingdom, an assembly which mirrors the concerns of the Lord's Prayer, and of the Lord who taught us to pray.

Coming together in unity at the Lord's table, we renew our identity as people of God's holy name. Our vision of God's will and reign lifts us above the daily grind. In confident hope we receive forgiveness and the daily bread for our life – unmistakable signs of the kingdom coming. We reconcile our differences in the name of Jesus, and we pledge to share generously what we have. Then we turn outward to the task God has given to us.

Entreating God's protection in the face of the opposition of "rulers and

226

authorities in the heavenly places" (Eph. 3:10), we move away from the table, into the world marked out with God's love. We are kept safe in times of testing by the power of the Spirit, as we go out, co-workers in Jesus' mission.

Along the way we encounter brothers and sisters. We find that we share the same task. Along the way together, we find people whom God is longing to invite to the Great Banquet.

The day of salvation is at hand. The banquet is prepared. The Lord himself invites us, saints and sinners, to come in with Abraham, Isaac, and Jacob. Let us join the festivities at his table.

Appendix A

Planning a Communion Service

IN THE twentieth century, virtually all Christian traditions have attempted to restore and enrich both roots of Christian worship—the Jewish one centering on the Scripture with prayers, and the uniquely Christian one centering on the service of shared bread-and-cup. Nowhere in the New Testament is there an order for Lord's day worship. But we can infer that certain activities were included: readings from Scripture, psalms or hymns, teaching and application to life, prayers, praise and thanks to God, holy kiss, bread-and-cup ceremony.

Justin Martyr describes Roman Christian worship of the mid-second century in some detail. But the text called the *Apostolic Tradition* of 215 gives the most detailed evidence of both structure and content. The worship was not fixed in its words, though a suggested form of words is given for much of the service. It is clear that people could pray extempore, and there was expectation of informal contributions to the worship. The *Apostolic Tradition* has served as inspiration and a prototype for twentieth-century liturgical renewals in all traditions.

1. The Basic Design of Christian Eucharist

This basic design of eucharistic worship, rooted in ancient Christian precedents, reflects a broad consensus shared across many denominations – Catholic, Anglican, Lutheran, Methodist, and free churches – who have been influenced by the liturgical renewal of the twentieth century.

A service which combines the two parts does not need to be lengthy or complicated. It doesn't have to be formal or wordy. But a communion service planned with awareness of both Jewish and early Christian precedents includes distinctive components. The service of the Word is followed by the communion service. The action always centers around the table.

The Service of the Word
Call to worship
Opening

The Communion Service
The peace
Offertory: receive gifts

Prayer hymn
Confession of sin
Assurance of pardon
Short prayer for the day
Old Testament reading
Psalm or hymn
Gospel reading
Sermon
Hymn
Prayers of intercession
Collection of gifts
Invitation to the communion
  table
Hymn (during which non-
  communicants leave)

Offertory prayer
Communion sentences
Words of Institution
Prayer of Thanksgiving
Memorial, invocation
Breaking the bread
Distribution
Taking of the bread and cup
Prayer of dedication
Lord's Prayer
Hymn
Dismissal[1]

2. A Baptist Pattern in England
(informal and participatory)

Call to worship
Hymn of praise
Prayers of adoration and confession
Members of congregation invited to read Scripture which exalts and
  praises God
Songs and hymns concentrating on Jesus' birth, life, death, and
  resurrection
Readings from Old and New Testaments
Prayer for illumination
Sermon
Prayer of response
Song of commitment
Words of invitation
1 Corinthians 11:23-26
Members invited to offer short prayers of thanksgiving for God's
  redemptive acts in Jesus
Leader giving the bread to the servers, and the congregation serving
  one another
Lord's Prayer
Leader initiating the serving of the wine in a similar way
Members invited to offer brief prayers of thanks, or to choose a song
  which concentrates on the risen or exalted Lord
(select features as desired, emphasizing the fellowship of believers)
  The Peace greeting exchanged
  New members received

News of the fellowship shared
Prayers for healing sought
Words of testimony and encouragement invited
Prayers offered for absent members, the wider church, and the
world
Hymn
The Grace or other benediction said together[2]

3. An Informal Breaking of Bread

Here is a still more informal approach to the Eucharistic Prayer, with a number of participants. Spontaneous songs and additional prayers may be led, but the five people designated know their sequence and the general content of their prayers, readings, and actions. This provides for informality and freedom and at the same time ensures a structural framework and strong biblical content.

After informal singing, Scripture readings, and a sermon or "prophetic discussion" of the texts, the congregation stands around the table. The large loaf or loaves rest unbroken on the table. One cup is filled, other cups are empty. A jug filled with wine stands on the table.

Person 1: *(taking up the bread, giving thanks, putting it down again)*
Leads in a prayer focusing on God, the Creator of life and Provider of all that sustains life.

Person 2: *(taking up the cup, giving thanks, putting it down again)*
Leads in a prayer focusing on Jesus, his life, ministry, death, resurrection–as Savior and Victor over evil.

Person 3: Gives thanks for the presence and work of the Holy Spirit.

Person 4: Reads or tells the narrative: from 1 Corinthians 11 or a Gospel parallel.

Person 5: *(breaking the bread, pouring the wine into the remaining cups, then lifting a cup and the plate of broken bread)*
Speaks the invitation.

Bread and cups are shared informally, with generous portions. People may pray or bless each other as they serve the bread and wine. Singing might break out or other music might accompany this informal service. A strong song with benediction would give a good corporate conclusion.

4. Breaking Bread at a Conference

This is an approach suitable for conferences, where people have brought packed lunches or food to share. It is a type of agape meal. All the food is generously displayed on the main table. A large tray with loaves of bread and goblets of wine stands at the center of the table.

First the leader explains the whole procedure:

Invitation to the Lord's table is spoken by voices 1 and 2.
The leader speaks the Lord's invitation.

The total group moves into smaller groups of from six to ten people. (Decide how many groups are needed. Give a numbered card ahead of time to a designated leader for each small group.) Each group leader moves to a designated area of the room. People gravitate into small circles around the card-holders. Let this be informal, no numbering off!

Group leaders go to the main table, each to get a small loaf of bread. They return to their groups and lead out in prayers of thanks. Others may also pray. The leader breaks and serves the loaf among the group; they keep breaking and serving the bread until it is all gone. They eat *all* of it.

All take part in the shared meal, perhaps with recorded music to give a festive tone.

At the close of the meal, all return to numbered groups again. Invitation words are spoken by voices 1 and 2 and the leader.

Group leaders bring the wine goblets from the main table into the small groups and give thanks; others may also pray as with the bread.

All share the cup around the circle. Drink *all* of it.

The overhead projector shows the closing words. The whole group may join hands to form one large circle. More songs or dances may follow, or recorded music may set the mood you want at the conclusion of the shared meal.

Here are suggested texts for the Breaking of Bread at a conference.

Invitation to break bread together

Voice 1: God says: "Ho, everyone who thirsts, come to the waters; and you that have no money, come, buy and eat! Come, buy wine and milk without money and without price. Why do you spend your money for that which is not bread, and your labor for that which does not satisfy? Listen carefully to me, and eat what is good, and delight yourselves in rich food."

(Isa. 55:1-2)

Voice 2: Jesus says, "Listen! I am standing at the door, knocking; if you hear my voice and open the door, I will come in to you and eat with you, and you with me." (Rev. 3:20)

Voice 1: Oh the joy of those who eat bread in the kingdom of God! (Luke 14:15)

Voice 2:   Give us today the bread that we really need.
(Matt. 6:11)

Declaration: (*all together*) Jesus, you are the bread of life. Whoever comes to you will never hunger, and whoever believes in you will never thirst. You are the bread that comes down from heaven, so that a person may eat of it and not die. Jesus, you are the living bread that came down from heaven. Whoever eats of this bread will live forever; and the bread that you give for the life of the world is your flesh.   (based on John 6:35, 50-51)

Breaking bread in groups

The meal

Invitation to share the cup

Voice 1:   Jesus said, "Let anyone who is thirsty come to me, and let the one who believes in me drink. As the scripture has said, 'Out of the believer's heart shall flow rivers of living water.'"
(John 7:37-38)

Voice 2:   Jesus said, "Those who drink of the water that I will give them will never be thirsty. The water that I will give them will become in them a spring of water gushing up to eternal life."
(John 4:14)

Declaration: (*all together*) Jesus, you are the fountain of life. This cup is the new covenant in your blood. It has been poured out for us for the forgiveness of our sins. We drink deeply of it in remembrance of you. And we look forward in eager anticipation to the day when we will drink it new with you in the kingdom of our Father. (based on Rev. 21:6; 1 Cor. 11:25; Matt. 26:29)

Sharing the cup

Concluding prayer: (*all together*)

In sharing bread and wine,
you have strengthened us, Lord Jesus.
Having eaten, we look to the future.
Maranatha! We long for your coming, O Lord!
Maranatha! We long for your coming, O Lord!
Maranatha! We await the coming of your justice,
salvation, and peace.
AMEN.[3]

Appendix B

Service Resources

1. A Seder Service

The young people of one church took this on as a special project, learning the background of the Seder, organizing details of the special foods, furnishings, games, stories, and music that accompany the Passover festival. They put on a feast for thirty-six people, just the size of a big family reunion. The Seder is a domestic, informal celebration which doesn't work so well on a grand scale. It is better to divide a large group into home-based feasts or to separate into smaller dining areas of a church building. It must be an atmosphere in which children feel at ease and in which they can play their important parts in the questions, stories, songs, and games.

You will need to explain the Seder to the children. Then they may help to prepare the decorations, food, and entertainments. They may make place cards, napkin rings, decorated drinking cups, and personalized Haggadoth. These would include their own names on the cover, drawings of the Exodus story, and a simplified order of events at the Seder.

Here is a description of the Seder written for Jewish children as they prepare for Passover, preceded by special words explained:

Pesach	Hebrew word for Passover, which refers to the Angel of Death passing over Jewish homes at the time of their liberation from slavery
Exodus	Greek word: going out from Egypt, place of slavery
Hametz	Hebrew word for any "leavened" type of food, cereals, or spaghetti, that would ferment; Jews may not eat such foods during the eight days of the Pesach festival
Haggadah	Hebrew word for a booklet of explanations about how to run a Passover meal
Seder	Hebrew word for Order, the name of the Passover meal
Kiddush	Hebrew word for the blessing said over the cup of wine
Matzah	Hebrew word for bread made without yeast, crisplike big crackers

The Story of Seder

Every year, we celebrate the escape of the Jewish people from Egypt for the eight days of Passover, starting with the Seder night dinner when we retell that story. *Seder* means order; everything that is done during the evening has to follow a certain order.

The celebration of *Pesach* takes place in spring. As the whole world wakes up from winter's sleep and everybody is full of spring energy, Jews prepare for Pesach. Many start several weeks before by cleaning their houses thoroughly, washing windows and curtains, and even painting. As the holiday approaches, people turn to the utensils they will be using during Pesach. They polish brass and silver pieces, and boil dishes and cutlery, pots and pans.

All this cleaning is done not only to make certain that every house will be sparkling for this important holiday, but also to insure that not even the smallest speck of hametz will be left anywhere. Hametz is the word for leavened bread and other foods such as cereal and spaghetti, which Jews are forbidden to eat during all eight days of the holiday.

Long before Pesach starts, Jews go to stores to buy foods that must or may be eaten. Of these, the most important is *matzah*. People also buy or bake cakes or cookies which are made out of ground matzah and matzah meal. Even birthday cakes have to be made out of matzah meal.

The night before Pesach starts, each house is inspected for the last time. A grown-up and children go around with a candle, feather, and tray to find and collect any hametz crumbs. Whatever hametz is found is burned by an adult the next morning.

All day the family is busy cooking, setting the table, and otherwise preparing for the Seder. When they come to the table that evening, they see things on it that usually aren't there at dinner on other days.

Next to each plate there is a booklet called *Haggadah*. The Haggadah tells exactly how to run the Seder; it also tells the story of Pesach.

While there is a glass for wine or grape juice next to each place setting, there is also an extra glass on the table. It is a special glass for Elijah the prophet. Elijah was a man who heard the voice of God, told the people what God said, and what will happen in the future. Jews believe that Elijah (*Eliyahu* in Hebrew) will bring peace to the world one day. Every Seder night Jews fill a glass of wine for him and leave open the door to the outside, hoping that he will visit and bring peace with him. In front of the person who conducts the Seder there is a Seder plate—a large plate divided into sections for different foods:

1. *Karpas*, a green vegetable such as parsley, which we dip in salted water before eating. The parsley reminds us of the new growth of spring and the salted water of the tears the slaves shed in Egypt.

2. *Maror*, a bitter vegetable such as lettuce or horseradish. It reminds us of the bitter days of slavery.

3. Roasted egg, which reminds us that in the days of the temple in Jerusalem, an animal was roasted (sacrificed) for God on each holiday.

4. Meat bone, which reminds us of the lamb the slaves roasted before leaving Egypt and of the lambs sacrificed in the temple every Pesach in later years, in addition to the regular sacrifice.

5. *Haroset,* a delicious mixture of ground walnuts, grated apples, sugar, and sweet red wine. The haroset reminds us of the clay the Jewish slaves used for building Pharaoh's cities.

The Seder starts with the *kiddush,* the blessing over the wine. After washing hands, the person who conducts the Seder turns to the Seder plate and gives everybody a taste of the salty karpas. He then turns to another plate which is covered with a special Pesach cloth.

Under the cloth there are three matzoth. He takes the middle matzah, breaks it into two halves, puts one inside a cloth, and sets it aside. Children at the table may steal it from him; if they don't the host hides it from them at the end of the meal. The lucky child who can steal or find it gets a gift. This piece of matzah is called *afikomen.* When it is found, we are supposed to eat the afikomen as part of the dessert.

After the host has hidden the afikomen, he calls on the youngest child at the table to ask the "four questions."

1. How is this night different from all other nights? On all other nights we eat bread or matzah; why do we eat only matzah tonight?

2. On all other nights we eat all kinds of herbs. Why do we eat only bitter herbs tonight?

3. On all other nights we don't dip some foods into other foods. Why do we tonight dip two things: parsley into salt water and bitter herbs into haroset?

4. On all other nights we eat sitting or reclining. Why do we only recline tonight?

When children and grown-ups listen carefully to the Haggadah reading which follows the four questions, they hear the answers to them. People take turns reading the Haggadah or singing some of the parts. The reading and singing are interrupted from time to time in order to taste the foods from the Seder plate and eventually to have the delicious meal. While people read, listen, sing, and eat, they recline comfortably on pillows on their chairs.

In the first years after the Jews left Egypt, they celebrated the Seder in a hurry. They did it that way because the Jewish slaves left Egypt in a hurry. However, over the years the rabbis realized that the story of Pesach is too important to rush; more time is needed to tell and explain it all. So people started having longer, unhurried meals while reclining on comfortable pillows. Taking one's time also reminds us that we are free people. Only free people can relax over a meal. We are grateful that we are free people and hope and pray that people who are not free today will be free very soon.[1]

2. A Didache Service

This service is set up in a simple form of prayers with responses. The prayers are from a handbook for church leaders called the *Didache* (Teaching). This handbook reflects the life and worship of Syrian Christian communities at the end of the first century. Scholars debate whether these are eucharist or agape prayers. The very debate points to the early interlacing of what later became distinctly separate forms. The prayers are clearly modeled on Jewish Berakoth, prayers of thanksgiving before and after meals.

The phrase "the kingdom, the power, and the glory are yours forever" appears in these *Didache* prayers. Some ancient biblical manuscripts include these words at the end of the Lord's Prayer as found in Matthew 6:9-13. This and other internal evidence show strong interaction between these Syrian communities and the Gospel of Matthew.

Notice that the "cup grace" precedes the "bread grace." This is the same order as in Jewish Sabbath meal blessings (cf. Luke 22:17). Create a happy atmosphere. Play taped instrumental music as people come in, and perhaps during the blessings and meal. There is no allusion in these prayers to the death of Jesus, or to his body and blood. The tone is upbeat and expectant of the Lord's triumphant return to his kingdom, which is being gathered in "from the four winds." The metaphor of broken bread scattered over the hills alludes to the sowing of wheat. The scattering and gathering motifs refer to a global church witnessing to God's reign breaking into human time and rejoicing in that reign. "Let Grace come" refers to Christ's coming.

The one who leads should have the full service in hand, but participants only need to see the responses. The *Didache* represents a time of free worship form, so that a written-out liturgy would give the wrong impression. Songs, Bible readings, testimonies, and prayers, including the Lord's Prayer, would expand the form if it seems too short.

Be sure to launch a joyful song immediately after the MARANATHA conclusion. For example, "Yours is the kingdom, yours is the power, yours is the glory evermore." Other songs of Hebrew flavor such as "Shalom aleichem" or "In the presence of your people" would fit well into this free-flowing service. Such variations would be fully in keeping with this text which concludes with the comment that others "may give thanks in their own way" (*Did.* 10:7).

In these early days, leaders were not bound to use prescribed texts. There was opportunity for wide participation "as the Spirit gives utterance" (Acts 2:4, KJV). A hymn based on this text is given below.

The Full Service for the Leader

Meal Prayers from the *Didache*

Leader: *(lifting the large, ceremonial cup)*
Blessed are you, O Lord our God, King of the universe.
You create the fruit of the vine.
We thank you, holy Father, for the holy vine of David, your
child, which you have revealed through Jesus, your Child.
(cueing in congregational response with eyes and hand)

Response: To you be glory forever!
*(sharing the common cup, or with all holding their own cups during
the blessing, then drinking together)*

Leader: *(lifting the loaf of bread)*
Blessed are you, O Lord our God, King of the universe.
You bring forth bread from the earth.
We thank you, our Father, for the life and knowledge which you
have revealed through Jesus, your Child.

Response: To you be glory forever!

Leader: *(breaking off and distributing generous pieces of the loaf;
telling all to eat as they receive their portions)*
As this broken bread was scattered over the hills and then was
brought together and made one, so let your church be brought
together from the ends of the earth into your kingdom.

Response: Yours is the kingdom, the power, and the glory forever!

Leader: *(after meal is served, at least the main course, the leader stands
up and prays)*
We thank you, holy Father, for your sacred name which you
have lodged in our hearts, and for the knowledge and faith and
immortality which you have revealed through Jesus, your Child.

Response: To you be glory forever!

Leader: Almighty Master, you have created everything for the
sake of your name, and have given all of humanity food and
drink to enjoy that they may thank you. But to us you have given
spiritual food and drink and eternal life through Jesus, your
Child. Above all, we thank you that you ...
(continue the prayer extemporaneously)

Response: To you be glory forever!

Leader: Remember, Lord, your church, to save it from all evil and to make it perfect by your love. Make it holy, and gather it together from the four winds into your kingdom which you have made ready for it.

Response: Yours is the kingdom, the power, and the glory forever!

Leader: May grace come and this world pass away!

Response: Hosanna to the God of David!

Leader: If any are holy, let them come. If not, let them be converted.

Response: Our Lord, come! Maranatha! Amen. (*Did.* 9:2 – 10:6)

A Hymn Based on the *Didache*

Father, we give you thanks, who planted
your holy name within our hearts.
Knowledge and faith and life immortal
Jesus your Son to us imparts.

Lord, you have made all for your pleasure,
and given us food for all our days
giving in Christ the bread eternal;
yours is the power, be yours the praise.

Watch o'er your church, O Lord, in mercy,
save it from evil, guard it still,
and in your love unite it, perfect it,
cleanse and conform it to your will.

As grain, once scattered on the hillsides,
was in the broken bread made one,
so may your worldwide church be gathered
into your kingdom by your Son.[2]

You may wish to reserve the dessert course until after the final prayers. You could have live or taped music with dessert and coffee. Provide a festive atmosphere. Remember that early Christians often met early in the morning, so you could readily adapt this form for breakfast meetings.

Responses for Participants in the Didache *Service*

Here are suggested responses for participants in the *Didache* service. The words could be projected overhead or written on large papers at the front. An assistant to the leader could point to the relevant response and lead out with a strong voice. Or you could supply an explanatory sheet at each person's place, like this:

Meal Prayers from the *Didache*

Response: *(at beginning of service, on cue from the leader)*
　　　　To you be glory forever!

Leader: *(after meal, at end of service)*
　　　　Remember, Lord, your church, to save it from all evil and to make it perfect by your love. Make it holy, and gather it together from the four winds into your kingdom which you have made ready for it.

Response: 　Yours is the kingdom, the power, and the glory forever!

Leader: 　May grace come and this world pass away!

Response: 　Hosanna to the God of David!

Leader: 　If any are holy, let them come. If not, let them be converted.

Response: 　Our Lord, come! Maranatha! Amen.

3. A Sixteenth-Century Anabaptist Communion Service

(Based on Hubmaier[3])

When all have assembled, the table shall be prepared, using ordinary bread and wine.

Confession: *(all kneel or be in appropriate physical attitude; in unison)*
　　　　Father, we have sinned against heaven and against you. We are not worthy to be called your children. But speak a word of consolation, and our souls will be made whole. God be gracious to us sinners.

　　　　May the almighty, eternal, and gracious God have mercy on all our sins and forgive us graciously. And when he has forgiven us, [may he] lead us into eternal life without blemish or impurity,

through Jesus Christ our Lord and Savior. AMEN.
(people sit)

Scripture reading and explanation: Luke 24:13-35. Alternative texts may include 1 Corinthians 10 or 11; John 13, 14, 15, 16, or 17; Matthew 3; Luke 3.

Open testimony and response to Scripture

Prayer: *(in unison)*

Stay with us, O Christ! It is toward evening, and the day is now far spent. Abide with us, O Jesus; abide with us. For where you are not, there everything is darkness, night, and shadow. But you alone are the true Son, light and shining brightness. Those for whom you light the way, they cannot go astray.

Self-Examination: *(in unison)*

Let us test and examine ourselves, and let us thus eat of the bread and drink of the drink.

Let us each ask ourselves:

Do I believe utterly and absolutely that Christ gave his body and shed his crimson blood for us on the cross?

Do I fervently hunger for the bread which comes down from heaven?

Do I thirst for the drink which flows into eternal life?

Do I desire to eat and drink in the spirit, faith, and truth which Christ teaches us?

Am I thankful both in words and in deeds toward God, for the abundant and unspeakable love and goodness shown through our Lord Jesus Christ?

Am I willing to say this publicly, making my pledge that I am willing to offer my body and blood for my fellow believers?

Exhortation: *(by leader)*

To fulfill the law, it is not enough to avoid sins and die to them. For we are called not only to forsake evil but to do good. We are called to do good to the neighbor. For Christ not only broke the bread, he also gave it to his disciples. And not only the bread, but also his own flesh and blood. So we must not only speak the word of love, hear it, confess ourselves to be sinners, and abstain from sin. We must fulfill love in deeds, as Scripture everywhere teaches us. In sum, God requires of us the will, the word, and the works of love. God will not be paid off or dismissed with words.

240

Silence and meditation, followed by the Lord's Prayer (*in unison*)

People: Our Father, who art in heaven ...

Pledge of Love

Leader: Whoever now desires to eat this bread and drink this drink of the Lord's Supper, let us rise and respond with heart and mouth in the Pledge of Love.

(all stand)

Brothers and sisters, if you desire to love God before, in, and above all things, in the power of his holy and living Word; if you desire to serve, honor, and adore God, and to sanctify his name; and to subject your sinful will to God's divine will which he has worked in you by the living Word, then let each say individually, "I desire it."

People: I desire it.

Leader: If you desire to love and serve your neighbor with deeds of love, to lay down for him or her your life; if you desire to be obedient to father, mother, and all authorities according to the will of God, and this in the power of our Lord Jesus Christ, who laid down his flesh and blood for us, then let each say individually.

People: I desire it.

Leader: If you will practice admonition toward your brothers and sisters, make peace and unity among them, and reconcile yourselves with all whom you have offended; if you desire to abandon all envy, hate, and evil will toward others, and willingly cease all action and behavior which causes harm, disadvantage, or offense to your neighbor; if you will love your enemies and do good to them, then let each say individually, "I desire it."

People: I desire it.

Leader: If you desire publicly to confirm before the church this pledge of love which you have now made, through the Lord's Supper, by eating bread and drinking of the cup, and to testify to it in the power of the living memorial of the suffering and death of Jesus Christ our Lord, then let each say individually, "I desire it in the power of God."

People: I desire it in the power of God.

Leader: So eat and drink with one another in the name of God the Father, the Son, and the Holy Spirit. May God accord to all of us the power and the strength that we may worthily carry out this pledge and bring it to its saving conclusion. May the Lord Jesus impart to us his grace. AMEN.

Thanksgiving: *(congregation standing; leader takes the bread; all in congregation lift their eyes and pray)*

People: We praise and thank you, Lord God, Creator of the heavens and earth, for all your goodness toward us. Especially we thank you that you so sincerely loved us and gave your most beloved Son for us, so that we who believe in Jesus may not be lost, but have eternal life. May you be honored, praised, and magnified now, forever, always, and eternally. AMEN.

Breaking and distribution of the bread

Leader: *(breaking the bread)* The Lord Jesus, in the night in which he was betrayed, took the bread, gave thanks, broke it, and said: "Take, eat. This is my body which is broken for you. Do this in my memory." Therefore, dear brothers and sisters, take, and eat also this bread in the memory of the body of our Lord Jesus Christ, which he gave unto death for us.

     (leader offers the bread into the hands of those present; people hold their fragment of bread, and then eat it together)

Sharing the cup

Leader: *(taking cup, speaking with lifted eyes)*
          God! Praise be to thee!

Likewise, the Lord Jesus took the cup after Supper and said: "This cup is a new testament in my blood. Do this, as often as you drink, in memory of me." Take, therefore, also the cup, and all drink from it in the memory of the blood of our Lord Jesus Christ, which was shed for us for the forgiveness of our sins.

     (leader passes the cup to the people, and all drink)

People: As often as we eat the bread and drink of the drink, we proclaim the death of the Lord, until he comes.

     (people sit down)

Conclusion

Leader: By eating the bread and drinking the drink in memory of the suffering and shed blood of our Lord Jesus Christ for the remission of our sins, we have had fellowship with one another. By eating the bread and drinking the drink in the Lord's memory, we have all become one loaf and one body. Our Head is Christ. We are called to be conformed to our Head and as his members to follow after him. [We are called] to love one another, to do good, to give counsel, and to be helpful to one another, each offering up our flesh and blood for the other.

And so I urge you, most dearly beloved in Christ, as table companions of Christ Jesus, to lead a Christian walk before God and all people. Remember your baptismal commitment and your pledge of love. Bear fruit worthy of the baptism and the Supper of Christ. May you in the power of God satisfy your pledge and promise, your sacrament and commitment. God sees it and knows your hearts. May our Lord Jesus Christ, ever and eternally praised, grant us the same. AMEN.

Dear brothers and sisters, watch and pray, lest you wander away and fall into temptation. We know neither the day nor the hour when the Lord is coming and will ask an accounting of our life. Therefore watch and pray. I commend you to God. May all of us say,

People: Praise, praise, praise to the Lord eternally! AMEN.

Leader: And so let us rise.
(people stand)
Go in the peace of Christ Jesus.

People: The grace of God be with us all. AMEN.

Notes

COMMUNION ACROSS THE CENTURIES
1. Last Supper to Church Supper
1. Paul Bradshaw, *The Search for the Origins of Christian Worship* (London: SPCK, 1992), 159-160.

2. Dennis E. Smith and Hal E. Taussig, *Many Tables* (London: SCM, 1990), 51-66.

3. Smith and Taussig, *Many Tables*, 63-64.

4. Hermas, *Vision* 3.9.2-4.

2. Jewish Blessings and Roman Banquets
1. Bradshaw, *Origins*, 15-16.

2. Joachim Jeremias, *The Eucharistic Words of Jesus* (Philadelphia: Fortress Press, 1977), 250.

3. Ibid., 109.

4. Ibid., 110.

5. The Passover is instituted in Exodus 12; the Festival of Unleavened Bread in Exodus 13:8-9.

6. E. H. van Olst, *The Bible and Liturgy* (Grand Rapids: Eerdmans, 1991), 39-40.

7. Smith and Taussig, *Many Tables*, 31-33.

8. See ibid., chapters 2 and 3, for a discussion of Christian transformation of banquet traditions.

3. Love Feasts
1. Geoffrey Wainwright, *Eucharist and Eschatology* (London: Epworth, 1963), 21; see also chapter 2.

1. Jeremias, *Eucharistic Words*, 118-119.

3. Rom. 16:16; 1 Cor. 16:20; 2 Cor. 13:12; 1 Thess. 5:26; 1 Pet. 5:14.

4. Jeremias, *Eucharistic Words*, 115-122.

5. I. Howard Marshall, *Last Supper and Lord's Supper* (Exeter: Paternoster, 1980), chap. 5.

6. Smith and Taussig, *Many Tables*, 58-63.

7. Pliny, *Letters* 10.96. These were addressed to Emperor Trajan.

8. Ignatius, *Letter to the Smyrnaeans* 8.

9. Tertullian, *Apology* 39.16-19. The date is ca. A.D. 200.

10. Trevor Lloyd, *Agapes and Informal Eucharists* (Bramcote, Notts: Grove, 1973), 10.

11. Augustine, *Orations* 6.4.

12. Clement of Alexandria, *Instructor* 2.1.4; Tertullian, *On Fasting* 16.

4. Early Christian Eucharist

1. Christians met before work, throughout the week, for communal teaching and prayers.

2. Josef Jungmann, *The Early Liturgy* (London: Darton, Longman, & Todd, 1960), 44.

3. Ibid.

4. *Apology* 1.13.

5. Origen, *Contra Celsum* 8.57.

6. Justin, *Dialogue with Trypho* 110.2-3.

7. *Didache* 9.2-4.

8. Justin, *Dialogue with Trypho* 41.

9. Justin, *Apology* 1.65.

10. Many scholars no longer ascribe authorship of *Apostolic Tradition*, a composite document, to Hippolytus.

11. *Apostolic Tradition* 4.

12. Clement of Alexandria, quoted in Jungmann, *The Early Liturgy*, 44.

13. Justin, *Apology* 1.13.

14. Johann Franck, 1649; trans. Catherine Winkworth, 1863. Meter 88 88D (Trochaic). From United Reformed Church hymnal *Rejoice and Sing* (Grand Rapids: Eerdmans, 1985), 446.

5. Medieval Mass and Divine Liturgy

1. John Chrysostom, *In Eph. hom.* 3.4.

2. Josef Jungmann, *The Mass of the Roman Rite: Its Origins and Development* (Dublin: Four Courts, 1953), 2:362.

3. Ibid., 363.

4. Peter of Blois (died ca. 1204), quoted in Jungmann, *Mass of the Roman Rite*, 2:364.

5. Ibid., 362.

6. Ibid., 362.

7. Ibid., 365-366.

8. J. G. Davies, ed., *The New Westminster Dictionary of Liturgy and Worship* (London: SCM, 1986), 139.

9. Jungmann, *The Mass of the Roman Rite* 1:179.

10. Jungmann, *The Early Liturgy*, 164-166.

11. William H. Willimon, *Word, Water, Wine and Bread* (Valley Forge, Pa.: Judson Press, 1980), 52.

12. Jim Forest, "The Attractions of Orthodoxy," *De Herault* (a Dutch Jesuit magazine), 1990, 6.

13. Ibid., 5.

14. Alexander Schmemann, *For the Life of the World* (Crestwood, N.Y.: St. Vladimir's Seminary Press, 1988), 29.

14. *The Orthodox Liturgy* (Oxford: Oxford Univ. Press, 1982), 35, 93-94.

6. Reformation: A Communion Revolution

1. For further discussion of Reformation eucharistic views see Robert E. Webber, ed., *The Sacred Actions of Christian Worship*, The Complete

Library of Christian Worship, vol. 6 (Nashville: Star Song, 1994), 211-214, 234-239.

2. Huldrich Zwingli, *The Latin Works of Huldreich Zwingli*, 2:49, cited in Webber, *The Sacred Actions*, 236.

3. John Calvin, *Calvin's Tracts*, 2:249.

4. James White, *Protestant Worship: Traditions in Transition* (Louisville: Westminster John Knox, 1989), 36.

5. Willimon, *Word, Water, Wine and Bread*, 65-66.

6. Ibid., 68.

7. Gregory Dix, *The Shape of the Liturgy* (Westminster: Dacre Press, 1945), 632.

8. Louis Bouyer, *Eucharist: Theology and Spirituality of the Eucharistic Prayer* (Notre Dame: Univ. of Notre Dame Press, 1968), 81.

9. C. W. Dugmore, *The Mass and the English Reformers* (London: Macmillan, 1958), 160.

10. H. Wayne Pipkin, *Zwingli: The Positive Value of His Eucharistic Writings* (Leeds: Yorkshire Baptist Association, 1984), 4.

11. Martin Luther, in Jaroslav Pelikan, ed., *Luther's Works* (St. Louis: Concordia, 1955-86), 53:63-64.

12. John Rempel, *The Lord's Supper in Anabaptism* (Scottdale, Pa.: Herald Press, 1991).

13. John H. Yoder, trans. and ed., *The Legacy of Michael Sattler* (Scottdale, Pa.: Herald Press, 1973), 45.

14. "The Schleitheim Brotherly Union" (1527), in Yoder, ed., *The Legacy of Michael Sattler*, 34-42.

15. Adapted by Eleanor Kreider from *Balthasar Hubmaier: Theologian of Anabaptism*, trans. and ed. H. Wayne Pipkin and John H. Yoder (Scottdale, Pa.: Herald Press, 1989), 403-404, and used by permission.

16. "Orthodox Confession" (1678).

7. Modern Developments: Innovation and Recovery

1. White, *Protestant Worship*, 53.

2. Quoted in Geoffrey Wainwright, *Doxology* (Oxford: Oxford Univ. Press, 1980), 333.

3. Ibid., 334.

4. Friederich Heiler, *The Spirit of Worship* (London: Hodder and Stoughton, 1926), 108.

5. Quoted in White, *Protestant Worship*, 107.

6. Horton Davies, *Worship and Theology in England*, 1690-1750 (London: Oxford Univ. Press, 1961), 5, 54.

7. Quoted in Davies, *Worship and Theology in England*, 3, 68.

8. For a brief description of another eighteenth-century rediscovery of the agape, see Graydon Snyder, "Love Feast," in *Brethren Encyclopedia* (Philadelphia: Brethren Encyclopedia, Inc., 1983-84), 1:762-765. Also see essays on the Brethren heritage of the Lord's Supper in *The Lord's Supper: Believers Church Perspectives*, ed. Dale Stoffer (Scottdale, Pa.: Herald Press, 1997), 148-192.

9. Frank Baker, *Methodism and the Love Feast* (Epworth: Epworth Press, 1957), 15, 25.

10. For fascinating detail, see Donald Durnbaugh, *The Believers' Church* (London:

Macmillan, 1968; Scottdale, Pa.: Herald Press, 1985), chap. 6.

11. Robert Haldane (1764-1842) and James Alexander Haldane (1768-1951).

12. Thomas Campbell (1763-1854), his son Alexander (1788-1866), and Barton Stone (1772-1844).

13. John Robinson at Delft Haven (1620), quoted in Daniel Wilson, *The Pilgrim Fathers* (1851), 358.

14. Quoted in White, *Protestant Worship*, 174.

15. Roy Coad, *A History of the Brethren Movement* (Exeter: Paternoster, 1968), 18-21.

16. Anthony Groves, *Memoir*, 48-49. See Coad, *Brethren Movement*, 24.

17. F. W. Newman, "Phases of Faith," 27, 33, 34. Quoted in Coad, *Brethren Movement*, 26.

18. Davies, *Worship and Theology in England*, 3, 243-245.

19. White, *Protestant Worship*, 200.

20. Davies, *Worship and Theology in England*, 5, 14.

21. Robert E. Webber, ed., *Twenty Centuries of Christian of Christian Worship*, The Complete Library of Christian Worship, vol. 2 (Nashville: Star Song, 1994), 134-140.

22. Ibid., 136.

23. Ibid., 137-139.

24. Robert and Julia Banks, *The Home Church* (Tring: Lion, 1986), 18-22.

COMMUNION: VARIATIONS ON THE THEME
8. Historic Themes Come Alive

1. Mark 14:24; Luke 22:20; 1 Cor. 11:25.

2. Deut. 12:5-7, 17-18; 14:23, 26; 15:20; 27:7.

3. *Didache* 10.6.

4. On the overlapping times, see 1 Cor. 10:11, "... to instruct us, on whom the ends of the ages have come." For further reading: Geoffrey Wainwright, *Eucharist and Eschatology* (London: Epworth, 1971), chap. 2; Thomas Finger, *Christian Theology: An Eschatological Approach*, vol. 2 (Scottdale, Pa.: Herald Press, 1989), chap. 13.

5. Wainwright, *Eucharist and Eschatology*, 60-70.

6. Ibid., 67.

7. Peter Lampe, "The Eucharist," *Interpretation* 48 (1994), 36-49. Also see Finger, *Theology*, 2:340-341.

8. Lampe, "The Eucharist," 36-49.

9. Rom. 16:16; 1 Cor. 16:20; 2 Cor. 13:12; 1 Thess. 5:26.

10. Eleanor Kreider, "Let the Faithful Greet Each Other: The Kiss of Peace," *Conrad Grebel Review* 5 (1987), 44.

9. Christ Is Present, the Mystery Is Revealed

1. John Meyendorff, *Byzantine Theology* (New York: Fordham Univ. Press, 1987), 29.

2. Alexander Schmemann, *Church, World, Mission* (Crestwood, N.Y.: St. Vladimir's Press, 1979), 60.

3. See Horton Davies, "The Eucharist as Mystery," in his *Bread of Life and Cup of Joy: Newer Ecumenical Perspectives on the Eucharist* (Grand Rapids: Eerdmans, 1993), 147-179.

4. Raymond Brown, *The Gospel According to John, XIII-XXI*, The Anchor Bible

(New York: Doubleday, 1970), 673-674.

5. William H. Willimon, *Word, Water, Wine and Bread* (Valley Forge: Judson Press, 1980), 58.

6. Kathy Carter et al., "Is the Church Aesthetically ... ?" *Regenerate* 5 (Nov. 1994), 10.

7. G. W. H. Lampe, "The Eucharist in the Thought of the Early Church," in R. E. Clements et al., *Eucharistic Theology Then and Now* (London: SPCK, 1958), 34.

8. Jean Lebon, *How to Understand the Liturgy* (London: SCM, 1987), 2.

9. Donald Baillie, *Theology of the Sacraments and Other Papers* (London: Faber and Faber, 1957), 54.

10. Communion Themes for Life in the Congregation

1. John H. Yoder, *Christology and Theological Method: Preface to Theology* (Elkhart, Ind., Goshen Biblical Seminary, n.d.), 221.

2. *Pope John Sunday Missal* (Leigh-on-Sea, Essex: Kevin Mayhew, 1978), 508.

3. *Alternative Service Book* (Oxford: Oxford Univ. Press, 1980), 187.

4. Rowan Williams, *Eucharistic Sacrifice: The Roots of a Metaphor*, Grove Liturgical Study 31 (Bramcote, Notts: Grove, 1982), 7-8.

5. Ibid., 29.

6. Yoder, John H., *Christology*, 221.

7. *Didache* 4.8.

8. Thomas Phelan, "Offertory," *New Westminster Dictionary of Liturgy and Worship* (Philadelphia: Westminster, 1986), 394-395.

11. Communion Themes for Mission

1. See Gustaf Aulén, *Christus Victor* (New York: Macmillan, 1958); Walter Wink, *Naming the Powers* (Philadelphia: Fortress Press, 1984).

2. Matt. 10:38; Mark 8:34ff.; 10:38ff.; Luke 14:27; John 15:20; 2 Cor. 1:5; 4:10; Phil. 1:29; 2:5-8; 3:10; Col. 1:24ff.; Heb. 12:1-4; 1 Pet. 2:21ff.; Rev. 12:11.

3. Yoder, *Christology*, 223.

4. Matt. 26:26-29; Mark 14:22-25; Luke 22:19-20; 1 Cor. 11:23-26.

5. In this section I have drawn from J. C. Thomas, *Foot Washing in John 13 and the Johannine Community* (Sheffield: JSOT Press, 1991); and J. C. Thomas, "Footwashing within the Context of the Lord's Supper," in *The Lord's Supper*, ed. Dale R. Stoffer (Scottdale, Pa.: Herald Press, 1997), 169-184. Cf. Brown, *The Gospel According to John*, XIII-XXI, The Anchor Bible.

6. Monica Hellwig, *The Eucharist and the Hunger of the World* (New York, NY: Paulist, 1976), 10.

7. Ibid., 23.

8. "Birkat Ha Mazon" (Various blessing), in Chaim Raphael, ed., *A Jewish Book of Common Prayer* (London: Weidenfeld and Nicolson, 1985), 103.

9. Wainwright, *Eucharist and Eschatology*, 19-21.

10. Ps. 23:5; Prov. 9:1-6; Song of Songs 5:1; Isa. 55:1-2; 25:6-9.

11. Wainwright, *Eucharist and Eschatology*, 18-58.

12. Exod. 16:4, 15; Ps. 78:24f.; Neh. 9:15.

13. Second Baruch 29:8, in the Pseudepigrapha.

14. Matt. 14:13-21; Mark 6:32-44; Luke 9:10-17; John 6:1-13.

15. Isa. 2:2-4; 25:6-9; 55:4ff.; 56:6-8; 60; 66:19-24; Hag. 2:6-9; Zech. 2:11; 8:20-23; 14; Tobit 13:11; 14:5-7.

16. John Wesley called the eucharist a "converting ordinance," indicating his understanding of its missionary character. This theme can be traced in Wesleyan eucharistic hymnody.

17. Wainwright, *Eucharist and Eschatology*, 30-35.

18. Joachim Jeremias, *The Lord's Prayer* (Philadelphia: Fortress, 1964), 23-27.

19. Yoder, *Christology*, 207-208.

20. John Driver, *Understanding the Atonement for the Mission of the Church* (Scottdale, Pa.: Herald Press, 1986), 71-209.

21. Lampe, "Eucharist," 36-49.

22. Paul Bradshaw, *The Search for the Origins of Christian Worship* (London: SPCK, 1992), 53-55.

COMMUNION SHAPES CHARACTER

12. The Language of Ritual

1. Matt 6:7 (KJV). NRSV: "Do not heap up empty phrases as the Gentiles do; for they think that they will be heard because of their many words."

2. John Gordon, "With This String I Divorce You," *Independent*, 6 Sept., 1995, 4.

3. Steve Faimaru, "Life Amid Death," *The Boston Globe*, 1 Aug., 1994, 6.

4. Daniel Berrigan, *No Bars to Manhood* (New York: Bantam, 1970), 16.

5. Richard Rohr, "The Spirituality of Subtraction," tape 3.

6. Alan Kreider, *Worship and Evangelism in Pre-Christendom* (Cambridge: Grove, 1995), 32-33.

13. Thanksgiving Sets the Tone

1. See Appendix B for a full Seder service.

2. From the opening essay by Marc H. Ellis and Otto Maduro, eds., *Expanding the View: Gustavo Gutiérrez and the Future of Liberation Theology* (Maryknoll, N.Y.: Orbis Books, 1989), 25.

3. A good example is *A Passover Haggadah as Commented Upon by Elie Wiesel* (New York: Touchstone, 1993).

4. Examples: Phil 2:5-11; Rev. 11:15-16; 213-4; Luke 1:46-55, 68-79.

14. An Open Table?

1. Used by the Church of England in the 1662 and 1928 *Book of Common Prayer*, and also in the 1980 *Alternative Service Book*, but with the words "this holy sacrament" rather than "the supper of the Lord." Congregational and Mennonite service books also include this invitation, but Mennonites use the words in italics.

2. From a Methodist service book and also quoted by Paul Beasley-Murray in *Faith and Festivity* (Eastbourne: Monarch, 1991), 64, in which Beasley-Murray suggests adding the Hebrews reading.

3. Ibid., 63-64. Beasley-Murray recognizes that the church should not ask more of people than Christ does, but surely believers should desire to obey Christ's command for baptism (Matt. 28:19-20).

4. Words by John L. Bell and Graham Maule © 1989 WGRG, Iona Community, Glasgow. Extract from the song "Jesus Calls Us," Metre 87 87D. Used by permission.

5. Used by permission of Hope Douglas J. Harle-Mould, Pastor and Teacher of Springboro (Ohio) Church of Christ.

6. Michael Forster, unpublished manuscript, "The Open Table," chap. 5, esp. 80.

7. Ibid., 84.

8. See examples above, in chapter 16, "Words and Stories at the Table."

9. David Holeton, *Infant Communion Then and Now* (Bramcote: Notts: Grove, 1981), 8.

10. Ibid., 15.

11. *Mediation Manual* (Akron, Pa.: Mennonite Central Committee).

12. Donald R. Steelberg, in a paper, "Children and Communion," written for a discussion conference on "Communion," 26 Jan. 1995, at Associated Mennonite Biblical Seminary, Elkhart, Ind.

13. In a conversation with Wood Green Mennonite Church, London, 12 Nov. 1991.

14. Marjorie Waybill, "Children," *Builder*, Aug. 1993.

15. A Community of Many Tables

1. Jeanne Hinton, *Communities* (Guildford: Eagle, 1993), 157.

2. Reta Halteman Finger, *Paul and the Roman House Churches* (Scottdale: Herald Press, 1993), 152.

16. Words and Stories at the Table

1. Jeremias, *Eucharistic Words*, 173.

2. *Alternative Service Book* (1980), 131-132.

3. Markus Barth, *Rediscovering the Lord's Supper* (Atlanta: John Knox, 1988), 88-95, supported by Heb. 8:5; Rom. 5:14; 1 Pet. 5:4; Rev. 8:3, 5; 11:19; 21:2.

4. Ibid., 88-95.

5. Rom. 8:1; John 6:35; Matt. 8:2-3; 1 John 1:3, 5, KJV.

17. Singing Our Communion Theology

1. Tertullian, *On the Soul* 9.4; *Apology* 39.18.

2. Joseph Gelineau, S.J., "Music and Singing in the Liturgy," in Cheslyn Jones et al., eds., *The Study of Liturgy*, rev. ed. (London: SPCK, 1992), 495.

3. Heb. 12:22; Rev. 5:9; 15:3-4; Heb.13:15.

18. Offering Ourselves and Our Gifts

1. Robert Webber, "The Lord's Supper: Is It to Be Solemn or Joyful?" *Worship Leader*, June/July, 1993, 10.

19. An Environment for Thanksgiving

1. See J. G. Davies, *Temples, Churches and Mosques: A Guide to the Appreciation of Religious Architecture* (Oxford: Oxford Univ. Press, 1982).

2. John Newport, "Space for Worship: A Baptist View," in Robert E. Webber, ed., Music and the Arts in Christian Worship, *The Complete Library of Christian Worship*, vol. 4, (Nashville: Star Song, 1994), 572.

3. Paul Beasley-Murray, *Faith and Festivity* (Eastbourne: MARC, 1991), 68.

20. Praying at the Table

1. Tertullian, *De oratione*.

2. *Apostolic Tradition* 37; also Cyprian, *De lapsis* 26.

3. *Martyrdom of Polycarp* 8.1.

4. *Didache* 8.4.

5. Josef Jungmann, *The Mass of the Roman Rite*, 1:336-337. The text is given in Latin.

6. Based on a prayer in *The Book of Common Prayer* (New York: Seabury, 1977), 456.

7. Quoted in Horton Davies, *Bread of Life and Cup of Joy* (Grand Rapids, Mich.: Eerdmans, 1993), 34.

8. *The University of Notre Dame Sunday Missal* (London: Collins, 1979), 46.

9. *The Alternative Service Book* (Oxford: Oxford Univ. Press, 1980), 131, 194, 140, 191.

10. This prayer is part of "Additional Eucharistic Prayers" (GS 1138B), debated by the General Synod in February 1996, but not authorized for liturgical use in the Church of England. Extract from *Patterns for Worship. A Report by the Liturgical Commission of the General Synod of the Church of England* (London: Church House Publishing, 1989), copyright © The Central Board of Finance of the Church of England, and reproduced by permission.

11. From the *Service Book*, © 1989 The United Reformed Church in the United Kingdom, and used by permission of Oxford University Press, 1989.

12. Church of Scotland, Committee on Public Worship and Aids to Devotion, *New Ways to Worship*, ed. David Beckett et al. (New York: Overlook, 1980), 35-36.

WHAT COMES FROM COMMUNION?

21. Character

1. "You are the body of Christ, and individually members of it" (1 Cor. 12:27); Alexander Schmemann, *The Eucharist* (New York: St. Vladimir's Press, 1988), 23.

2. Christopher Rowland, "A Response: Anglican Reflections," in Paul Fiddes, ed., *Reflections on the Water* (Oxford: Regent's Park Press and Smith and Helwys, 1996), 128.

3. Stanley Hauerwas, *The Peaceable Kingdom* (London: SCM, 1983), 110.

4. Vincent Donovan, *Christianity Rediscovered* (Maryknoll, N.Y.: Orbis, 1982), 125.

5. Hauerwas, *Peaceable Kingdom*, 107.

22. Unity

1. Nicholas Lash, "Credal Affirmation as a Criterion of Church Membership," in J. Kent and R. Murray, eds., *Church Membership and Inter-Communion* (London: Darton, Longman & Todd, 1973), 51.

2. Wainwright, *Doxology* (Oxford: Oxford Univ. Press, 1980), 298.

3. Ken Read, "A Restorationist View of the Lord's Supper," in Robert E. Webber, ed., *The Sacred Actions of Christian Worship*, The Complete Library of Christian Worship, vol. 6 (Nashville: Star Song, 1994), 242-244.

23. Mission

1. Jürgen Moltmann, *The Church in the Power of the Spirit* (London: SCM, 1977), 244.

2. Gen. 12:1-3. The Abrahamic covenant is reiterated four times in Genesis.

3. Luke 22:20b; 24-27; 24:46-48. Wilbert Shenk, *Write the Vision. The Church Renewed* (Leominster: Gracewing, 1995), 81-84.

4. Moltmann, *The Church in the Power of the Spirit*, 246.

5. Alpha was initiated by Nicky Gumbel, Holy Trinity Brompton, Brompton Road, London SW7 1JA. Information and resources are available.

6. Moltmann, *The Church in the Power of the Spirit*, 249.

Appendix A: Planning a Communion Service

1. Stephen Winward, *Celebration and Order* (Didcot, Oxon: Baptist Union of Great Britain, 1981), 14.

2. "The Lord's Supper: The Third Pattern," from *Patterns and Prayers for Christian Worship*, © 1991 The Baptist Union of Great Britain (1991), 74-75; used by permission of Oxford University Press.

3. A type of agape service in the Workshop lay-training program as led by its director, Noel Moules.

Appendix B: Service Resources

1. Extract from *The Complete Family Guide to Jewish Holidays*, by Dalia Hardof Renberg (London: Robson, 1987), 139-142; used by permission of Robeson Books.

2. Based on the *Didache*. Meter, 98 98f, Bland Tucker (d. 1984). From United Reformed Church hymnal *Rejoice and Sing* (Grand Rapids: Eerdmans, 1985), 444. Permission requested from Church Pension Fund, Church Hymnal Corporation, New York City.

3. Prepared by Eleanor Kreider, based on Balthasar Hubmaier's *A Form for Christ's Supper* (1527), adapted from *Balthasar Hubmaier: Theologian of Anabaptism*, trans. and ed. H. Wayne Pipkin and John H. Yoder (Scottdale, Pa.: Herald Press, 1989), 393-408, and used by permission.

Hubmaier, as a Roman Catholic priest in Nikolsburg, Moravia, had been an effective and popular preacher, devoted to pilgrimage piety and to the veneration of Mary. He was a professor of theology and later an administrator in the University of Ingolstadt. He was priest in the largest parish church in the city. Hubmaier became an Anabaptist and was rebaptized in April 1525. He was burned at the stake in Vienna in March 1528. This entire service, prepared for and used in Hubmaier's parish, expresses important Anabaptist emphases on leadership, community, mutual love, and discipleship.

Index

Agape Meal, 20–21, 23, 34–39, 40, 42, 117, 166, 237–238
"Agnus Dei", 185, 187
Alpha, 220, 223-224
Anabaptists, 59, 61–62, 120, 160
Anglo-Catholic Movement, 76
Apostles' Creed, 218
Apostolic Constitutions, 47
Apostolic Tradition, 37, 43, 117–118
Atoning power of Christ's death, 85, 97, 110, 130–132

Banquet, 25
  Christian, 31
  funeral, 38
  Messianic, 18–19, 34–35, 91–92, 114, 128, 218, 220, 225
  Roman, 25, 29–31
Baptism, 48, 50, 67, 102, 115–116, 121, 123, 151–153, 156, 217
Beatitudes, 55, 127–128
Berakah, 25, 147, 236
Bible reading(s), 142, 143, 179
Blessing, 25, 27, 32–33, 90, 147
Blood, 93, 96–97, 101, 106, 111–114
Boundaries, 37, 115
Bread and wine, 198
Breaking bread, 18, 23, 27, 35–36, 166
Brethren (Plymouth), 73
Building(s), 194–195

Calvin, John, 59, 60–61, 67
Campbell, Alexander, 72
Campbell, Thomas, 72
Canon of the Mass, 50, 60
Cantillation, 183
Change(s), 172
Character, 213
Character of Christ, 135, 215, 220

Child communion, 159–160
Children, 157, 163
Christian Churches (Disciples of Christ), 71
Christus Victor, 119
Chrysostom, John, 46
Church of England, 69, 74, 76, 176, 208
Clement of Alexandria, 38, 41, 44
Clerical, 46–47
  order, 46–47
  power, 57, 65
Communion, 58–59
  close, 150
  frequency of, 57–59, 63, 65, 71, 78
Community, 52
Confession, 53, 106, 150
Convergence Movement, 80
Covenant, 28, 93, 97, 111
Cranmer, Thomas, 67
Creation healed, 125
Cup of blessing, 23, 28, 30, 96–97, 101, 106, 111–112

Darby, John Nelson 74–75
Death of Christ, 100, 123–124
Didache, 40, 42, 95, 203, 236–239
Discern the body, 21–22
Discipleship, 52, 62–64, 92, 100, 120, 150
Discipline, 75, 114–115, 150, 220
"Do this", 18–21, 26, 91, 164

Eastern Orthodoxy, 54–55
Enlightenment, 67–68
Eucharist, shape of, 57, 78
Eucharistic worship, 38–39, 220, 228
Excommunication, 116

Feet-washing, 122, 140
Filioque, 54
Forgiveness, 106, 220
Free worship, 34, 38, 79

Generosity, 22, 34
Gloria in excelsis, 184
Groves, Anthony, 73

Hallel Psalms, 28
Healing, 108, 204
Health, 22
Hermas, 22
Hodayah, 25
Holy Spirit, 52, 100–101, 148, 208
Home Church Movement, 82–83
Hope, 93, 119, 218
Hospitality, 23–24, 34, 36, 169
Hubmaier, Balthasar, 62
  Pledge of Love, 63–64
Hussites, 158
Hymn themes, 181–182

Inclusion, 31–32, 128
Inclusive, 154–156, 161
Individualism, 51–52, 77, 97, 161
Infant baptism, 158–159
Institution narrative, 18, 57, 60, 65, 91,
  111, 173, 179–180
Inter-communion, 216–218
Invitation, 221
  to the Lord's Table, 221

Justice, 20–23, 38, 45, 118, 125
Justin Martyr, 41–44, 117

Kingdom of God, 34, 51, 55–56,
  92–95, 99, 125, 218, 226
Kiss of peace, 98, 140, 202
Koinonia, 23, 35, 71, 95–96, 106
Kyrie eleison, 203

Last Supper, 17–18, 26–28
Lay presidency, 72, 158, 221
Liberation, 147, 220
Liturgical Movement, 78
Lord's Prayer, 27, 129, 202, 224
Love Feast, 70. *See also* Agape Meal

Low Mass, 49
Luther, Martin, 59–61, 67

Manna, 128
Maranatha, 94
Marpeck, Pilgram, 62
Masai, 214
Memory, 18–19, 21, 23, 24, 38, 63, 91,
  100
Mennonite(s), 150, 160
Methodism, 70
Mime, 171, 189
Mission, 220–221
Mood, 146, 148, 162, 188
Moving around, 199
Music, instrumental, 187–188
Mysterium tremendum, 47
Mystery, 99, 105, 129

New covenant 28, 97, 111–113, 156,
  221, 224

Oblation, 116
Offering(s), 40, 116
  bread and wine, 190
  money, 192
Open invitation, 154
Open table, 72, 151, 223
Origen, 41

Parable(s) 143–144, 174–175
Passover 18, 20–21, 23, 25, 27–29,
  32–34, 94, 114, 147
Peace, 97, 125, 140
Penitential system, 48, 53
Pentecostals, 77
Philips, Dirk, 62
Pledge of Love, 63–64. *See also*
  Hubmaier, Balthasar
Pliny, 36–37
Poets, 183
Polycarp, 203
Post-resurrection meals, 19, 36
Prayer(s), 127, 237–239
  corporate, 148
  intercessions, 202
Presence of Christ, 99–101
Proclamation, 95, 126, 130

Psalms in the eucharist, 186

Real meal(s), 17–18, 20, 23–24, 129, 161
Reconciliation, 97, 108, 151
Reformer(s), 58–60, 65, 67
Restoration group(s), 71, 218
Resurrection, 56
Return of Christ, 94–95
Ritual(s), 25, 33, 91–92, 112, 136–144

Sabbath meal, 147
Sacrament, 102
Sacrifice, 50–51, 106
   Christ's, 109,114
   emphasis, 50–51, 110–111
   Old Testament, 109
Sanctus, 185
Schleitheim Confession, 63
Seder, 28, 33, 147–148, 233–235
Sermon(s), 130, 143
Service, 130
Sharing, 19–20, 22–23, 34, 37–38, 45, 95, 110, 117–118, 125, 169
   act of, 95
Singing, 188
Stone, Barton, 72

Story, 33, 43, 91–92, 131, 161, 176–178, 214
Swiss Anabaptist Congregational Order, 63
Symbol, 102

Table, 197
Taizé community, 217
Tertullian, 37–38, 117
Thanksgiving, 23–26, 29, 40–41, 205
Tradition(s), 135, 138, 142, 157, 158–161, 165
Transformation, 51
   of selves, 89
   of society, 51
Transsignification, 218

Unity, 21, 23, 52, 54, 63, 73–75, 95–98, 150, 216–219
Unworthy, 22, 46–47, 48, 65, 149, 150, 178, 220

Vine and branches, 100, 121
Visuals, 200

Wesley, John 70–71, 221

Zwingli, Huldrich, 59–63, 69